Modern Canada 1930-1980's

Readings in
Canadian Social History
Volume 5

Edited by
Michael S. Cross
and Gregory S. Kealey

McClelland and Stewart

McClelland and Stewart Limited
The Canadian Publishers
25 Hollinger Road
Toronto, Ontario
M4B 3G2

Canadian Cataloguing in Publication Data
  Main entry under title: ·
    Modern Canada, 1930-1980's

  (Readings in Canadian social history; v. 5)
  ISBN 0-7710-2460-6

  1. Canada – Social conditions.   2. Canada – Economic
  conditions – 20th century.   I. Cross, Michael S.,
  1938-   II. Kealey, Gregory S., 1948-
  III. Series.

  FC600.M62 1984   971.064   C83-099312-6
  F1034.2.M62 1984

Printed and bound in Canada by Webcom Ltd.

Contents

General Introduction
– The Series

The emergence of social history has been perhaps the most significant development of the last fifteen years in Canadian historical writing. Historians young and old have brought new approaches and new perspectives to Canada's past, revealing areas previously overlooked and offering new interpretations of old areas. The result has been what historian Ramsay Cook has called the discipline's "golden age." This five-volume series of readers in social history is intended to make the fruits of that "golden age" readily available to teachers, students, and general readers.

Modern social history is an approach rather than a specific subject matter. Where once social history was seen as what was left over after political and economic history was written, social history now is a "global" discipline, which can embrace politics and economics as well as the history of social groups or charitable institutions. The ideal of social history is to write the history of society, to study all of the ways in which people, groups of people, and classes of people interact to produce a society and to create social change. Such a global picture may never be drawn but its goal of an integrated history underlies recent study in Canada. The social historian, then, may write about a small subject over a limited period of time. However, that historian must be conscious of the links to the larger reality; of how local politics, say, indicate the relations of social classes, how they react with ideological assumptions of provincial politicians, how they affect local social customs.

It is a new field and that means its effort has been scattered. Canadian social history has embraced everything from the study of women's groups to computer analysis of population changes, to the history of disease. It also has been marked by some sharp differences of opinion. The editors of this series, as practitioners and partisans, make no claim to objectivity in assessing these differences. Broadly, some historians treat social history as an extension of previous historical writing and share its assumptions about the general sweep of Canadian development: its liberal-democratic character; its fluid class structure; its peaceful and orderly growth. Others, however, break from that interpretation and argue for a different picture: a more rigid and influential class structure; a greater degree of conflict and violence; an emphasis on the working class. Which interpretation will prevail remains to be seen. The essays chosen for the series attempt to present as many viewpoints as possible, but the overall structure clearly reflects the judgement of the editors, which favours the second approach, the "working class" approach.

Rather than being structured along the traditional political divisions, the volumes in the series have been organized around dates which seemed most appropriate to social history.

I New France to the Conquest, 1760

II Pre-Industrial Canada, from the Conquest to the end of the imperial economic system, 1760 to 1849

III The Age of Industry, from the coming of the railway to the full flowering of industrialism, 1849 to 1896

IV The Consolidation of Capitalism, from the beginnings of economic monopoly to the Great Crash, 1896 to 1929

V The Emergence of the Welfare State, from the origins of large-scale state intervention to the present, 1930 to 1981.

Again, the internal divisions of the volumes have been chosen to illustrate basic themes that represent building blocks in social history. Not all themes could be included and some historians might argue with the particular choices made here. We would suggest several rationales for the selection: these themes seem important to us; the volume of writing and research on them, completed and underway, suggests that many others find them important; and they have proven useful in teaching social history.

Different periods and the availability of good literature require some variance from volume to volume. The general structure, however, is consistent. Each volume begins with an essay on the major economic developments of the period, for we work from the assumption that changing economic forms underlie most social changes. The second theme is that of social structure and social institutions, of the classes and groups of Canadian society and the way in which they interact. This theme will embrace subject matter as diverse as politics, religion, and land-holding patterns.

Certain groups have emerged to centre stage historically in recent years. One is workers, the third theme in each volume. Workers and their work have been perhaps the area of richest development in historical writing in the last decade; social history has made its most profound impact in reshaping historical knowledge in this area. The fourth theme is one in which social history has had a similarly important influence, if only because interest in it is so recent. That is violence and protest, now receiving close attention from historians, sociologists, and criminologists. Violence and protest involved many Canadians and touched the lives of many more, and therefore are significant in their own right. However, they also provide a sharply defined picture of the structures and values of the society in which they occurred. The things people consider important enough to fight and protest about give us some indication of the values of particular groups. The attitudes of the leadership of society emerge in the fifth theme, social control. This theme studies the checks placed on violence and protest and inappropriate behaviour, as well as the institutions created to mould appropriate behaviour.

Along with workers, the other group to receive due attention from social history is women. No area, perhaps, was so neglected for so long as the study of women, outside of occasional writing on the suffrage movement. Recently, however, there has been a flood of literature, not just on feminism and women's organizations, but on women's productive and reproductive work. In a field devoted to creation of an integrated picture of society, this is a welcome and exciting development. Some of the trends in women's history, and some of the major achievements, are illustrated in these volumes.

The structure adopted here is offered as a useful one which will open to teachers and to students an exciting area of Canadian studies. It makes no claim to comprehensiveness; it is very much a starting point for that study. The additional readings suggested will help to move beyond that starting point and to introduce the controversies which cannot be reflected adequately in the small number of essays reprinted here. These volumes, however, do serve as a report on some approaches we have found helpful to students of social history and on some of the best literature available in this new field. More, they are collected on the premise that the investigation of social change in Canadian history, the ideas exposed and the questions raised, may allow students to understand more fully the nature of the Canadian society in which they live.

M.S. Cross
G.S. Kealey
Halifax and
St. John's,
July, 1981

Introduction
to Volume 5

Every generation believes that it lives in a period of unusually rapid change.Those who have experienced the evolution of Canadian society since 1930 may have more reason than most for holding that opinion, however. Depression, war, post-war boom, technological revolution, upheaval in male-female and family relationships, the coming of the microchip world – the forces of change have been overwhelming. The essays in this book touch on some of the major themes in this complex process of social alteration.

The clearest marks on the period are the long, deep scars left by depression and war. The "Great Depression" is usually described as extending from the stock market crash of October 1929 until the outbreak of World War II in September 1939. For parts of Canada the agony was more extended. In western Canada the economy had begun to shake in 1928, with unstable world markets for wheat and the beginning of a devastating drought in Saskatchewan. The grain exchange in Winnipeg collapsed, with plummeting wheat prices, a few days before the New York stock market crashed into panic in 1929. The Maritimes had suffered a quiet depression for most of the 1920's because of low fish prices and a declining industrial base. Many Canadians during the 1920's, a period of very uneven growth and a weak union movement, were already poor, desperately poor by the standards of the 1980's. Yet things got much worse for most Canadians after October 1929. By 1933 national income had declined by 50 per cent; in drought-tormented Saskatchewan the gross provincial income fell by 72 per cent as the price of wheat sagged from $1.65 to 30 cents a bushel over the four years. Some 15 per cent of the Canadian population was on direct government relief, at a time when the qualification for relief was absolute destitution. With unemployment between 20 and 30 per cent, tens of thousands of young men rode the rails from place to place, vainly searching for somewhere that economic conditions were better. Even the coming of war did not bring immediate respite. Unemployment remained high until the war effort moved into high gear in 1940.

This unparalleled economic disaster challenged many of the assumptions upon which Canadian society had operated. The belief that opportunity existed for all, that hard work would produce economic success, was difficult to sustain when millions were denied employment and driven into poverty by the mysterious illness of the economic system. The virtue of unregulated capitalism was no longer apparent to all. A variety of political movements, of the right, centre, and left, emerged in the 1930's, all calling into question some or all of the tenets of the traditional economy. They reflected an important change in the attitudes of the Canadian people. The misery of the depression produced growing demands for government action, first to provide basic relief for the unemployed, eventually to create a buttress of security against the irrationalities of the old economic order.

Governments moved ponderously to respond to these demands. By 1940 the most basic was met with the establishment of a national unemployment insurance scheme. The war then accomplished what the depression could not; it convinced government that the demands of the people could and must be met. The idealism and sacrifice of war made it clear that the country could not be permitted to sink back into the degradation of the depression. And the success of government management of the war economy was proof that government had the resources and the capability to protect its citizens. Government initiatives to do so took two forms. One was action to smooth out economic cycles, to avoid depression, by fiscal policy, encouragement of private enterprise, and, where absolutely necessary, direct government operation of certain industries such as petrochemicals. The other was the creation of the "welfare state." Family allowances, federal support for housing construction, and funding for universities – these and other programs marked a wide extension of government responsibility in the immediate post-war years. They would be followed by even more dramatic extensions, beginning in 1958 with hospital insurance. The Canada Pension Plan, medicare, and a myriad of other welfare schemes were spun out, the compelling legacy of depression's misery and war's idealism.

The creation of the welfare state was one of the central realities of the period. It is important for the obvious reasons that it assured a minimal standard of living for Canadians and that it led to an enormous increase in the size and influence of government. It is important in other ways as well. The welfare state was the governmental expression of a more general concern with security and greater social justice, which itself was a reaction to the depression and war. The lust for security was seen on the international scene, where Canada sought guarantees against the return of war, first on a world-wide basis in the founding of the United Nations in 1945, then more narrowly and militarily in the North Atlantic Alliance in 1949. It was seen at home, where Canadians attempted to expunge memories of privation in the materialism of a "consumer society." It was seen in the great emphasis placed on education and on the young. The desire to make life secure for the new generation, to make certain that one's children had an easier life, was a motivation behind many of the characteristic features of post-war society: the provision of an elaborate, expensive educational system; the emergence of "permissive" models of child-rearing (in Canada, as in the United States, perhaps only the Bible exceeded the book sales of Dr. Spock's *Baby and Child Care*); the exodus to the suburbs in the search for a better environment for children.

It was a painful paradox for many when, in the 1960's, some of their children rebelled against consumerism, security-consciousness, and their middle-class environment. The student revolts on university campuses and the large demonstrations against the Vietnam War after 1965 had very specific targets, whether authoritarian educational systems or a war of dubious morality. They also were understandable outgrowths, along with the hippie movement and the drug culture, of society's development since 1945. To many, it seemed, the concern with security and consumption had made the world more comfortable physically but not necessarily more satisfying. And to many it appeared that if greater security had been achieved, the twin desire for social justice had been forgotten. And it perhaps should not have been surprising that the young – the focus of so much attention, those for whom the world was to be made better – should have shared society's estimate of their importance and attempted to mould that world themselves.

The welfare state and the consumer society were also important for what they did not do. The young critics were correct. Despite a rising standard of living and extensive social security programs, wealth was not substantially redistributed across Canadian society. Comparisons in 1950 and thirty years later showed little change in the distribution of national income; the gap between rich and poor had not narrowed. Indeed, that gap may even have widened during the depression of the 1930's. While millions were unemployed, some profited greatly from declining prices and the opportunity to buy property cheaply. What the later elaboration of the welfare state did, then, was not to transfer a larger proportion of national income to the disadvantaged. Rather, it provided a safety net against the worst of economic misfortunes and, in the process, obscured the fact that the gap between rich and poor was not closing.

If the social reality of income distribution did not change, many other aspects of Canadian society did. Population shifted. Devastated by the depression, Saskatchewan lost population and did not fully stabilize until the latter half of the 1970's. The Maritimes and Newfoundland, which joined confederation in 1949, continued to decline in population in comparison with the rest of the country. British Columbia and Alberta, buoyed by burgeoning resource industries, especially after 1960, grew rapidly in both population and wealth. The industrial centre of the country, Ontario and Quebec, grew in the post-war boom but stagnated when Canadian industry weakened after about 1968 and showed signs of serious illness after the world oil crisis of 1973. Despite the overall growth of the Canadian economy through most of the period, the unevenness of that development led to questioning of the system. That questioning often had social as well as purely economic sources.

The essays in this book explore the roots and nature of some of these critiques of Canadian development. Paul Phillips and Stephen Watson discuss the extent and influence of foreign ownership, which was debated heatedly throughout the period and was the subject of three landmark commissions of inquiry: the Royal Commission on Canada's Economic Prospects, which reported in 1957 under the chairpersonship of Walter Gordon, who later became Liberal Finance Minister; the task force on foreign ownership led by economist Melville Watkins, which reported in 1968; and another task force headed by cabinet minister Herb Gray, whose report was leaked to the press in 1971. Despite all the studies, foreign ownership in the Canadian economy remained, like the weather, something that was much talked about but about which little effective was done. The studies and debates were far from simple economic ones. The issue was closely connected to concern over the survival of a distinctively Canadian culture. Foreign influence, in an age of television (which came to Canada with the first CBC stations in Toronto and Montreal in 1952), mass advertising, and more influential popular entertainment – all of which were heavily influenced by American culture – extended well beyond the gates of the branch plants.

Foreign ownership was only one issue in a continuing debate over economic policy. David Wolfe's article assesses the impact of the most powerful economic theories of the last fifty years, those of English economist John Maynard Keynes. Inspired in part by Keynes, the intervention of government during World

War II to strike a working balance between the economic interests of capital and workers was controversial. Equally controversial was the federal government's retreat from Keynes in the 1970's in its new preoccupation with inflation and the needs of business.

Michael Behiels explores the reaction of Quebec intellectuals to the impact of the modern economy in their society. From the beginning of the "Quiet Revolution" in 1960 until the Quebec referendum on sovereignty association in 1980, that province's struggle for economic, cultural, and linguistic distinctiveness was at the forefront of Canadian concerns. It produced dramatic changes outside Quebec as well as within. Controversies over the federal government's adoption of bilingualism marked the 1970's but, despite a good deal of opposition, relations between the two major linguistic groups did shift substantially toward greater equality in federal and provincial civil services and in acceptance of French as a working language. Quebec's insistence on its need for greater financial resources to accomplish its cultural goals helped to produce a reassertion of provincial authority in the 1960's and 1970's; this somewhat checked the flowering of federal power begun during World War II.

Another group of questioners was women. Ruth Pierson and Marjorie Cohen's article discusses the emergence of women into the work world as a result of manpower shortages during the war. They demonstrate the strength of traditional attitudes, as women were rapidly shepherded back into the home at war's end. If the quasi-liberation of World War II had been a false start, it was nevertheless true that the economic and social conditions of the period after 1945 inexorably altered the traditional confinement of women to the domestic sphere. Sectors of the economy where some women had been employed, such as education, secretarial and clerical fields, and food and other services, grew rapidly, making more room for women workers. Mechanization of housework made it somewhat easier to combine outside work with the domestic chores that remained largely the responsibility of women, even women employed outside the home. Although an ever-growing proportion of the work force, women remained underrepresented in skilled and prestigious jobs. They also earned much less than men, with no apparent narrowing of the gap between male and female wage levels throughout the period. Given these facts, it was to be expected that some women would question the apparent sexual inequalities in society. The "women's liberation movement," as it came to be called in the 1960's, expressed concern not only over economic disparities but over the whole range of male-female relationships. As Quebec's questioning reached a culmination in the election of a Parti Québécois government in 1976, so women's questioning was focused during International Women's Year in 1975.

Equally dramatic, at times, were the protests of labour, chronicled here by Wayne Roberts and John Bullen and by Wallace Clement. As with all societies, however, Canada has avoided social dislocation and limited questioning of socio-economic structures through social control. One important instrument of social control has been the educational system. Along with its skill-training and cultural-enrichment functions, the education system transmits to the young an appreciation of the values of society. In this collection Paul Axelrod discusses higher education, which grew even more rapidly than the rest of the educational system. All levels of schooling, however, flourished in the atmosphere of the post-war world. Education was seen as an important guarantee of security for individuals, who could expect better and higher-paying jobs as a result of their education, and for society, given the conventional wisdom that a better-educated population speeded economic development. Only at the end of this period was this relationship between education and economic return seriously questioned.

The preoccupation with education since 1945 illustrates many of the characteristics of modern Canadian society, including the desire for economic security and a richer cultural life. It illustrates, too, modern society's hope for the young and faith in the expert. At its core for many Canadians who lived through depression and war is a desire for more equal opportunity. The failure to provide that opportunity, as equally and as quickly as our social rhetoric seemed to promise, stimulated the questioning by labour, women's groups, and others. It generated restlessness, too, in a sector of society almost invisible for generations, the native peoples. There was a striking parallel between native demands and those of the Canadian regions, especially Quebec. Natives began to ask for the individual and collective opportunity that society's rhetoric promised to all. They sought to use the tools of modern society to achieve it, through employment of the expertise of educated professionals to argue land claims – just as Quebec nationalism was driven by the new professionals. Yet they sought to retain traditional values while sharing the largesse of the modern economy, again a balancing act very similar to that of the Québécois. The delicacy of that balancing act was shown in the painfully slow progress the native peoples made toward their goals.

Not only native Canadians but most Canadians struggled with the balance between change and continuity. The much greater emphasis put on cultural survival was one element in the balance. From the Royal Commission on National Development in the Arts, Letters and Sciences (the Massey Report) of 1951, which led to such initiatives in "high culture" as the creation of the Canada Council, to the growing popularity of genealogical research, the desire to retain one's roots in an era of change was apparent.

The impact of change, education, and new ideas often made this desire difficult. Religion, for example, struggled to maintain an institutional relevance in the period. The church was still central in Canadian life in the 1930's, even in politics. The leadership of Quebec nationalism came from a priest, Abbé Lionel Groulx. In Alberta, Social Credit was as much a revival meeting as a political party under the lay preacher William Aberhart. The social democratic CCF was fuelled by the social conscience of Protestantism and led by a former minister, J.S. Woodsworth. Religion moved from the centre of society in the materialistic post-war world. This was shown by the severing of the links of church and state – the secularization of education in Quebec, the easing of governmental restrictions on Sunday sports and entertainment, and the like. It was shown, too, in the debates within the churches over modernization of ritual and the role of churches in social action. Religion was affected, as well, by the demographic changes of the period. English Canada, once British and Protestant, was inundated by European immigrants. By the 1980's, this immigrant tide had made Canada a majority Catholic country.

Writing about the immediate past is never easy because the insights derived from the longer view are not available. It is more difficult yet when dealing with a bewildering pace of change. In this volume we have chosen to commission new essays rather than to reprint published articles, as in previous books in the series. All our authors have published innovative work on modern Canada; we chose them because of their fresh perspectives on our recent past.

The topics that these authors have explored were ones on which they had special expertise, as well as being ones that they and the editors thought important. They do not add up to the sum of Canada's social experience since 1930. We hope that they do begin the process of answering the most fundamental historical questions: who are we as a people and how did we become what we are?

I
Economic Overview

In the two following essays, our authors try to make sense out of the Canadian economy, an effort which at the moment seems beyond the capacity of the federal government. The magnitude of the current economic crisis demands an historical comprehension of its origins. In the first essay, Paul Phillips and Stephen Watson survey the depressing state of the Canadian economy in the post-war period and analyse the decisions of the C.D. Howe-directed Liberals in favour of resource extraction. In the following contribution, David Wolfe chronicles the decline of the "social contract" of the 1945 White Paper on Employment and Income. The recent destruction of this post-war settlement in Canadian government economic policy has its echoes in social and labour policy, as we shall see elsewhere in this volume.

The crisis of the Great Depression and the valiant national war effort in the fight against fascism left Canadians committed to the struggle for social and economic democracy in 1945. In those years before the advent of the Cold War and with the recent memory of a northern alliance with the Soviet Union, Canadians showed little suspicion of either government centralization or nationalization. The demands for social programs found some support even among the Liberal mandarins in Ottawa, many of whom had been influenced by both Keynesian and social democratic ideas. Yet the prevailing ideological commitment to capitalism and to continentalism led to the willing dismantling of a plethora of Canadian war industries that had represented a potential basis for post-war economic advance. The sale of these national assets at bargain-basement prices, often to United States corporations, should have seemed contradictory to the new social contract. Yet this apparent contradiction was unimaginable to C.D. Howe or his ilk. Thus, in the late 1940's, a wave of capital concentration under private control commenced, a surge that saw the corporate control of new Canadian giants, such as Argus Corporation formed by brewing magnate E.P. Taylor in 1945, solidified over large segments of the Canadian economy. The close ties between these corporate monoliths and the Canadian government, on both its political and civil service sides, has often been chronicled. Indeed, the careers of many Canadian cabinet ministers and important mandarins from the King, St. Laurent, Pearson, and Trudeau years illustrate this point only too well.

In the 1950's, after the advent of the Cold War, the total Canadian commitment to NATO, to Norad, and to the concomitant Joint Defence Sharing contracts marked the demise of more than the possibility of an independent foreign policy. The massive extent of continental integration was hardly even noted until the rise of economic nationalism in the 1960's. While dealing with one major problem of the Canadian economy – foreign control – too often economic nationalism has not addressed the undemocratic nature even of Canadian domestic corporate capital. Neither the Foreign Investment Review Act nor the National Energy Program is adequate to deal with this question, although Petrocan has been an important and much-needed innovation.

FURTHER READING:
For uncritical acclaim of C.D. Howe, see the biography by Robert Bothwell and William Kilbourn (Toronto, 1979). A survey of material on the emergence of Canadian economic nationalism would include: Kari Levitt, *Silent Surrender: The Multinational Corporation in Canada* (Toronto, 1970); *Foreign Ownership and the Structure of Canadian Industry* (Ottawa, 1968), popularly known as the Watkins Report; *A Citizen's Guide to the Gray Report* (Toronto, 1971); Philip Resnick, *The Land of Cain: Nationalism in English Canada, 1945-75* (Vancouver, 1977); and Wallace Clement, *Continental Corporate Power: Economic Elite Linkage Between Canada and the United States* (Toronto, 1979). Contrasting views are offered in John Richards and Larry Pratt, *Prairie Capitalism: Power and Influence in the New West* (Toronto, 1979); Jorge Niosi, *The Economy of Canada – A Study of Ownership and Control* (Montreal, 1979, 1982) and his *Canadian Capitalism – A Study of Power in the Canadian Business Establishment* (Toronto, 1981). An interesting recent debate on these topics is Philip Resnick, "The Maturing of Canadian Capitalism," *Our Generation,* 15, 3 (Fall, 1982), 11-24; and Jorge Niosi, "Response," *Our Generation*, 15, 4 (Spring, 1983), 51-5.

Paul Phillips and **Stephen Watson** are economists at the University of Manitoba. **David A. Wolfe** teaches political science at the University of Toronto.

From Mobilization
to Continentalism:
The Canadian Economy in
the Post-Depression Period

by Paul Phillips and Stephen Watson

INTRODUCTION

The Great Depression of the 1930's was a traumatic experience for Canada. The century that was to belong to Canada was less than a third old when the economy came crashing down amid unemployment among the wage-earners, drought among the western farmers, and despair among most citizens. The depression that originated in America and spread through most of the western industrial world seemed to be particularly serious in Canada, bringing to an end the great vision of a vibrant, economically integrated nation, *a mari usque ad mare*. The dreams of the architects of Confederation had at least temporarily been shattered.

In fact, even without the depression, the great expansion of the Canadian economy that had been associated with the National Policy had reached its end. This was symbolized by the return to the provinces in 1930 of what remained unalienated of the western land that the federal government had retained control of prior to this time to subsidize railway construction and to entice settlers into the region. Regardless of current criticism of the National Policy, that it resulted in an artificial economic structure (criticism that is by no means universally accepted), there can be little doubt that it was a remarkably successful *development* strategy in terms of welding the diverse economic regions of British North America into an economic and political unit.[1]

An analytic look at the National Policy reveals its internal logic. Its essence was to socialize under the federal government the investment costs of the development strategy. The primary vehicles were: land grants, direct subsidies, and monopolistic markets to finance railway construction; subsidies (bonuses), patent protection, and tariff protection to underwrite manufacturing investment. The investment that resulted, culminating in the great western wheat boom, has been well-documented.[2]

But the West was settled and agriculture had spread to virtually all arable areas by the late 1920's. Not one but three transcontinental railway systems had been built, and in the 1920's branch lines were extended to most communities in the region. The National Policy, having achieved its goal, was abandoned. Only its vestigial remnants were left – the tariff system, the Crow's Nest Pass rates, federal regulation of the transport and grain-handling systems, and the now publicly owned Canadian National Railways.

The depression, therefore, hit Canada at a time when the country was in a development policy vacuum, although this was little recognized at the time as international trade collapsed and with it investment. Government economic intervention came from the politics of necessity, not of design. Even Conservative Prime Minister Bennett's eleventh-hour conversion in 1935 to the necessity of social security programs was a victim of the deluded, politically motivated Judicial Committee of the British Privy Council. On the other hand, government intervention in the form of investment in commerce, communications, and transportation was more successful, as evidenced by the formation under the Conservatives of the Bank of Canada and the Canadian Wheat Board, both at first in essence public support for private capital. Later in the decade, the Liberals formed the Canadian Broadcasting Corporation and Trans Canada Airlines. Other rescue policies, such as the aid given to the attempted cartelization of the pulp and paper industry, were less successful.

As the decade neared its end and the depression showed little sign of imminent disappearance, the government, now under the otherworldly Liberal, Mackenzie King, cast around for new policy alternatives. His fishermen included Royal Commissioners Rowell and Sirois, whose Report on Dominion-Provincial Relations was ready just as war was engulfing the world. Concerns about economic development and stabilization policy gave way to a preoccupation with war mobilization. Ideological debate on investment policy took a back seat to gearing up the Canadian economy for the European war.

THE WAR ECONOMY

The start of World War II pushed the government to embark on a program for economic development that, for boldness and scope, was matched only by Confederation and the National

Policy. The object of wartime economic policy was victory in war, not economic development, but the resulting growth in the Canadian economy was very impressive. The real Gross National Product in 1944 was 80 per cent larger than it had been in 1938. Moreover, the real growth in GNP in the peak year of 1942 – 18.6 per cent – was twice as high as the highest growth rate achieved since 1945: 9.4 per cent in 1955. The unemployment rate, which had been 20 per cent or more (depending on the estimate) during the worst part of the Great Depression and at least 11 per cent in 1939, fell as low as 1.4 per cent during the war. Real investment during the five years 1940 to 1944 was 68.7 per cent higher than in the preceding five years.[3]

In addition to a high rate of growth, there were also significant changes in the Canadian economy. The dominance of natural resource production declined in the face of rapid growth in the manufacturing sector. In the years 1926 to 1939, manufacturing accounted, on average, for only 22.6 per cent of Gross Domestic Product. This ratio reached a peak of 32 per cent during the war as the real GDP in manufacturing increased by about 125 per cent from 1938 to 1943. Moreover, much of the increased manufacturing output came from industries that had hardly existed before the war, and these new industries tended to be relatively advanced ones such as aircraft, synthetic rubber, and electrical instruments.

Another important change was the increased size of the federal government. Its expenditures rose from 9.2 per cent of GNP in 1938 to 44.6 per cent in 1944, although this had declined to about 12 per cent by the late 1940's. What was of greater importance perhaps was the increased size of the federal government as compared to provincial and local governments. The federal government accounted for 40 per cent of all government expenditure in 1938, and 87 per cent in 1944. This only declined to 56 per cent in the late 1940's before starting to rise again.

The economic policy that rendered these results entailed a high degree of federal government intervention in the economy. In part, the difference between the government's wartime policy and its policy in other periods was simply a matter of degree; government in Canada has often undertaken to promote development by building infrastructure, supplying capital assistance to private firms, or setting up Crown corporations. It simply did these things on a larger scale during the Second World War. Some aspects of wartime policy, however, were quite different in nature from what has been done at other times. Most significantly, the government took direct responsibility for a large part of new investment. Certainly, the government has invested heavily in economic development in other periods – the CPR and the St. Lawrence Seaway are just two examples – but the difference in the Second World War was that the government's investment was not concentrated in one large project. It was spread through several sectors of the economy and many projects. In fact, it is possible to consider the government's policy as an example of the socialization of investment called for by John Maynard Keynes. (Briefly, socialization of investment is the determination of the level and structure of investment by the government reflecting collective socio-economic priorities, rather than by the private sector reflecting corporate profit maximization.) This makes it all the more interesting given that, in spite of the policy's success, it was abandoned at the end of the war in favour of what has been called "bastard Keynesianism," where the government attempts to influence investment using only broad levers of monetary and fiscal policy through which it hopes to affect the profit levels of private investment.

The economic problem facing the government during the war was to increase rapidly the supply of everything required for the war effort. And that covered just about everything produced in the economy: arms, ammunition, tanks, ships, airplanes, communications equipment, uniforms, eating utensils, blankets, rope, food, fuel. . . . The list was effectively endless. In other words, the war forced the country to embark on a program of intensive economic development.

Despite the undoubted commitment of the King government to private enterprise, it did not believe that mobilization of an economy for high-speed development could be left solely to private initiative. Had the government so believed, it would simply have placed orders for the things that were needed and waited for the private sector to produce them. In fact, the government instituted what we might call socialism, capitalist style; during the war, Canada had a centrally planned economy in which market mechanisms were largely superseded by administrative decisions, while ownership of most of the productive capacity was left in private hands.

The locus of the government's planning and control of the war economy was the Department of Munitions and Supply (DMS), established under C.D. Howe, in April 1940. DMS soon acquired responsibility for most major aspects of the war effort. The major exception was price control, although there was close co-operation between the Wartime Prices and Trade Board and DMS. The powers and responsibilities of DMS were so broad that it is difficult to summarize them. It is easier to consider the major subdivisions of DMS separately.

The Wartime Industries Control Board was composed of fifteen controllers, each responsible for a particular key industry such as steel, base metals, power, aircraft, motor vehicles, machine tools, and so on. The job of each was to ensure that adequate supplies of the goods within his purview were available for the war effort. They did this in two ways: by pursuing various measures to increase production, and by restricting the non-essential use of controlled commodities. Their powers were virtually unlimited and included the rights to purchase, expropriate, manufacture, ration, and whatever else proved necessary. Most controllers were also appointed as administrators of the Wartime Prices and Trade Board for purposes of controlling prices.

Let us take the metals controller as an example. Two basic mechanisms were employed to increase the production of base metal ores and fabricated products. First, a Crown company, Wartime Metals Corporation, was formed to supervise the rehabilitation of mines that were uneconomic prior to the war and, less frequently, to develop new mines. In most cases, the corporation contracted with private mining companies to do the work on a management fee basis. Second, on the advice of the controller, the government constructed new plants or additions to existing plants for the purpose of fabricating metal products. Most of these plants were operated by private firms on behalf of the government.

The other job of the metals controller was to restrict and regulate the consumption of metals so that as much as possible was available for war use. For example, the use of aluminum was prohibited in the manufacture of cooking utensils, electrical conductors, and aluminum foil, other than for essential war needs. Most of the dozens of orders issued by the metals controller were much more specific so that Order MC 17, for example, restricted the use of copper and zinc in lithography, photoengraving, and electrotyping. MC 22 prohibited the use of any base metal, except in the form of wire or cable, in the manufacture of organs.

Another major division of DMS was the Production Board and eleven associated production branches. Each branch was responsible for a particular class of supplies such as aircraft, chemicals and explosives, or army vehicles (the exception being the Economics and Statistics Branch, which produced the data necessary for centralized economic planning). The branches took whatever action was necessary to ensure that the required items were forthcoming. This involved a variety of activities including the building and running of factories owned by the Crown, contracting with private firms for the production of finished goods or components, sponsoring applications by private firms for government capital assistance, drawing up blueprints and design specifications, procuring machine tools or other equipment for manufacturers, running training schools to provide the necessary skilled labour, procuring purchase orders from the armed forces of Canada and other countries, and so on.

For example, the Aircraft Production Branch supervised the expansion of the Canadian aircraft industry from an average output of about forty aircraft a year before the war to an annual average of 4,031 over the three years 1942 to 1944. The branch oversaw the investment by the government of $83.3 million in aircraft production capacity, including $8 million in the government-owned Victory Aircraft company, which operated the largest single airplane factory in the country and produced the famous Lancaster bomber. One other aircraft manufacturer – Federal Aircraft – was government-owned but the other companies that received federal investment funds were private. These included DeHavilland, Canadian Vickers, and Boeing of Canada. The branch also established training facilities for labour and operated an Overhaul and Repair Division that serviced 6,500 airframes and over 30,000 engines, as well as assembling 2,500 British aircraft.

Much of the department's influence over the war effort was effected through Crown corporations. The minister had full discretionary power over these corporations and delegated broad responsibilities to them. An important advantage of Crown corporations was that they were less constrained than a regular government department or agency. They were also a form of organization familiar to the private-sector businessmen who were usually appointed to head them.

It should be emphasized that most of the wartime Crown corporations were not directly involved in production. Of the twenty-eight wholly government-owned companies established during the war, only nine actually operated plants. The other nineteen fulfilled administrative and purchasing functions. For example, the Wartime Metals Corporation oversaw fourteen mining projects, but all of the actual testing, mine rehabilitation, and production was done by private mining companies under contract to Wartime Metals Corporation. The role of WMC was to identify the projects to be undertaken, contract with private firms to do the work, arrange financing, and provide general supervision. Except for one lawyer and a former Quebec Minister of Mines, all the directors and officers of WMC had been seconded to the corporation by private mining companies.

For example, the president of WMC was also president of Hollinger Consolidated Gold Mines.

The foregoing description of DMS gives some idea of the means by which the government organized the wartime economic expansion. But we must also step back and look at the larger picture to see the government's role in the economy.

The engine of economic growth is investment. What the government did during the Second World War was to increase sharply the volume of investment. For the most part, it did so directly by investing government funds rather than indirectly via tax incentives and such (although these indirect methods were used to some extent). The sharp increase in the government's direct investment is reflected in Figure 1, which shows investment by government departments, enterprises, and institutions as a percentage of total public and private investment. Public investment was 25 per cent or less of the total prior to the depression and rose to a peak of 36 per cent in 1932 as a result of a more rapid decline in private than public investment. But in each of the four years 1940 to 1943, public investment rose almost vertically until, in 1943, it accounted for 42 per cent of the total. (The public investment figures include all levels of government, but the wartime increases are mainly attributable to the federal government.) Note that this increase in the *relative* amount of public investment occurred even though the absolute amount of private investment was also increasing: between 1939 and 1942, nominal private investment increased by 80 per cent; nominal public investment increased 201 per cent.

Prior to the war boom, large flows of public investment were associated with a few major infrastructure projects such as transportation systems or hydroelectric power development. Thus, there are at least two ways in which public investment during the war differed from past experience. First, investment was not concentrated in a few projects, but was widely disbursed over many projects. Second, much of the investment went not to infrastructure development, as was traditional, but to the manufacturing sector, which had always been the preserve of private capital.

Between September 1, 1939, and December 31, 1945, the federal government invested $718 million in 247 Crown plants that manufactured items required for the war effort ranging from blankets to Lancaster bombers. The government retained ownership of almost all of the plant and equipment in which it invested, at least until the end of the war. However, only a fairly small proportion of this productive capacity was actually operated by the government. Fifty-six per cent of the government's

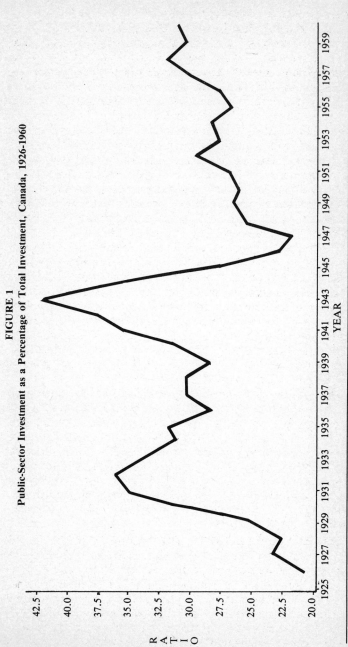

FIGURE 1

Public-Sector Investment as a Percentage of Total Investment, Canada, 1926-1960

SOURCE: M.C. Urquhart and K.A.H. Buckley, *Historical Statistics of Canada.*

direct investment in war production facilities was spent on Crown plants operated by private firms for a management fee. Another 23 per cent was spent on alterations and extensions to privately owned and operated plants, although the government retained ownership of all extensions or new equipment it paid for. Plants operated by Crown corporations accounted for only 13 per cent of the investment, and the remaining 8 per cent was spent on plants operated by government departments.

As an exercise in economic development, this policy was unique. Instead of merely trying to create conditions favourable to investment or plying potential investors with tax inducements – practices that may or may not produce the desired results – the government acted directly to increase the flow of investment in the manufacturing sector. On the other hand, instead of trying to create Crown corporations to operate all the new plants and equipment, which would have entailed a still larger expansion of the government sector at a time when skilled people were in extremely short supply, the government simply contracted with private firms to operate the new capacity. Thus, the government was able to achieve both certainty of outcome and efficiency of operation.

It should be noted that the government's investment in manufacturing accounted for only a portion of its investment during the war. There was also a large volume of investment in housing, transportation, defence installations, and so on. Some of the results of the government's wartime economic policy are summarized in Table 1.

TABLE 1
Performance of the Canadian Economy during World War II

	% Increase GNP	% Increase GDP in Manu- facturing	Unemployment Rate
1939	7.4	7.4	11.4
1940	14.1	28.9	9.2
1941	14.4	37.3	4.4
1942	18.6	30.2	3.0
1943	4.0	10.9	1.7
1944	4.0	–0.7	1.4

SOURCE: Statistics Canada, National Income and Expenditure Accounts.

That the government's wartime economic policy was successful did not mean that it was carried over into peacetime. At the earliest possible date most aspects of the war economy were dismantled. The government's economic policy for the post-war period was set out in a White Paper entitled "Employment and Income with Special Reference to the Initial Period of Reconstruction" (commonly referred to as the White Paper on Employment and Income), presented to Parliament in April 1945 by C.D. Howe.

THE "AMERICAN BOOM" IN CANADA

The White Paper on Employment and Income and the accompanying Proposals of the Government of Canada to the Dominion-Provincial Conference on Reconstruction (the Green Book) were the blueprint of post-war economic policy and marked a distinct break both with the interventionist, entrepreneurial mobilization policies of the wartime period and the ad hoc crisis-response policies of the 1930's. The prime concern of the federal government was to ensure that the depression "would never happen again." Hence, the focus was on fiscal and monetary policies to stabilize the economy, policies based at least in part on the economic theories advanced by British economist John Maynard Keynes in 1935. The opening statement of the White Paper, which set out as the primary object of government policy the maintenance of a high and stable level of income and employment, established the tone.

Stabilization held centre stage in the government's post-war plans, yet the two policy papers included also the framework of a larger economic development policy. While maintaining the earlier National Policy's reliance on staple exports as the engine of growth and on imported capital to finance the investment required to expand staples production, these policy statements departed in a very important way from the earlier policy framework. As the architect of the policy, W.A. Mackintosh, has written:

> From 1942 on, the Government of Canada has pressed strongly for postwar international arrangements which would increase the freedom of movement of trade and capital. Realizing the extent to which international trade contributed to our national income and the import of capital had assisted national development, the government pressed strongly for the elimination of all extraordinary and bilateral trade restrictions and control of capital movements such as had made the decade of the thirties so destructive of international economic relations. Increased freedom and multilateral trade were the major points of the Canadian case.[4]

Though tariffs in fact came down only very slowly over the following decades, the policy vision was in marked contrast to that of the previous century. Canada had come to rely even more heavily on natural resource exports for its growth. This was reflected in the policy papers not only by the abandonment of the concept of a protected manufacturing sector, but also by the emphasis on federal expenditures for the conservation and development of natural resources. Also unlike the National Policy period, control of natural resource development was not within the powers of the federal government but resided with the provincial governments. Hence, the federal government's role was viewed essentially as only facilitory.

In any case, the Canadian economy, and indeed the international economic constellation, in 1945 was very different from what it had been in the last decades of the nineteenth century. In the earlier period industrialization was just beginning and the manufacturing sector was dominated by small, competitive firms. The vehicle of staples expansion was seen to be agriculture, carried out by thousands of independent producers. The government's interest in supporting capital formation was concentrated on the commercial and transportation needs of this industry and in supporting the manufacturing industries catering to this staples-induced expansion. The source of finance was the bond markets of Britain; the market for exports, the industrial populations of Europe.

How different the conditions in 1945. The resources were under provincial jurisdiction and required immense capital investments within the control of large, multinational, primarily American corporations, and the market was the voracious industrial sector in the United States. Federal aid to investment was in two forms: infrastructure (including transportation and mineral surveys) and tax incentives. The provincial governments proved even more generous in their support of resource capital, forgoing all but minimal royalties, ignoring the conservation of renewable resources (such as reforestation), and permitting the resource companies to foul the environment. At the same time the provinces were building roads and providing the social services, such as education and health facilities, in the new resource communities. The *social capital* was provided by governments at both levels; the *profitable, productive capital* came from the multinational resource companies. The government's role was passive, quite in contrast to its role both in the National Policy period and in the mobilization period.

But in other ways, the economic environment was also very different by 1945. Canada was predominantly a rural, agricultural country in 1879. Even by 1939, much of the country remained rural and agriculture-oriented. Policy had to take cognizance of the numbers of independent producers. The wartime mobilization and government entrepreneurship changed all that. In 1939 less than 16 per cent of the labour force was employed in the manufacturing sector. By the end of the war, this percentage had risen to over 26 per cent. In fact, manufacturing reached its zenith in 1944 in terms of the percentage of the labour force employed in this sector. At that time it appeared that a major transformation had been achieved in the Canadian economy, from being "hewers of wood and drawers of water" to being a modern, industrial society based on a predominant industrial sector complete with the belching smoke of steel mills, the continuous clatter of production lines, and the metallic roar of heavy machinery. The apparent transformation can be seen in the figures in Table 2. Manufacturing exceeded in employment growth all other industry groups except forestry over the wartime period. In the following decade, by comparison, employment in manufacturing stagnated while only forestry and agriculture had slower (in fact, negative) employment growth.

TABLE 2
Indexes of Employment by Industry Group

Industry Group	1939	1945	1956	1968	1970
Agriculture	100.0	83.0	59.4	48.9	36.5
Forestry	100.0	201.9	160.4	141.7	104.7
Mining	100.0	87.8	130.9	128.2	143.3
Manufacturing	100.0	177.6	191.3	194.5	237.4
Construction	100.0	86.8	212.6	202.7	218.0
Transportation, communications, and utilities	100.0	143.8	197.8	185.8	208.6
Trade	100.0	123.9	205.4	222.3	308.7
Finance, insurance, and real estate	100.0	114.2	202.2	231.1	342.8
Service	100.0	142.8	220.2	257.1	474.1
Industrial composite	100.0	147.8	200.8	197.5	249.3

SOURCE: *Canada Year Book*, various issues. The year 1970 is not entirely comparable due to a change in industrial classification.

The immediate post-war period, however, produced a number of major changes that made this vision of an industrial society transitory. One was the conversion of government policy from its interventionist, entrepreneurial role in the wartime economy to "Keynesian" intervention only at the broad level of fiscal and monetary policy.[5] From governmental control of the pace and direction of investment, the determination of capital formation was returned to the private sector subject only to the broad influences of macro-economic policies.

The second major change was the rapid deregulation of the wartime economy, which had the concomitant effect of returning to the provinces control of economic development policy tied to resource exploitation. A very important aspect of this must be recognized. Provincial economic policy could only influence the supply of resources. Demand lay outside provincial policy purview. During the war period, excess demand was tightly controlled by the federal government. With deregulation and the withdrawal of the government from its entrepreneurial role, it increasingly came under the control of foreign demand and, to a much lesser extent, domestic demand as influenced by general economic conditions, in turn affected by federal fiscal and monetary policies. Because of the slow recovery of Europe and its shortage of hard currency, this meant that external demand in the Canadian economy was increasingly dominated by American needs.

The third major change was also a consequence of wartime regulation and the preceding decade of depression and enforced abstinence from consumption. During the depression there was no lack of desire for the new consumer goods that had appeared in mass production form in the twenties, particularly automobiles, household appliances, and radios. The problem was lack of ability to pay. Wartime prosperity brought the ability to pay but not the supply of goods. Rationing, enforced saving, taxation, and the conversion to military production meant either that consumer goods were not available or that income generated by the expansion in employment was not available for consumption. Deregulation, the freeing up of wartime savings, and the industrial slack created by the end of hostilities changed all of that.

At the same time the industrial capacity created by government in the period of national emergency was being sold off, at low prices, to the corporate interests that had operated it during the war. As the labour force, male and female, was being demobilized not only from the military but also from the war-related industries, pent up consumer buying power was released. The initial effects were, as could be expected, salubrious for Canadian industry. The post-war depression that had been feared by so many did not appear. In fact, except for 1946 when the economy paused in transition, the opposite occurred, a major post-war boom.

The basis of this boom was twofold. In addition to the consumer demand in Canada was a burgeoning demand from the United States for industrial raw materials. The reasons for this demand were in part similar to those that propelled consumer demand in Canada. Consumer buying power was released in the United States, which created an enormous demand for raw materials that could not be met, or could be met only at much enhanced prices, from American sources. However, as the decade progressed a second major factor emerged – rearmament. The Cold War between the two wartime allies, the United States and the Soviet Union, provided the rationale for continuing high levels of military expenditure in the United States and, consequently, a continuing high level of demand for strategic Canadian raw materials.

Thus, in a very real sense, the economic boom in Canada was heavily initiated by American demand. In addition, however, we designate it as the "American boom in Canada" (a term suggested by Tom Kent) because consumer demand in Canada was in large part met by branch plants of U.S. corporations, some of them wartime plants purchased from the Canadian government. The boom faltered in the closing years of the fifties but, supported by Vietnam War expenditures, reasserted itself in the sixties. By the early seventies it had run its course, as the North American economy increasingly encountered stagflation exacerbated by the oil pricing shocks after 1973. The great post-war boom can be said to have ended by the early years of the seventies.[6]

There were two major results of this boom. One was the rapid extension of American multinational control of Canadian manufacturing. The second was a massive expansion of American investment into Canadian resource industries. Both operated to make the Canadian economy increasingly dependent on the American economy. Both also operated to reinforce the regional disparities that had been a feature of the Canadian economy since Confederation. Regional prosperity became increasingly a function either of the location of branch plants or of the location of raw materials in demand by American industry, neither of which were particularly responsive to national or provincial economic policy.

SECONDARY MANUFACTURING

The entry of American corporations into the Canadian market long predates the post-war boom. The movement of United States capital into Canada was well underway by the late nineteenth century, propelled on by the continental expansion of large companies. Still, by 1900 American *direct* investment (i.e., investment in ownership of firms) was only $175 million and was dwarfed by the amount of British *portfolio* investment (i.e., investment in the form of loans), which stood at $1 billion.[7] Even by 1939 U.S. direct investment in Canada was less than both British and U.S. portfolio investment. (See Table 3) No major change occurred during the wartime period except for the decline in Canadian indebtedness to Britain, which was forced to call in its loans to help pay for the war.

TABLE 3

Foreign Investment: Selected Years, 1939-1970
(millions of dollars)

Source		1939	1946	1952	1960	1970
U.K.	direct	366	335	544	1,535	2,503
	portfolio	2,110	1,335	1,342	1,824	1,518
U.S.	direct	1,881	2,428	4,530	10,549	21,403
	portfolio	2,270	2,730	3,467	6,169	13,511
All foreign countries						
	direct	2,296	2,826	5,218	12,872	26,358
	portfolio	4,617	4,355	5,167	9,342	17,679
U.S. as a % of total						
	foreign investment	60.0	72.0	77.0	75.0	79.3

SOURCE: F.H. Leacy, ed., *Historical Statistics of Canada,* 2nd ed. (Ottawa, 1983).

Indeed, even in the few years immediately following the war the inflow of foreign capital was modest. This inflow became a virtual tidal wave as the 1940's ended. In 1939, 38 per cent of the Canadian manufacturing industry was foreign-controlled (32 per cent by Americans). By 1948, this had risen to only 43 per cent, of which 39 per cent was American-controlled. Fifteen years later, however, 60 per cent of Canadian manufacturing was foreign controlled, 46 per cent by American interests. By the early 1970's foreign control of manufacturing appears to have reached its peak, in 1970 Canadians controlling only 39 per cent of our industry, Americans 47 per cent. (In contrast, by 1977 Canadians controlled 46 per cent of manufacturing capital, Americans 42 per cent.)

The influx of foreign capital into Canadian manufacturing was in part a manifestation of another major transformation taking place, the rising dominance of very large, oligopolistic corporations. (Oligopoly means "few sellers.") Much of this came from the internal growth of existing firms, many of them American branch plants. This was the age of rising advertising expenditures to differentiate one manufacturer's products from those of its rivals, particularly as television began to invade the homes of the nation during the fifties.

Alternatively, a number of these giant firms were the result of a rising post-war tide of mergers and takeovers of smaller firms, in many cases foreign takeovers. The statistics are given in Table 4. Cyclical peaks occurred in 1945-46, 1955-56, 1959-61, and 1968-72, at the end of periods of economic expansion. It should also be noted that the peak period of foreign mergers was the late fifties and the decade of the sixties, the highest year being 1960, when almost half of all mergers were foreign-controlled. (The number drops significantly after Canada passed the Foreign Investment Review Act in 1972.)

TABLE 4
Merger Activity in Canada, 1945-74

	Number	Yearly Average	Foreign	% Foreign
1945-49	289	57.8	76	26.3
1950-54	398	79.6	113	32.7
1955-59	698	139.6	271	38.8
1960-64	959	191.8	383	39.9
1965-69	1,572	314.4	574	36.5
1970-74	1,838	367.6	604	32.9

SOURCE: D.N. Thompson, "Mergers, Effects, and Competition Policy: Some Empirical Evidence," Table 1.

Post-war manufacturing growth was also characterized by a profound regional concentration, perpetuating the uneven distribution that had existed since the deindustrialization of the Maritime region between the 1890's and the 1920's. By 1929 over 80 per cent of Canada's net value of manufacturing was concentrated in the industrial heartland of Ontario and Quebec. In 1939, the figure was 82.4. Concentration declined marginally during the war, to 80.5 per cent in 1945, then increased to almost 82 by 1950. It continued between 81 and 82 per cent through the fifties and sixties, standing at 81.4 per cent in 1970. In the seventies, energy-related processing in the West has served to decrease the concentration slightly. Also, over the post-war period manufacturing activity has increasingly located in Ontario at the relative expense of Quebec.

Why has this pattern been perpetuated? The simplest explanation is the historical one – the advantages of being first and strategically located in relation to transportation systems, resources, and the American industrial belt. The latter influence has been shown to be extremely important in that branch plants of American firms tend to locate as near as possible in Canada to their American head offices.[8]

There are other consequences for Canada's manufacturing industry of its branch plant structure. The domestic market is generally too small for manufacturers to reach efficient levels of production when there are similar numbers of major producers in the ten-times-larger American economy. This is perhaps best demonstrated by the dilemma faced by the Canadian automobile industry in the 1950's and early 1960's. During the 1920's the American companies had expanded in Canada to service the Commonwealth market, which was protected by imperial preferences. Almost 40 per cent of Canadian-produced cars were exported. The liberalization of trade, the growth of the British, French, and German car industries, and the problems of convertability in the sterling bloc after the war reduced the market virtually to domestic demand. By the end of the fifties Canada was plagued by an inefficient industry producing too many models of too many cars at too high a cost for too small a market. Two options were available: reorganization of the industry to produce one line of Canadian cars, or integration of Canadian production into the North American market by rationalizing the industry on a continental basis with the creation of an automobile free-trade area subject only to certain guarantees to Canada regarding investment and employment.

The Canadian government under Lester Pearson chose the continentalist alternative with passage of the Auto Pact in 1965. In that year exports of automobiles had fallen to $36 million and the trade deficit on cars and parts had risen to $551 million. For the rest of the decade, the Auto Pact appeared to be the salvation of the industry. The deficit declined with increasing rationalization, and by 1970 an actual overall surplus was achieved. But this merely served to obscure the nature of the rationalization. Canada was increasingly assembling cars from imported parts with semi-skilled labour while more skilled and technical activities were increasingly concentrated in the United States. By the mid-seventies the harvest of the process was being felt as Japanese competition, skyrocketing energy prices, and American non-tariff barriers pummelled the industry. The result was a return to massive and rising trade deficits on automobiles and parts.

The automobile industry is somewhat unique in Canada in that it is one of the few major secondary manufacturing sectors formally integrated and rationalized on a continental basis. (The other major exceptions are farm machinery, in which free trade exists, and military hardware production under the Defence Production Sharing Agreement of 1959.) Nevertheless, the problems it illustrates are present in other sectors of secondary manufacturing: the low levels of technology, of decision-making, of skilled and technical jobs, of research, development, and technical innovation, of exports, and of efficient production. It is not accidental that in this period Canada consistently has one of the worst records for research and development of any country in the western industrialized world, with total R&D expenditures averaging around 1 per cent of Gross National Product, one-half the average level of the leading industrial nations.

Canada has traditionally imported a great deal of its manufactures, but the post-war period saw an intensification of this reliance on imports, particularly those involving advanced technology and machinery. Figures for imports' share of the Canadian market are available for 1966 and 1976. Selected industries are reported in Table 5.

The results of this reliance on imports show up in trade fig-

TABLE 5
Import Shares of the Canadian Market
(selected end-product manufacturing industries)

Industry	1966	1976
Low-technology sector	11.1	17.4
Rubber and plastics	19.5	21.9
Leather	13.6	35.0
Textiles	24.4	26.9
Knitting	12.8	36.9
Clothing	4.9	14.9
Furniture and fixtures	5.2	12.3
High-technology sector	34.4	40.1
Machinery	65.8	71.1
Metal fabricating	11.7	15.5
Transport equipment	38.9	68.9
Electrical products	22.3	34.4
Chemicals	23.6	29.8
Total all sectors	**21.6**	**29.6**

SOURCE: Richard Starks, *Industry in Decline,* Table 2-2.

ures. The average trade deficit in end products in the 1960-62 period was $1.9 billion. By 1970-72 it had doubled to $3.9 billion and by 1976-78 had ballooned to over $10 billion.[9] Machinery alone accounted for approximately a third of these deficits. The United States was the prime supplier of these end products: 77 per cent in the early sixties rising to almost 80 per cent a decade and a half later.

It is clear from the foregoing that the post-war period in Canada has seen a marked reversal in its industrial structure compared to the rapid expansion of manufacturing in the hot-house conditions between 1939 and 1945. But if the three decades or so since the allied victory saw a progressive deterioration in Canada's secondary manufacturing base, what was the foundation of the long post-war boom? The answer, of course, was the resurgence of growth in the "new staples," or, as Aitken entitled his study of the process, *American Capital and Canadian Resources.*[10]

THE RESOURCE SECTOR

The real basis of the American boom in Canada in the post-war decades was the wave of investment that accompanied the expansion of the resource sector, more particularly oil and gas and mining. The characteristics of these staples, along with pulp and paper, are very different from those of earlier staples that dominated the evolution of the Canadian economy prior to the industrial period. The characteristic of the earlier staples was that they were *trades*. The dominant form of capitalist enterprise in the fish, fur, and timber staples was the merchant trader. Production was largely carried out by independent producers. The traders could command control of a major proportion of the profits of the staples because they controlled the necessary merchant capital. Staple agriculture in both the mid-nineteenth century and in the wheat boom period differed in two respects: in the sheer number of independent commodity producers and the consequent requirement for social and economic infrastructure that a large, widely dispersed population required; and in the requirement for heavy fixed investment in transportation facilities. It should again be noted that capitalist enterprise was not involved in grain production but in the grain trade and in transportation, although, as we have already noted, from the third decade of the nineteenth century, industrial capital was increasingly attracted to the manufacturing industries servicing the production and consumption needs of the agricultural producers.

In contrast, the new staples (lumber, pulp and paper, mining, and energy) were markedly different in their economic characteristics. They were staples industries, not staples trades. Capitalist enterprises were not limited to controlling the movement and sales of the natural resource but rather were the basic producing/processing unit. Command of surplus was due to control of *industrial* capital, very large quantities of which were required for development of these new resources. Indeed, these capital requirements have grown steadily with evolving technology. These characteristics are key to understanding the nature of the long post-war boom and the role of American capital in the process.

Certainly, the movement of American capital into resource industries in Canada in the post-war period was massive. In 1936 U.S. direct investment in mining, smelting, and petroleum amounted to around $350 million, some 43 per cent of the amount invested in manufactures and representing approximately 40 per cent of total investment in Canada in these industries. However, this absolute figure is greatly misleading because a very significant part of our manufacturing sector is devoted to processing natural resources for export. This includes pulp and paper, metal refining, lumber and sawmilling. (In fact, until over a decade after the war, petroleum and natural gas refining, exploration, and development were included in manufacturing statistics.) As a rough estimate, around 12 per cent of manufacturing employment and 16 to 18 per cent of manufacturing value added were in export processing in the early 1950's. Twenty years later, the figures were marginally less. Because of their capital intensity, the processing industries' share of capital employed would be considerably higher.

In any case, the movement of American capital into resource-based industries at both the extractive and processing levels was considerable, though not until several years after the end of the war. Aitken gives the following description of this influx:

The book value of total investment in Canadian industry increased by approximately $17.4 billion in the period 1926-1954; more than one-third of this increase represented nonresident investment, and almost all of this one-third came from the United States. In mining and smelting, nonresident financing contributed 65 per cent of total capital expansion in this period, while in manufacturing . . . the proportion was over 50 per cent. Between 1946 and 1953 approximately one half of Canada's net capital imports from the United States went into petroleum development; total United States investment in the Canadian petroleum industry reached $1,144 million at the end of 1953, as compared with only $177 million at the end of 1945. By the end of 1953, 56 per cent of the capital employed in Canadian mining, smelting, and petroleum exploration and development companies was nonresident owned, as compared with 39 per cent in 1948 and 36 per cent in 1926. . . . . Approximately 78 per cent of the total inflow of direct capital investment from the United States in the period 1946-1955 went into the petroleum, mining, and pulp and paper industries. . . . In the Canadian petroleum industry the proportion of nonresident control [1955] (in terms of capital invested) is 95 per cent; in mining, smelting, and refining, 75 per cent; and in manufacturing, 57 per cent. United States interests account for the bulk of nonresident control in each case.[11]

Much the same point, and for the later post-war period to the seventies, is made in Table 6, which traces the degree of foreign control of the major resource industries. American investment continued to expand until the end of the sixties, which marks the effective end of the American boom in Canada.

TABLE 6
Non-resident Control of Selected Resource Industries, 1939-1975 (per cent)

Industry	1939	1948	1963	1970	1975
Mining and smelting	42	40	59	70	60
Petroleum and gas	n/a	n/a	74	76	74
Pulp and paper	n/a	n/a	n/a	53	45

SOURCES: Kari Levitt, *Silent Surrender* (Toronto, 1970), Table 2; *Canada's International Investment Position*, various issues.

What was the basis of this expansion of resource capital into Canada? Even more than with secondary manufacturing, it was the continentalization of the North American market, a move encouraged by the policy adopted in the White Paper and Green Book. On the American side it reflected the growing demand from industry for increased supplies of raw materials that were militarily and politically secure, not just to meet expanding markets but also to replace depleted domestic supplies. The importance of Canada was brought out clearly in the U.S. president's Materials Policy Commission (better known as the Paley Report) in 1952. The United States was forecast to be running low on a number of key resources. On almost half of these key resources, Canada was considered to be the prime future source.

Included were iron ore, nickel, copper, lead, zinc, aluminum, fluorspar, and asbestos. Also considered were joint developments of hydroelectricity. Such forecasts were supported by the empirical evidence, as indicated in American reliance on natural resource imports in 1956.[12]

A second measure, this time from Canadian data, is Canada's export dependence on a small number of raw and processed materials, primarily to the United States, a dependence that declined during the Second World War but rose quite dramatically in the immediate post-war decade and remained at high levels in the following decade. Various measures of this dependence are given in Tables 7 and 8. What is noticeable is that in the post-war decade, staples increased in importance in exports, the decline in the old staples being offset by the rise in the new. At the same time, and in large measure because of this, exports have become increasingly concentrated to the United States. (In Table 8, figures are given both including and excluding exports of automobiles and parts in order to eliminate the distortion in the historical comparison brought about by the Auto Pact.)

TABLE 7
Forty Leading Domestic Exports, 1939-1960

Exports by Type	% of 40 Leading Exports				% of All Exports			
	1939	1946	1955	1960	1939	1946	1955	1960
New staples (raw and processed forest and mineral products)	62.2	52.1	68.8	68.4	42.4	34.5	57.6	58.3
Old staples (agriculture, fish, and furs)	29.2	33.4	19.3	17.0	19.9	22.1	16.2	14.5
Total staples	91.5	85.6	88.2	85.4	62.3	56.6	73.8	72.8
Manufactured products	8.5	14.4	11.8	14.7	5.8	9.5	9.9	12.5
Leading 40 exports	100.0	100.0	100.0	100.0	68.1	66.1	83.7	85.3
Exports to U.S.					41.6	38.8	60.0	56.4

SOURCES: *Canada Year Book*, various issues; Urquhart and Buckley, *Historical Statistics of Canada*.

We have assumed throughout that this resource boom in the long expansion after the war had, in fact, the characteristics of a classic staples boom. In other words, economic growth is di-

TABLE 8
Exports by Type, 1960-72

Type	1960-62 (Incl. Autos and Parts)	1960-62 (Excl. Autos and Parts)	1970-72 (Incl. Autos and Parts)	1970-72 (Excl. Autos and Parts)
Food and animals	20.3%	20.5	11.9	15.5
Crude and fabricated materials	70.4%	71.1	52.6	68.6
End products	9.1%	8.2	35.3	15.8
Special transactions	.2%	.2	.2	.3
Exports to U.S.	56.1%	56.4	67.0	58.7

SOURCE: Lukin Robinson, *Canada's Crippled Dollar*, various tables.

rectly related to the expansion of the natural resource base and the investment directly related to this expansion. As well, a ripple effect from this resource-based expansion is seen in the Canadian economy in the social and economic infrastructure (e.g., schools, new towns, hospitals, roads, and other transportation facilities), in suppliers to the resource industries (e.g., mining and logging equipment), and in consumer demand created from the incomes generated in the resource industries (e.g., housing, commercial outlets, and service establishments). It first must be recognized that natural resource exports are a very significant part of our total economy. Exports accounted for 27 per cent of GNP in 1946 and approximately 20 per cent through the fifties and early sixties, rising to around 25 per cent by 1970. (By way of comparison, exports were consistently higher than *total* government expenditures at all levels throughout the period, and in the early years of the post-war boom were almost twice as large.) Considering that staples are the biggest part of exports, therefore, their impact on the growth and welfare of the economy is obviously very considerable.

More sophisticated econometric attempts have been made to demonstrate this relationship. The most thorough and exhaustive study was *The Canadian Economy* (1961) by Richard Caves and Richard Holton. It is worth quoting their conclusion as to the nature of the post-war expansion: "Growth of investment and income have been closely geared both to the current level of exports and to the general outlook for export industries bolstered by a remarkable series of natural resource discoveries." [13]

In less abstract and general terms, the staples-induced "American boom in Canada" can be illustrated by a specific case, the St. Lawrence Seaway. Negotiations to deepen and develop the seaway, which for centuries had been the dominating economic highway of Canadian staples, had been going on with the United States since the First World War, but agreement could not be reached until after the Second World War when a combination of factors finally forced the Americans' hand. One of these factors was the growing need of the American Northeast for hydro power; another was the declining domestic reserves of iron ore for the American steel industry. What precipitated agreement was the decision by the Canadian government in 1951 to go it alone with construction of an all-Canadian system. In 1954 a bilateral agreement was reached and construction began. The seaway was completed at a cost in excess of $1 billion in 1959.

The prime purpose of this enormous expenditure was the movement of staples exports: grain eastward-bound; iron ore from Sept Isles west to the U.S. industrial heartland; oil and coal to Quebec; newsprint and pulpwood to American Great Lakes ports. More than 55 per cent of the tonnage handled in its early years was grain and iron ore.

The iron-ore development is a further example of the process by which the natural resource sector fed investment. The ore was mined at Knob Lake, some 358 miles north of the St. Lawrence River, which required the construction of a railway, the building of the town of Schefferville, the transformation of Sept Iles, construction of docks, and the building of a hydro dam to provide power for the expanded community. The system came on stream in 1954. As Aitken has noted, the northern Quebec-Labrador frontier "is Canadian only in a geographical and political sense; economically, it is a frontier of United States resource investment."[14] (Perhaps symbolic of the end of the American boom was the abandonment of Schefferville by the U.S.-owned Iron Ore Company of Canada in 1983.)

THE LEGACY OF DEPENDENCE

After mobilizing its domestic resources for the successful prosecution of the war, Canada embarked on a policy of continental economic integration. One should not minimize Canada's considerable accomplishments during the wartime period under central government economic planning. Canada became a truly industrial economy, but with the end of hostilities the country abandoned its regime of direct investment and output control in favour of general policies of manipulating the levers of aggregate demand. The intentions were clear in the White Paper and the Green Book. Whether the implications were foreseen and evaluated or even considered is another question.

The consequences of the abandonment of any industrial development policy after the war, other than opening the Canadian economy to increased dependence on natural resource exports within a continental system, were considerable. One was to open the country to a degree of foreign ownership unique in the industrial world. Second was to allow a long-term decline in secondary manufacturing within an inefficient, branch plant structure. Third was to leave prevailing regional disparities up to the lottery of resource distribution. Fourth, and perhaps fundamental to subsequent economic problems that besieged the Canadian economy in the seventies and since, it has reinforced dependency of the Canadian economy and, more specifically, investment, on an external economy over which Canada has little or no influence. The legacy, therefore, is an economy that has no structural coherence – not a national economy but a number of regions that are part of a continental configuration, subject to the political and economic predilections of a foreign power and definitely not *maître chez nous*. Aitken's judgement of 1959 remains true, forty years after the war.

> The nation that today is Canada has never been master of its own destiny; as a satelitic staple-producing economy, it reflected, and still reflects, in its rate of development the imperatives of more advanced areas. . . . the influence of the United States upon the character of Canadian development is in the direction of perpetuating Canada's traditional status as a staple-producing economy.[15]

Perhaps Canada could not have escaped unscathed the integrating forces that emerged with the new world economic order that resulted from the post-war negotiations, the international economic institutions of the International Monetary Fund, World Bank, and General Agreement on Tariffs and Trade, and the developing hegemony of the American economic empire. Nevertheless, the accomplishments of the World War II period showed what an independent nation, mobilized in a national purpose, could do.

NOTES

1. V.C. Fowke, "The National Policy – Old and New," *Canadian Journal of Economics and Political Science*, 18 (1952), 271-86.

2. K.A.H. Buckley, *Capital Formation in Canada, 1896-1930* (Toronto, 1955).

3. This section is based on the forthcoming Ph.D. thesis by Stephen Watson.

4. W.A. Mackintosh, "Canadian Economic Policy from 1945 to 1957 – Origins and Influences," in H.G.J. Aitken *et al., The American Economic Impact on Canada* (Durham, N.C., 1959), 62.

5. H. Scott Gordon claims that post-war government policy, while paying lip service to Keynesian theory, actually was not and in most years finance ministers pursued a balanced budget, definitely a non-Keynesian goal. See Gordon, "A Twenty Year Perspective: Some Reflections on the Keynesian Revolution in Canada," in S.F. Kaliski, ed., *Canadian Economic Policy Since the War* (Toronto, 1966).

6. For evidence of this periodization, see D.M. Gordon, Richard Edwards, and Michael Reich, *Segmented Work, Divided Workers* (New York, 1982).

7. K. Levitt, *Silent Surrender* (Toronto, 1970), 66.

8. D.M. Ray, "Regional Economic Development and the Location of U.S. Subsidiaries," in Paul Phillips, ed., *Incentives, Location and Regional Development* (Winnipeg, 1975).

9. For a detailed discussion, see Lukin Robinson, *Canada's Crippled Dollar* (Toronto, 1980).

10. H.G.J. Aitken, *American Capital and Canadian Resources* (Cambridge, Mass., 1961).

11. H.G.J. Aitken, "The Changing Structure of the Canadian Economy, with Particular Reference to the Influence of the United States," in Aitken *et al., American Economic Impact,* 10-11.

12. See Aitken, *American Capital and Canadian Resources*, Table 30.

13. Richard Caves and Richard Holton, *The Canadian Economy* (Cambridge, Mass., 1961), 112.

14. Aitken, *American Capital and Canadian Resources,* 85.

15. Aitken, "The Changing Structure of the Canadian Economy."

The Rise and Demise of the Keynesian Era in Canada: Economic Policy, 1930-1982

by David A. Wolfe

INTRODUCTION

In the years since the Great Depression of the 1930's, the relation between the state and the economy has changed dramatically in all advanced capitalist countries, including Canada. This change is illustrated most clearly by the increase in the level of government spending. In 1930, governments accounted for 19.2 per cent of all spending in the Canadian economy. By 1982, total government expenditure rose to 47.4 per cent of gross national expenditure. This significant change in the economic role of the state arose largely in response to the experience of the Great Depression and World War II. During the depression, levels of economic output, employment, and international trade fell at an unprecedented rate. The result was untold suffering for millions of people throughout the advanced capitalist countries. The hardship and suffering wrought by the depression resulted in political and social instability, which led to the rise of fascism and the start of World War II. The war, in turn, precipitated a massive industrial mobilization, organized and co-ordinated by the state, which restored the vitality and dynamism of world capitalism with a rapidity inconceivable at the height of the depression. The starkness of the contrast between the stagnation of the depression years and the intense economic activity of the war years made a strong impression on the political thinking of democratic electorates throughout the industrial countries. Traditional assumptions about the limited political role of the state were shattered, to be replaced by the belief that the state could, and should, assume responsibility for sustaining high levels of employment and economic growth.

This change in political thinking affected all segments of advanced capitalist society. Businessmen, who had clearly benefited from the wave of prosperity induced by the government's wartime role, were willing to accept a limited extension of this role into the post-war period. Salary- and wage-earners came to view the expanded role of government as a guarantee of the adequate jobs and incomes they had been denied during the depression. The resulting consensus over the appropriate role of the state in the economy created a new political compromise between business and labour, which emerged in the form of the welfare state. The terms of the compromise left the investment decision-making process in the hands of private enterprise in exchange for the adoption of economic policies to provide stable levels of employment and income for the mass of wage-earners. The key feature of the welfare state was the acceptance of an explicit obligation by the state to provide assistance and support for those individuals who were unable to participate in the labour market adequately enough to provide for their basic needs. This commitment included the institution of social insurance programs to deal with old age, unemployment, ill health, and a variety of disabilities. The post-war compromise also involved an explicit commitment by the state to recognize and support the democratic rights of trade unions to bargain collectively to improve the wages and living standards of their members and, in some instances, to participate directly in the determination of public policies. [1]

The theoretical and ideological justification for the post-war welfare state was provided by the writings of the British economist, John Maynard Keynes. Keynes' ideas represented an attempt to unite the principle of continued private control of the investment and production processes of a capitalist economy with public demands for a change in the market-determined pattern of employment and income. He analysed the causes of the Great Depression in terms of a lack of investment and a falling level of demand. Keynes argued that in conditions of heavy unemployment, the government was required to use its fiscal policy – its taxing and spending decisions – in such a way as to offset the fall in the level of private demand. Keynes' insistence that the fiscal policies of government could be used to stabilize the cyclical fluctuations of the private market economy provided the theoretical rationalization for the introduction of techniques for the democratic management of capitalist economies. More significantly, Keynesianism provided a theoretical framework that justified the interest of workers in higher wages as being of general benefit to the economy by sustaining levels of aggregate demand. The Keynesian policy prescriptions also legitimated higher levels of spending on social insurance, not as charity, but as "automatic stabilizers" built into the economy, which would buoy up aggregate demand in periods of cyclical downturn. In effect, it

> was Keynesianism that provided the ideological and political foundations for the compromise of capitalist democracy. Keynesianism held out the prospect that the state could reconcile the private ownership of the means of production with democratic management of the economy. . . . Democratic control over the level of unemployment and the distribution of income became the terms of the compromise which made democratic capitalism possible.[2]

Canada has generally been recognized, by economists such as John Kenneth Galbraith, as among the first advanced capitalist countries to embrace the principles of Keynesianism.[3] While there is a certain element of truth to this assertion, it ignores the specific way Keynesian ideas were interpreted and applied in Canada. It overlooks also the difference between the way the post-war compromise was implemented in Canada and the way it was implemented in other advanced capitalist countries. The adoption of Keynesian ideas in Canada was based on several prior assumptions. The most important of these was the assumption that Canada had always been, and would remain, an open trading economy specializing in the export of resource staples. Consequently, Canada could only hope to apply Keynesian policies in a liberalized post-war trading environment that would stimulate the export of its resource products. Thus, in adopting Keynes to the Canadian context, government leaders and their economic policy-advisers fashioned a uniquely Canadian synthesis of the more general Keynesian theory with the traditional staples approach to Canadian economic development.[4]

The strong emphasis placed on the contribution of Canada's staple exports to the realization of the Keynesian goals of high levels of employment and growth introduced an important element of instability into the implementation of the post-war political compromise. In all the advanced capitalist countries, the introduction of Keynesian policies led to growing conflicts between the demands of labour for full employment and steadily rising real wage levels and the demands of business for adequate profit levels. The ability of the state to reconcile these competing claims progressively deteriorated over the period after the end of World War II. The visible manifestation of this deterioration was the gradual emergence of higher levels of unemployment simultaneous with spiralling rates of inflation (a phenomenon termed "stagflation"). Canada's stagflation problem was compounded by the instability introduced by its continued reliance on a high level of staple exports and steadily rising levels of manufactured imports and foreign investment. This pattern of growth resulted in a steadily worsening balance-of-payments problem that seriously constrained the government's ability to pursue the goals of the Keynesian welfare state. In the years after 1975, the commitment to the Keynesian welfare state was gradually eroded and the political compromise between business and labour abandoned. Canada now faces an economic and political crisis strongly parallel to that of the Great Depression.

DEPRESSION, WAR, AND RECONSTRUCTION

The countercyclical fiscal policies, which were an integral part of Keynes' theoretical approach, represented a radical departure from the historic pattern of Canadian budgetary policy. In the period from Confederation to the depression, public finance in Canada was closely tied to the level of staple exports and the pre-eminent role of the state in the construction of major transportation projects, such as the Canadian Pacific Railway. Fiscal policy was characterized by a strongly cyclical pattern that tended to reinforce, rather than offset, the swings in the economy. Strong upswings in the level of exports contributed to a higher level of national income (and aggregate demand). This, in turn, would induce a boom in business investment and a rise in the level of imports into Canada. The higher level of imports generated a rise in government revenues, which were derived almost exclusively from customs duties. In periods of rising exports, the government was induced by the buoyance of its revenues to undertake ever more ambitious transportation projects. However, the overcommitment of the government's resources in these boom periods invariably intensified the upswing of the business cycle and left the government saddled with a crushing burden of debt when the boom came to an end. In the downswing of the cycle, the government would react in the exact opposite fashion. As exports and the level of domestic investment began to fall, revenues would decline. The government would cut back on its expenditures in an effort to balance its budget, further reducing aggregate demand and intensifying the cyclical downswing. Thus government policies tended to exacerbate, rather than mitigate, the effects of cyclical swings in the economy.[5]

Although Canadians were accustomed to dramatic fluctuations in their economic fortunes, the impact of the Great Depression was particularly severe. With the onset of the depression, exports declined precipitously, inducing a sharp drop in the level of national income. Unemployment rose steeply, reaching a peak in 1933 when more than 19 per cent of the labour force was listed as officially out of work (Table 1), and thousands more had simply given up looking for work. A large proportion of business and government investment in the export industries and transportation network in previous decades had taken the form of bonded debt. The impact of the depression made the weight of these debt obligations particularly burdensome. Government expenditures rose rapidly over the first half of the decade as the cost of relief for the unemployed and assistance to impoverished provincial and municipal governments was added to the existing fixed debt charges. At the same time, government revenues fell because the lower level of imports into the country generated a lower level of customs duties. Remaining true to the orthodox economic principles of the day, the government attempted to balance its budget by raising tariff rates, the sales tax, and personal and corporate income taxes. As a result of these measures, by 1933 budgetary revenues had ceased to fall, and by 1936 they had been restored to the 1929 level, despite the 30 per cent decline in the national income that had occurred in the interim.[6]

TABLE 1
Economic Indicators, 1930-1982

	Gross National Expenditure (constant 1971$s) % change	Consumer Price Index % change	Unemployment Rate	Labour Compensation per unit of output* % change
1930	−4.3	−0.7	9.1	—
1931	−12.7	−9.6	11.6	—
1932	−10.4	−9.1	17.6	—
1933	−6.7	−5.0	19.3	—
1934	12.1	1.8	14.5	—
1935	7.8	0.6	14.2	—
1936	4.4	2.0	12.8	—
1937	10.0	3.1	9.1	—
1938	0.8	1.1	11.4	—
1939	7.4	−0.8	11.4	—
1940	14.1	4.1	9.2	—
1941	14.4	5.6	4.6	—
1942	18.6	4.7	3.0	—
1943	4.0	1.7	1.7	—
1944	4.0	0.7	1.4	—

TABLE 1 (continued)
Economic Indicators, 1930-1982

	Gross National Expenditure (constant 1971$s) % change	Consumer Price Index % change	Unemployment Rate	Labour Compensation per unit of output* % change
1945	–2.5	0.5	1.6	—
1946	–2.7	3.4	2.6	—
1947	4.3	9.3	1.9	12.3
1948	2.5	14.4	1.6	10.7
1949	3.8	3.0	2.0	2.9
1950	7.6	2.9	2.7	0.0
1951	5.0	10.6	1.5	9.4
1952	8.9	2.4	2.0	5.2
1953	5.1	–0.9	2.1	1.9
1954	–1.2	0.6	4.0	0.3
1955	9.4	0.1	3.8	–3.3
1956	8.4	1.5	2.9	3.1
1957	2.4	3.2	3.3	5.6
1958	2.3	2.7	6.0	0.5
1959	3.8	1.1	5.4	0.1
1960	2.9	1.2	7.0	2.7
1961	2.8	0.9	7.1	–0.5
1962	6.8	1.2	5.9	–0.5
1963	5.2	1.8	5.5	0.8
1964	6.7	1.8	4.7	0.1
1965	6.7	2.4	3.9	3.0
1966	6.9	3.7	3.4	5.4
1967	3.3	3.6	3.8	5.1
1968	5.8	4.0	4.5	1.1
1969	5.3	4.6	4.4	4.5
1970	2.5	3.3	5.7	5.1
1971	6.9	2.9	6.2	3.3
1972	6.1	4.8	6.2	3.8
1973	7.5	7.6	5.5	6.9
1974	3.6	10.9	5.3	13.3
1975	1.2	10.8	6.9	15.3
1976	5.5	7.5	7.1	8.6
1977	2.1	8.0	8.1	6.1
1978	3.6	8.9	8.4	4.0
1979	2.9	9.1	7.5	7.4
1980	0.5	10.2	7.5	11.6
1981	3.1	12.5	7.6	10.6
1982	–4.8	10.8	11.0	—

* Commercial non-agricultural industries.
SOURCES: F.H. Leacy, ed., *Historical Statistics of Canada*, 2nd ed. (Ottawa, 1983), Tables F55, K8, D132; Statistics Canada, *Aggregate Productivity Measures, 1946-72* (Ottawa, 1974), 38; Department of Finance, *Economic Review, April, 1983* (Ottawa, 1983), Reference Tables 4, 43, 26, 36.

Both Conservative and Liberal governments continued to subscribe to this perverse logic of "balance the budget" orthodoxy almost to the end of the depression. The first hint of Keynesian ideas only began to creep into government policy with the budgets of 1938 and 1939. The persistence of these conservative economic ideas about the appropriate role of the state reveals the limited impact that the massive levels of unemployment had on Canadian politics during the depression years. The formation of the social democratic Co-operative Commonwealth Federation (CCF) in 1932, the activities of the Workers' Unity League, and the spread of the Congress of Industrial Organizations from the United States into Canada were all indicative of the political unrest of the period. However, their direct impact on the policies of the dominant Liberal and Conservative Parties was quite limited. The social, economic, and political pressures that had built up during the depression only came to a head during the war years.

The staggering dimensions of the war effort necessitated an increase in virtually every area of government activity. The Canadian state assumed a degree of control over the economy never equalled in the country's history. The government's role in the industrial mobilization included policies designed to subsidize the cost of building new plant and equipment or expanding and modifying existing plant and equipment to produce the needed war supplies. This was done through the use of accelerated depreciation allowances and direct capital subsidies to the firms that were contracted to produce munitions. Another form of government involvement was the creation of numerous Crown corporations to produce munitions for which there was no available domestic supplier. The government also intervened directly with the allocative mechanism of the market in aid of the war effort. It imposed a series of controls over a wide array of key commodities that were vital to the war effort. Furthermore, through a number of combined administrative agencies, the government controlled the allocation of key commodities and industrial products between Canada and the United States. This produced an unprecedented degree of integration between the two North American economies. The exigencies of the war effort also involved an expansion of the regulatory role of the government – the most notable aspects were the imposition of mandatory wage and price controls and the gradual extension of the industrial relations system.

The transformation of the Canadian economy and the economic role of the state induced by the war had significant effects on Canadian society and politics. The economic expansion generated by the war produced a dramatic increase in the overall size and relative strength of the organized labour movement. With the strong demand for labour created by the war, the CIO-backed organizing campaign initiated in the 1930's began to pay large dividends as plant after plant in the burgeoning industrial sector was unionized. Total union membership more than doubled during the war years. This strengthened the influence of the central trade union organizations, such as the newly formed Canadian Congress of Labour. It also attracted the attention of political leaders and policy-makers, who became concerned over the prospects of a repetition of the outbreak of labour strife that had followed the end of World War I. The increased size and strength of the labour movement were reflected in another important development – the astounding rate of growth of support for the CCF. During 1943 and 1944, the election of the CCF as the official opposition in Ontario, its victory in several federal by-elections, its surpassing of the two major parties in public opinion polls, and its success in the Saskatchewan provincial election had a far-reaching impact on the policies and positions of the two established parties.

The profound social, economic, and political changes were also reflected in the cultural values and political attitudes of Canadians. The intense social strains generated by the waging of modern warfare tend to call into question the existing distribution of power and resources in society. Few Canadians questioned the need for the numerous sacrifices demanded by the war effort, but many feared that the war would be followed by a return to the conditions of economic misery prevalent during the depression. The importance of this issue was indicated by the increasing amount of attention it received in the popular press and by the results of government opinion surveys. By 1943, the question uppermost in people's minds was the government's plans for after the war.[7]

The implications of this change in popular attitudes and concerns were not lost on the leaders of the governing Liberal Party. From mid-1943 onwards, Prime Minister Mackenzie King became increasingly preoccupied with the growing strength of the labour movement and its political allies in the CCF. King could foresee the potential effects this development might have on the Liberal Party's electoral fortunes; to prevent it, he engineered a dramatic change in government policy with respect to planning for post-war reconstruction and the introduction of social welfare reforms. King and the Liberals were aided in their efforts by a new coterie of young economists who had been recruited to government service by the Deputy Minister of Finance, W.C. Clark. This group, which included W.A. Mackintosh, R.B. Bryce, Louis Rasminsky, A.F.W. Plumptre, and J.J. Deutsch, played an instrumental role in aiding the diffusion of Keynesian ideas throughout the upper echelons of the Ottawa bureaucracy. Mackintosh, in particular, played a crucial role as the chairman of a subcommittee of the prestigious Economic Advisory Committee in co-ordinating the cabinet's plans for post-war reconstruction.[8] These plans were outlined in the Speech from the Throne read to Parliament on January 27, 1944, which declared that the primary object of post-war domestic policy would be "social security and human welfare." The government committed itself to aim for the establishment of a national minimum of social security with regard to such matters as employment, nutrition, housing, and protection from unemployment, the effects of accident, ill-health, and old age. In sum, the speech was far-ranging and innovative in the degree of government involvement it promised in order to ease the transition from wartime to peace, to guarantee full employment in the post-war economy, and to provide a national minimum of social security for all Canadians.[9]

The government's planning for post-war reconstruction continued throughout 1944 and 1945, on both the domestic scene and at the international level. Crucial pieces of legislation in the areas of family allowances, housing, veterans' rehabilitation, subsidies for agricultural products, and insurance for overseas exports were all enacted. Canada played a critical role also in the international negotiations that led to the signing of the Bretton Woods Agreement in July 1944, which established the international financial arrangements that were to govern the post-war economy. By early 1945, some of the government's advisers felt that an official statement of the underlying principles governing the approach to post-war planning was required. W.A. Mackintosh convinced the Minister of Reconstruction, C.D. Howe, of this need and the result was the White Paper on Employment and Income, read to the House of Commons on April 12, 1945. The White Paper recorded the government's official commitment to the Keynesian principle of countercyclical fiscal policy and the idea that it should construct its budgets with an aim to safeguarding the economy against recurrent inflation and deflation. It outlined the four main sources of national income (or aggregate demand) that must be encouraged to sustain stable economic growth – export trade, private investment in capital stock, private consumption expenditures, and government expenditures – and went on to detail the measures the government had implemented in each of these areas.

While the White Paper followed the main outlines of Keynes' argument throughout, its distinctive feature was the emphasis it placed on the contribution of exports to the maintenance of high levels of employment and income in Canada. It argued that the successful application of a full employment policy would depend largely on Canada's ability to recapture its pre-war export markets and to find new markets overseas. The White Paper started from the assumption that prosperity and business confidence in Canada had always been associated with strong export markets. Any undue emphasis on other measures to sustain economic growth, such as public works projects, might only prove to be counterproductive in that they might serve as storm signals to undermine business and consumer confidence. For this reason, the White Paper considered the new arrangements that had been reached to reconstruct the international economy (the Bretton Woods Agreement and the negotiations for a new international trade agreement) to be critical for the success of a post-war full employment policy in Canada. In effect, the White Paper constructed a rather unique synthesis of the traditional Canadian staples-led approach to economic development with the Keynesian theory of demand management and fiscal stabilization.[10]

KEYNESIAN POLICY IN A CONTINENTAL ECONOMY

During the early years of the post-war era, many of the changes that had occurred during the war became entrenched as permanent features of the Canadian economy. Among the most important of these was the increased strength and collective bargaining power of the organized labour movement. The demands of labour for a more equitable collective bargaining system had been recognized by the government in 1944 with the introduction of new provisions to govern the certification of unions and compel employers to bargain with unions. The unions were unable to translate these legislative gains into real wage increases during the war due to the operation of the government's wage controls. The end of the war was followed by a concerted effort on the part of the unions to break out of the structure of wartime wage controls. This effort commenced with an industry-wide strike in the lumber industry in the summer of 1946 and was followed by major strikes in metal mining, rubber, automobiles, electrical appliances, textiles, and steel. The strike wave of 1946 and 1947 played a crucial role in the establishment of a new industrial wage structure throughout the economy. It created new breakthroughs and patterns in wages and hours of work for many of the key industries. The post-war period also represented an important period of consolidation and further expansion for the trade union movement as membership rose to one million by 1949. In addition to the significant wage gains, the security of most union members was greatly enhanced by the new provisions of collective bargaining legislation and by improvements in other aspects of the industrial relations system. The government's formal commitment to a policy of high employment further reduced the fear and insecurity that organized labour had felt in the face of the massive unemployment levels of the depression. The greater degree of collective bargaining power enjoyed by the unions, combined with the greater degree of security created by the commitment to high employment levels, introduced a new dimension into the post-war political economy with important implications for the operation of Keynesian policies.[11]

The government's plans for post-war reconstruction had assumed that the pattern of Canada's export trade before the war would be restored after its end. Canada had traditionally enjoyed a substantial surplus in its export markets in Europe and other overseas countries, which had been used to offset the high level of imports from the United States, thus maintaining an overall surplus in the balance of trade. To this end, Canada had introduced the Export Credits Insurance Act and extended a large loan to the United Kingdom to allow traditional customers in European markets to resume their purchase of Canadian exports. This expectation was dealt a severe blow in the years immediately following the war by the slow rate of economic recovery in Europe and the low level of Canadian exports to those markets. The problem was compounded by the massive inflow of imports from the U.S. to supply the needs of the large-scale capital investments being undertaken by Canadian industry and to meet consumer demand. It was further exacerbated by the large payments made to Britain and other European countries under the loan agreement and the Export Credits Insurance program. The result was that Canada experienced a shortage of foreign exchange that reached crisis proportions by the end of 1947 (Table 2).[12]

In response to this crisis, the government introduced the Emergency Exchange Conservation Act, which imposed temporary controls on a variety of imports from the U.S. It pressed the U.S. government also to allow European countries to make "off-shore" purchases of Canadian goods with funds allotted to them under the European Recovery Program (Marshall Plan).

TABLE 2

Canada's Balance of International Payments, 1930-1982

	Merchandise Trade Balance	Current Account		Current Account Balance	Capital Account		Capital Account Balance	Net Official Monetary Movements
		Interest & Dividends	Services Balance		Long-term Flows	Short-term Flows		
1930	-93	-289	-214	-337	392	-19	373	36
1931	21	-282	-182	-174	87	54	141	-33
1932	97	-265	-182	-96	33	60	93	-3
1933	164	-226	-161	-2	-37	33	-4	-6
1934	164	-211	-90	68	-91	27	-64	4
1935	206	-206	-77	125	-151	32	-119	6
1936	342	-236	-94	244	-237	-2	-239	5
1937	265	-226	-78	180	-157	-17	-174	6
1938	195	-241	-85	99	-95	13	-82	17
1939	193	-249	-61	128	-104	13	-91	37
1940	196	-261	-53	151	-102	-46	-148	3
1941	468	-226	19	501	53	14	67	568
1942	1,109	-203	-21	106	-787	7	-780	-674
1943	1,471	-202	-269	690	-315	-11	-326	364
1944	2,192	-193	-1,187	60	224	-10	214	274
1945	2,032	-171	-519	689	-46	25	-21	668
1946	571	-242	-111	363	-715	86	-629	-266

TABLE 2 (continued)

Canada's Balance of International Payments, 1930-1982

	Merchandise Trade Balance	Current Account			Capital Account			Net Official Monetary Movements
		Interest & Dividends	Services Service Balance	Current Account Balance	Long-term Flows	Short-term Flows	Capital Account Balance	
1947	188	-273	-118	49	-721	4	-717	-668
1948	432	-255	-7	451	43	-2	41	492
1949	293	307	-142	177	-29	-20	-49	128
1950	7	-381	-341	-319	610	431	1,041	722
1951	-151	-337	-377	-512	666	-98	568	56
1952	485	-261	-299	187	455	-605	-150	37
1953	-60	-242	-378	-448	649	-239	410	-38
1954	18	-277	-436	-424	599	-51	548	124
1955	-211	-312	-442	-687	414	229	643	-44
1956	-728	-382	-599	-1,372	1,490	-70	1,420	48
1957	-594	-441	-806	-1,451	1,320	26	1,346	-105
1958	-176	-447	-836	-1,137	1,153	93	1,246	109
1959	-421	-491	-953	-1,487	1,179	297	1,476	-11
1960	-148	-485	-959	-1,233	929	265	1,194	-39
1961	173	-551	-1,029	-928	930	290	1,220	292
1962	184	-581	-995	-830	688	296	984	154
1963	503	-630	-996	-521	637	29	666	145

Year								
1964	701	-678	-1,111	-424	750	38	788	364
1965	118	-764	-1,277	-1,130	833	455	1,289	158
1966	224	-822	-1,438	-1,162	1,228	-425	803	-359
1967	566	-916	-1,137	-499	1,415	-896	519	20
1968	1,471	-906	-1,752	-97	1,669	-1,223	446	349
1969	964	-915	-2,024	-917	2,337	-1,355	982	65
1970	3,052	-1,022	-2,099	1,106	1,007	-583	424	1,663
1971	2,563	-1,141	-2,398	431	664	-318	346	896
1972	1,857	-1,048	-2,527	-386	1,588	-983	605	336
1973	2,735	-1,260	-2,971	108	628	-1,203	-575	-467
1974	1,689	-1,553	-3,706	-1,460	1,041	443	1,484	24
1975	-451	-1,953	-4,686	-4,757	3,935	417	4,352	-405
1976	1,388	-2,498	-5,760	-3,842	8,007	-3,643	4,364	522
1977	2,730	-3,658	-7,444	-4,301	4,217	-1,337	2,880	-1,421
1978	4,007	-4,696	-8,992	-4,935	3,111	-1,475	1,636	-3,299
1979	4,118	-5,241	-9,746	-4,962	1,905	4,746	6,651	1,908
1980	8,488	-5,384	-10,831	-1,096	907	-1,306	-401	-1,280
1981	7,351	-6,474	-14,258	-5,346	558	6,004	6,562	1,426
1982	17,746	-9,303	-16,501	2,669	8,561	-11,925	-3,364	-695

SOURCES: *Historical Statistics of Canada*, 2nd ed., Tables G57-115; Department of Finance, *Economic Review, April, 1983* (Ottawa, 1983), Tables 68, 71, 74.

The Liberal government felt that the long-term solution to the crisis required a restructuring of Canada's export trade in such a way as to maintain a more even balance with the level of imports from the U.S. In the first round of negotiations concluded under the General Agreement on Tariffs and Trade (GATT) in 1947, Canadian negotiators succeeded in winning tariff reductions and lessening quotas on Canadian resource exports to the U.S. The tariff concessions on Canadian staple exports gained under GATT were welcomed by C.D. Howe:

> As the mineral reserves of the United States are diminished, it was logical that attention will turn increasingly to Canadian mineral and associated hydro power resources. The new tariff rates are a great step forward in achieving an economic integration of North American resources, to the mutual advantage of the northern and southern halves . . . .[13]

Other important policy initiatives of the Liberals included increased tax incentives for resource exploration and development as well as the negotiation of increased sales to the U.S. stockpile of strategic metals and minerals in the late 1940's.[14]

In the 1950's, Canada's merchandise exports rose dramatically, largely as a result of the increased flow of resources to the U.S. Prior to World War II, less than 40 per cent of total Canadian exports went to the U.S., but by 1956 the proportion had risen to nearly 60 per cent. The rising level of exports was accompanied by a large amount of U.S. direct investment in the Canadian economy, particularly in such resource industries as nonferrous metals, forest products, and petroleum. This investment was accompanied by a substantial increase in the flow of U.S. imports into Canada, largely machinery and capital equipment required for the expansion being undertaken in the resource and other industries. The flow of imports was so great that Canada continued to experience a deficit in merchandise trade in the mid-1950's; however, this was more than offset by the massive inflow of capital, thus avoiding a recurrence of the exchange crisis of the preceding decade (Table 2).

The continued growth of the Canadian economy in the mid-1950's, along with the steady increase of U.S. investment, had important effects on the implementation of fiscal and monetary stabilization policies. The sustained economic expansion of this period was accompanied by a steady rise in the annual rate of inflation (Table 1). The government began to shift the focus of its stabilization policies away from a concern with unemployment to controlling the persistent drift toward inflation. The government became reluctant to apply the major tax and expenditure levers of fiscal policy to counteract an anticipated economic downturn for fear of aggravating the rate of inflation. It began also to place greater reliance on monetary policy as a supplementary instrument of stabilization policy. This emphasis was due to the conviction of the independent-minded governor of the Bank of Canada, James Coyne, that the inflationary problem was primarily the result of a strong demand for investment funds. Coyne believed that the problem of inflation and the current account deficit on the balance of payments were both linked to the country's excessive reliance on an inflow of U.S. funds to finance its capital investments. He felt the most sensible policy response was to restrict the amount of investment funds available through credit controls and restraints on the rate of growth of the money supply.

In the period from late 1954 on, the Bank of Canada applied this policy with increasing vigour. By the end of 1956, these measures began to take hold as a serious credit squeeze developed throughout the economy. The success of this policy produced a decline in the rate of inflation by 1957; but it coincided with a fall in the rate of investment, which signalled the onset of the first major post-war recession. The lower rate of economic growth persisted throughout the tenure of the first post-war Conservative government under John Diefenbaker from 1957 to 1963. The impact of Coyne's restrictive monetary policies was compounded by the deflationary effects of Finance Minister Donald Fleming's fiscal policies, hence prolonging the economic recession. Coyne's obsession with the balance of payments and his provocative statements on the need for more fiscally conservative and nationalist economic policies eventually led to his dismissal by the Diefenbaker government. His policies of the late 1950's, however, provide the first clear indication of the constraints on the ability of Canadian governments to implement Keynesian demand management policies. The growing conflict between the management of the current account deficit and the maintenance of stable levels of employment and prices revealed the potential contradictions between the marriage of Keynes and the staples orientation of the Canadian economy that had been attempted in the White Paper on Employment and Income.[15]

The end of the recession accompanied the defeat of the Diefenbaker government in 1963. Several factors contributed to the economic recovery. The reduced value of the Canadian dollar, pegged at $.925 U.S. by the Conservatives in 1962, provided a strong boost for Canadian exports. Furthermore, the expansionary economic policies adopted by the Kennedy and Johnson administrations in the U.S., in a vain attempt to wage the war in Vietnam and a domestic war on poverty simultaneously, also provided a strong stimulus to the Canadian economy. The increased demand for Canadian goods in the U.S. produced strong surpluses in Canada's merchandise trade throughout the rest of the decade and into the 1970's (Table 2).

Two additional factors contributed to the improved trade performance. One was the signing of the Canada-U.S. Auto Pact in 1965. In the years before the Auto Pact, Canada had experienced a constant deficit on its trade in motor vehicles and parts with the U.S. Under the terms of the Auto Pact, U.S. manufacturers increased their assembly operations in Canada and by the early 1970's this resulted in the achievement of a modest surplus on Canada's overall trade in motor vehicles and parts. The second factor was the rising level of energy exports – principally petroleum and natural gas – from Canada to the U.S. because of declining U.S. energy reserves. Canada's trade balance in energy commodities shifted from a deficit of $155 million in 1966 to a surplus of $183 million in 1970.[16]

The new Liberal government under Lester Pearson also introduced more expansionary economic policies. The publication of the *First Annual Review* of the Economic Council of Canada, which advocated the goals of full employment and economic growth, justified the pursuit of these policy goals. The fiscal policies adopted by the Liberals in the mid-1960's reflected this approach. As a consequence of both the external stimuli to growth and domestic policies, the annual rate of increase of Gross National Expenditure (GNE) averaged between 5 and 6 per cent during the mid-1960's (Table 1). The cycle of renewed economic expansion was marked, however, by a degree of industrial strife and wage militancy not seen since the end of the war. Membership growth in the trade union movement had been relatively static from the mid-1950's to 1964. In the next four years it increased by more than 500,000 (largely due to the extension of collective bargaining rights to the federal public service). The labour movement drew a greater sense of strength from the increase in its size and the rapid growth of the economy. This strength was manifested in an unprecedented increase in strike activity in the mid-1960's.

The union militancy of the mid-1960's must be understood in the context of the poor performance of the Canadian economy in the late 1950's and early 1960's. During the years of the recession, employers took a much tougher position in bargaining and sought to regain some of the wage concessions made in the postwar period. Unions achieved significantly lower wage gains than they had in the previous decade. The rising militancy of the 1960's was in part attributable to the release of pent-up demands that had accumulated during the years of the recession.

The new aggressiveness of the labour movement's wage demands created considerable concern among the Liberal government's economic policy-makers. They felt that the economy had reached a state of virtual full employment in 1965. As the steady pace of expansion continued, they became increasingly preoccupied with the rise in the rate of inflation from 1.8 per cent in 1964 to 4 per cent in 1968 (Table 1). Attempts to restrict the rate of price increases while maintaining the level of employment through the use of traditional fiscal and monetary policies failed. The policy-makers became convinced that Canada was experiencing a new type of cost-push inflation, generated by the organizational strength of unions and corporations and their expectations that governments would prevent a severe recession. The government's conviction led to the introduction of the ill-fated Prices and Incomes Commission (PIC) experiment in 1969. The PIC attempted to persuade both labour organizations and business associations to agree to a one-year program of voluntary wage and price restraint. In conjunction with more restrictive fiscal and monetary policy, the agreement by business representatives voluntarily to restrain prices succeeded in bringing the rate of inflation down in 1970. The experiment ended in failure, however, largely due to the militant noncompliance of the labour movement. [17]

While the restrictive fiscal and monetary policies adopted in 1969-70 helped reduce the rate of inflation, they had an unanticipated effect on the balance of payments and the exchange value of the Canadian dollar. In response to the sharp reduction in the rate of growth of the money supply, engineered by the Bank of Canada, Canadian interest rates rose substantially, widening the gap with those in the U.S. This induced a large inflow of capital from the U.S. into Canada in response to the higher rates. In conjunction with the improved performance in Canada's balance of merchandise trade at this time, the overall improvements in the balance of payments placed strong upward pressure on the exchange value of the Canadian dollar. In early 1970, the government was forced to free the dollar from its fixed exchange rate of $.925 (U.S.) and it quickly floated upward to near parity with the U.S. dollar. Over the next two years, the continued strong performance of Canada's merchandise trade created a strong balance of payments position, which sustained the upward pressure on the dollar. The Bank of Canada became concerned that any further appreciation of the dollar would undermine Canada's export prospects and slow down the rate of economic growth. At the same time, the Liberal government, anticipating the approaching federal election, shifted its concern from inflation back to unemployment, which had risen during 1970 and 1971 (Table 1). To reduce the upward pressure on the dollar and to facilitate a faster rate of economic growth, the Bank of Canada eased its monetary restraint and lowered interest rates. As a result, the money supply, defined in terms of currency and demand deposits, increased from a rate of growth from 2.2. per cent in 1970 to 12.7 per cent in 1971, 14.3 per cent in 1972, and 14.5 per cent in 1973.[18]

The shift to a more expansionary monetary policy in the early 1970's was accompanied by a more stimulative fiscal policy and by continued strong demand for Canadian exports on world markets. Into the buoyant economic climate of these years was injected one more significant factor: a strong improvement in Canada's international terms of trade as a result of the commodities price boom of 1972-74. During these years the prices paid for resource commodities rose much more rapidly than the prices paid for manufactured goods. Because such a significant proportion of Canada's exports consisted of resource products, while the major proportion of its imports were manufactured goods, this shift contributed to a strong resurgence of the rate of economic growth. From 1971 to 1973 the rate of increase of GNE averaged over 7 per cent. The rate of increase of the Consumer Price Index rose as well, from 2.9 per cent in 1971 to 10.9 per cent by 1974 (Table 1).

The rapid rise in consumer prices was largely a product of the increase in international commodities prices. The appreciation of the Canadian dollar and the improvement in Canada's terms of trade contributed to the realization of a higher dollar value for a given volume of exports and thus to a higher level of national income and aggregate demand in the economy. At the same time, commodity price increases also affected the cost of raw materials used in production in Canada and the cost of imported goods. A study done by the Conference Board of Canada estimated that in the period from 1972 to 1975 almost 45 per cent of the overall increase in the price level could be accounted for by increases in material costs and imported goods. The author of the study noted:

The sources of inflationary pressure experienced during the 1970s have significant implications for domestic stabilization policy. In its early stages, the inflation was not solely the result of excess demand in Canada, and therefore the scope

for moderating the rate of price increase by traditional demand management policies was limited. The principal point
here is the vulnerability of the Canadian economy to inflation
from external sources. More than 40% of the inflation in
Canada during the 1970s originated outside the country. The
important role played by international prices makes the
achievement . . . of a rate of price increase in Canada which is
significantly lower than in the rest of the world exceedingly
difficult.[19]

Once again, the contradictions between the demand management concerns and the export orientation of the Keynesian
policy synthesis were revealed in the economic difficulties of the
mid-1970's.

The problems were further compounded, however, by the impact the inflationary spiral of the early 1970's had on domestic
wage developments. A scant four years after the abandonment
of the Prices and Incomes Commission experiment, the Liberal
government found itself confronted with an almost identical
situation – only with substantially higher rates of inflation. During the early part of the economic upswing, wage increases had
lagged well behind the rate of price increases. This lag was partly
due to the fact that many unions were locked into two- and
three-year contracts that did not allow for the dramatic price
rises that occurred. By 1974, the level of strike activity had
begun to rise as unions attempted to recoup the real wages they
had lost and to protect themselves against further losses in the
future years of the contract. The renewed wage militancy displayed by unions in the mid-1970's once again became a major
source of concern to the government. In the budget speech of
November 1974, the Minister of Finance, John Turner, warned
that the sum total of the nation's resources, "the real national
pie," was not equal to all of the demands being placed on it by
different groups. He followed up this warning in early 1975 with
a round of talks with the major labour organizations, business
executives, and other representative groups in Canadian society
aimed at developing a consensus on the need for voluntary income restraints. The talks broke down, much as they had in
1970, largely because of the conviction of the labour organizations that the restraints proposed by the Liberal government
were inherently unequal with respect to the treatment of wages
and other sources of income.[20]

By the summer of 1975, the government's concern over the de-
teriorating economic situation had increased. The OPEC price
revolution of 1973, itself an important part of the international

TABLE 3

Structural Changes in Income, 1930-1982

(per cent distribution of net national income by component)

	Labour Income	Corp. Profits before Taxes	Dividends Paid to Non-residents	Interest and Investment Income	Farm Income	Unincorporated Business Income	Inventory Valuation Adjustment
1930	64.3	7.4	-4.1	3.1	8.0	15.8	5.5
1931	72.5	4.9	-4.5	2.6	2.8	16.5	5.2
1932	76.3	1.2	-5.0	3.0	4.0	16.3	4.2
1933	77.1	7.3	-4.2	2.4	2.8	15.5	-0.9
1934	71.3	10.8	-3.8	2.7	6.1	14.3	-1.4
1935	69.2	11.7	-3.9	3.1	7.2	14.2	-0.7
1936	67.9	14.3	-4.8	2.6	6.0	15.1	-1.1
1937	66.5	15.6	-4.3	2.5	7.3	14.7	-2.3
1938	64.0	12.9	-4.4	1.7	9.0	15.1	1.7
1939	63.1	16.7	-4.2	1.9	8.7	15.1	-1.3
1940	63.3	17.0	-3.7	2.3	9.5	14.0	-2.4
1941	64.3	18.0	-2.7	2.5	7.3	13.1	-2.5
1942	61.7	16.3	-2.1	2.3	11.5	11.8	-1.5
1943	66.0	14.8	-1.8	2.6	8.1	11.3	-1.0
1944	64.2	13.0	-1.6	2.3	11.4	11.3	-0.6
1945	64.7	13.1	-1.5	2.4	9.4	12.3	-0.4
1946	62.2	15.7	-2.1	1.8	11.0	14.1	-2.7
1947	63.8	17.5	-2.4	1.8	10.4	14.2	-5.4
1948	63.6	16.5	-2.1	2.0	11.0	13.0	-4.1
1949	63.6	15.1	-2.4	2.2	9.1	13.3	-0.8

1950	62.9	17.9	-2.8	2.7	8.9	12.9	2.6
1951	62.6	18.3	-2.2	2.7	10.9	11.5	-3.7
1952	62.0	15.8	-1.8	2.7	9.6	11.1	0.6
1953	64.9	14.8	-1.6	2.9	7.3	11.7	—
1954	67.3	13.8	-1.7	3.1	4.6	12.5	0.4
1955	65.6	15.9	-1.8	3.5	5.1	12.5	-0.8
1956	66.3	16.1	-1.8	3.6	5.3	11.6	1.0
1957	69.1	14.0	-2.0	3.9	3.6	11.7	-0.2
1958	68.0	13.9	-1.8	4.0	4.2	11.9	0.2
1959	69.0	14.3	-1.9	3.8	3.6	11.6	-0.4
1960	69.8	13.4	-1.7	3.9	3.6	11.1	-0.1
1961	70.5	13.7	-2.1	4.3	2.8	10.9	-0.1
1962	69.4	13.7	-1.9	4.4	4.3	10.4	-0.3
1963	69.0	14.2	-1.9	4.5	4.5	10.3	-0.6
1964	69.1	15.5	-2.1	4.6	3.5	9.8	-0.4
1965	70.1	15.3	-2.0	4.6	3.4	9.4	-0.8
1966	70.5	14.5	-1.8	4.5	4.2	8.9	-0.7
1967	72.7	13.7	-1.8	4.7	2.5	8.8	-0.7
1968	72.0	14.2	-1.5	4.8	2.4	8.7	-0.6
1969	72.6	13.7	-1.4	5.1	2.4	8.6	-1.0
1970	74.1	12.0	-1.5	5.3	1.9	8.4	-0.3
1971	74.1	12.3	-1.5	5.5	2.2	8.4	-0.9
1972	73.5	13.6	-1.3	5.7	2.1	7.7	-1.3
1973	71.7	16.3	-1.3	5.7	3.2	7.0	-2.5
1974	71.4	17.6	-1.4	6.7	3.4	6.1	-3.7
1975	72.9	15.1	-1.4	6.7	3.0	5.9	-2.3
1976	73.7	13.5	-1.2	7.5	2.2	5.7	-1.4
1977	74.9	13.0	-1.3	8.2	1.8	5.7	-2.1

TABLE 3 (continued)
Structural Changes in Income, 1930-1982
(Per Cent Distribution of Net National Income by Component)

	Labour Income	Corp. Profits before Taxes	Dividends Paid to Non-residents	Interest and Investment Income	Farm Income	Unincorporated Business Income	Inventory Valuation Adjustment
1978	73.4	14.3	-1.6	8.9	2.0	5.5	-2.6
1979	71.9	16.6	-1.5	9.3	1.9	5.2	-3.5
1980	72.1	15.9	-1.4	9.7	1.7	5.1	-3.1
1981	73.9	12.8	-1.5	10.5	1.7	5.2	-2.7
1982	76.2	8.2	-1.3	11.2	1.8	5.3	-1.4

SOURCES: Statistics Canada, *National Income and Expenditure Accounts, 1: The Annual Estimates, 1926-1974* (Ottawa, 1976) 96-7, 196-7, 296-7; Department of Finance, *Economic Review, April, 1983* (Ottawa, 1983), Reference Table 12.

commodities price boom, had triggered a generalized recession throughout the advanced capitalist economies. By 1975, the impact of the recession had begun to be felt in Canada. The rate of increase of the GNE fell from 7.5 per cent in 1973 to 1.2 per cent (Table 1). In spite of the growing slack in the economy, union wage demands showed no signs of abating. The government was subjected to substantial pressure from business interests, who were alarmed by the shift in the distribution of national income from corporate profits, interest, and dividends to wages and salaries (Table 3). The government felt also that the large wage increases being won were driving the cost structure of the Canadian economy out of line with those of its major trading partners, principally the U.S. The Department of Finance's Index of Competitiveness, reproduced in Figure 1, indicates that unit labour costs, measured against a currency weighted average of unit labour costs of Canada's major trading partners, rose substantially from the mid-1960's to 1976. While the government was partly correct in attributing this shift to the substantial increase in unit labour costs in the 1970's (Table 1), it was also attributable to the appreciation of the exchange value of the Canadian dollar.

FIGURE 1
Canada's Competitiveness in the Manufacturing Sector, 1960-1982
(Competitive Index 1970 = 100)

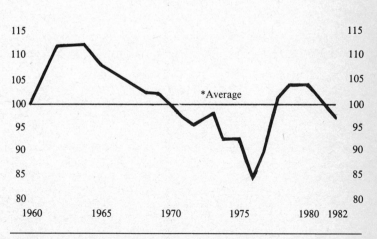

* Weighted average of unit labour costs of competing countries relative to unit labour costs in Canada, the unit labour costs being expressed in U.S. dollars.

SOURCE: Department of Finance, *Economic Review, April, 1983* (Ottawa, 1983), 56.

The government was equally concerned over the dramatic deterioration in Canada's balance of international payments, which occurred in the context of the international recession. While the demand for Canadian exports declined on world markets in late 1974 and 1975, the Canadian demand for imports remained strong due to the delayed onset of the recession and the higher levels of income in the domestic economy. The merchandise trade balance fell from a surplus of $3 billion, reached in 1970, to a deficit of $451 million in 1975. At the same time, the deficit on the current account had risen as well, largely due to the growing amounts of interest and dividends being paid on the foreign capital invested in Canada since the 1950's. The overall result was that Canada recorded a record deficit of $4.757 billion on the current account of the balance of payments in 1975 (Table 2).

In response to the economic difficulties encountered in 1975, the government displayed a growing scepticism about the efficacy of Keynesian policies. At the outset of the recession in 1974, fiscal and monetary policy had become somewhat more expansionary in an attempt to sustain levels of employment and income. By the fall of 1975, the government was convinced that this attempt had made the economic situation even worse. In the budget speech of May 1976, Mr. Turner's successor, Donald S. Macdonald, proclaimed that the fiscal stimulation applied in late 1974 had intensified the inflationary spiral and worsened the balance of payments position.[21] The Keynesian formulae, which had guided post-war economic policy, were no longer regarded as valid.

THE END OF THE KEYNESIAN ERA

Keynesianism had fallen victim to both the internal and external economic contradictions it had contained since its inception. The assumption underlying the post-war political compromise was that demand management policies could assure a profitable basis for the accumulation process and simultaneously could guarantee the wage and income security of the working population as a whole. The implementation of the post-war political settlement resulted in a substantial alteration of the historical conflict between capital and labour over the distribution of income. The gradual emergence of inflation as the primary economic problem of the post-war period resulted from the intensified efforts of trade unions to improve their real wage levels and the response of corporations to maintain their profit levels.

These economic problems were compounded even further in a dependent staples-producing economy such as Canada's. The profound cyclical fluctuations in the Canadian economy tied to the external demand for staple exports added a degree of uncertainty to the wage and profit calculations of unions and corporations.[22] This uncertainty intensified the competitive struggle over the distribution of the national income as was evidenced in the 1972-75 period. At the same time, the problems of demand management policy were complicated by the concerns of the balance of payments and the attempt to stabilize the currency's rate of exchange. These concerns repeatedly frustrated the goals of Keynesian demand management policies.

In a series of dramatic moves in the fall of 1975, the government signalled the abandonment of Keynesianism in favour of more conservative alternatives. The first of these was the announcement by the governor of the Bank of Canada of the bank's conversion to a gradualist strategy of monetary restraint to bring inflation under control through steady decreases in the rate of growth of the money supply. This new policy was announced in a speech by the governor, Mr. Bouey, to the Canadian Chamber of Commerce in Saskatoon in September 1975.

> The last time this country began to emerge from recession into recovery with a persisting problem of substantially escalated labour costs was as recently as 1970, only five years ago. In those days a policy aimed at trading off a bit more inflation in order to get a bit more employment was still the conventional economic wisdom. . . . And now we find ourselves back at square one with higher unemployment rates, with higher underlying rates of cost and price inflation, and with higher interest rates. For more than 20 years almost every country in the western world has given rapid growth and high unemployment much higher priority in its policies than the preservation of the value of money. This approach worked well for quite a while, but it will not work well any longer. . . . We now have no option but to contain inflation and inflationary expectations if we are to have any realistic hope of achieving sustained economic growth.[23]

The specific policy option that followed from this philosophical conversion was the establishment of narrowly defined specific target ranges for the rate of growth of the money supply (currency and demand deposits). The initial target range was set by the bank in November 1975 between 10 per cent and 15 per cent. The targets were gradually lowered at regular intervals over the

next few years to a range between 4 per cent and 8 per cent in
1982. In establishing this policy, the bank made it clear that
other aspects of monetary policy, such as the level of interest
rates and the exchange rate, would be subordinated to this
primary goal.[24]

The second component of the Liberal's post-Keynesian policy
orientation was the introduction of the Anti-Inflation Program
on October 14, 1975. The *Attack on Inflation* consisted of four
related strategies: fiscal and monetary policies to reduce the rate
of inflation; government expenditure restraint aimed at keeping
the rate of increase in government spending to less than that of
GNE; structural policies to deal with the supply of energy, food,
and housing; and a prices and incomes policy that established
guidelines for determining wage and price increases. The *Attack
on Inflation* reiterated the theme struck by Governor Bouey.
"The government's clear determination not to accommodate
continued high or increasing inflation must be embodied . . . in
the settings of fiscal and monetary policy."[25] With respect to the
issue of the overall size of government spending in the Canadian
economy, it announced, "The federal government shares the
view that the trend of total spending by all governments in
Canada should not rise more quickly than the trend of gross national product."[26] Taken together, these two aspects of the government's new economic strategy indicated that the traditional
Keynesian notion of discretionary changes in fiscal and monetary policy to offset fluctuations in the economy was dead and
buried; it had been supplanted by a return to the traditional Vic-
torian "balance the budget" orthodoxy, which had prevailed
during the depression.

The centrepiece of the *Attack on Inflation* was the compre-
hensive set of guidelines introduced to control the rate of increase of wages and prices. The Anti-Inflation Board (AIB) was
created to monitor wage and price increases in the economy. It
was empowered to restrain increases in prices, profit margins,
compensation, and dividends for firms with more than 500 employees, the federal, provincial, and municipal governments,
and professionals. Rather than controlling prices directly, the
program hoped to limit the rate of price increases indirectly by
restraining wages and profit margins. The emphasis in the program was on flexibility and administrative simplicity. Although
the government argued at the time that the program was designed to effectively restrain both wage and price increases, its
critics argued that the controls over wages were considerably
more stringent than those over prices. The actual experience of
wage and salary earners under the program was to provide am-
ple support for this criticism.

The Liberal government's new economic strategy achieved mixed results at best. The Bank of Canada's policy of monetary targeting was highly successful in attaining its primary goal. The rate of growth of the money supply fell consistently after 1975. From an annual rate of increase of 13.6 per cent in 1975, it was reduced to a rate of increase of 2 per cent in 1982, well below the target range established by the bank. Whether the strategy of gradualism was equally successful in controlling the rate of inflation is another question. In the initial period following the adoption of the Anti-Inflation Program and the strategy of gradualism, the CPI fell substantially. In the late 1970's and early 1980's, however, the rate of price increases shot back up to double-digit levels, in spite of the fact that the size of the money supply was being tightly controlled. This growing divergence between the rate of growth of the money supply and the rate of price increases led many observers to question the effectiveness of the bank's strategy.[27]

The impact of the strategy of gradualism on the stability of the exchange rate and the problems of the balance of payments were even more questionable. The shift in monetary policy in late 1975 led to a rapid rise in both short and long-term interest rates. By March of 1976, the difference between Canadian and U.S. short-term rates had increased from just under 2 per cent to almost 5 per cent. This rise in interest rates encouraged a massive rise in the level of corporate and government borrowing in the U.S.[28] Long-term capital flows into Canada jumped from $1 billion in 1974 to $8 billion in 1976. The effect of this sudden influx of foreign capital into Canada was to maintain the exchange rate of the dollar at a much higher level than was warranted by the increasing deficit on the current account. The dollar remained above parity with the U.S. dollar until late in 1976. This policy both hindered the recovery of Canadian exports on world markets and increased the size of the current account deficit due to the rapidly rising cost (in interest and dividends) of servicing the massive foreign borrowings, more than $9 billion by 1982 (Table 2).

The effects of the other element of the restraint policy, the Anti-Inflation Program, were equally as dubious. The wage and price guidelines were much more effective in limiting wage gains than they were in restraining prices. The rate of increase of labour compensation per unit of output fell from 15 per cent in 1975 to 4 per cent in 1978 (Table 1). Several econometric studies have attempted to assess the direct impact of the AIB on this decline. A study carried out by the Conference Board of Canada concluded that by the third quarter of 1978 wage levels in Canada would have been 7.7 per cent higher in the absence of controls.[29] A study done for the Anti-Inflation Board itself also concluded that the controls program had a significant effect in lowering the level of wage increases during the period of its existence.[30] In reality, the controls program effected a substantial redistribution of income from labour to capital. By restraining wage increases much more effectively than it restrained profit margins or price increases, the controls contributed to shift the national income away from labour toward profit and dividends (Table 3). The combined effect of both the controls program and the government's tight monetary policies also produced the improvement in Canada's international competitive position that they were seeking. The fall in the Department of Finance's Index of Competitiveness was stopped in 1976 and by 1979 it had climbed back to a higher level than it had enjoyed in the mid-1960's (Figure 1).

The overall costs of the government's restraint strategy have been extremely high. On the one hand, it introduced a policy of wage and price controls to restore Canada's international competitive position and restrain domestic demand to reduce the growing deficit in merchandise trade. At the same time, a gradualist monetary policy was introduced to achieve the same goals. The cumulative results have been substantially higher interest rates, massive capital inflows, and a further deterioration of the current account due to the inflated costs of servicing the foreign debt. Although the devaluation of the dollar and an improvement in export markets gradually led to a better trade balance in the early 1980's, a higher and higher level of exports was required each year to finance the spiralling service account deficit. At the same time, interest rate differentials between Canada and the U.S. had to be maintained to ensure a continued inflow of capital to keep the overall balance of payments in equilibrium. By the early 1980's, the Bank of Canada was virtually raising interest rates on a reflex basis in direct response to changes in U.S. rates without regard for the consequences for the domestic levels of employment and income. The gradualist chickens came home to roost with a vengeance in late 1981 and 1982. Interest rates peaked at levels in excess of 20 per cent, triggering the most severe recession since the 1930's. Real GNE declined by almost 5 per cent in 1982 (Table 1), the official unemployment rate reached 12.7 per cent (while unofficial estimates placed it closer to 20 per cent), and a total of 1,231,000 jobs were lost in the Canadian economy between August 1981 and December 1982.[31]

The recession of the 1980's eventually corrected the problems of inflation and the deterioration of the balance of payments, but at a terrible social and economic cost in terms of lost output and higher rates of unemployment. The Liberals' abandonment of Keynesianism also cost them dearly at the polls in the general election of 1979. However, they were quickly given an opportunity to return to power by the parliamentary blundering of the new Conservative government. In the election campaign of 1980, the Liberal Party attempted to fashion a new political platform to replace the abandoned framework of the post-war Keynesian compromise. The new platform attempted to trade off a continued adherence to the monetary gradualism and expenditure restraint espoused by the Bank of Canada and conservative business interests with a more interventionist approach to promoting industrial development in key sectors of the economy. The entire package of policies was legitimated with a strongly nationalist appeal the Liberals hoped would garner them the support the welfare state policies had drawn in the past.

The centrepiece of the new political framework was the National Energy Program (NEP) of October 1980 and an industrial development strategy keyed to the construction of energy megaprojects.[32] The government hoped that the increased revenues it derived from the NEP would provide sufficient funds to realize a more balanced budget and simultaneously enable it to finance major industrial development projects. The onslaught of the world recession in 1982 left this strategy in shambles. Energy prices fell rather than rose, leaving the government with even larger budgetary deficits than had been anticipated. Most of the megaprojects were abandoned by their sponsors in the face of the plummeting world demand for energy. Business interests in Canada were overwhelmingly incensed by the nationalism of the new policy and the general electorate alienated by the immense social costs of the recession. The attempt to fashion a new political consensus appears to have been stillborn.

CONCLUSION

The shift from Keynesianism to monetary gradualism in 1975 signalled the end of the post-war era in Canadian economic policy and the abrogation of the post-war political compromise. The delicate balance that the post-war compromise attempted to strike between the economic interests of capital and wage and salary earners was replaced by a one-sided preoccupation with the concerns of business and the requirements of capital accumulation. With the demise of the Keynesian era and the onslaught of the new depression, the fundamental distributional issues that lie at the heart of a capitalist economy are once again emerging at the forefront of political debate. For most of the post-war period these issues were suppressed by the prospect of a "democratic capitalism" that the Keynesian compromise seemed to hold out. As that prospect fades farther into the distance, it is not surprising to see renewed struggles between capital and labour emerging at the centre of the political stage. The political struggle within each national economy is complicated by the global restructuring of the international capitalist economy, which is occurring in the context of the current economic crisis. Most attempts to resolve the current impasse have emphasized nationalist solutions involving an attempt to insulate the economy from international pressures or a strategy for competing more effectively in the emerging New International Division of Labour. Given the growing degree of interpenetration in the world economy, the prospects of success for such a strategy are highly doubtful. The global nature of the current crisis differentiates it from the Great Depression of the 1930's; any political resolution of the current crisis must commence with this fundamental reality of post-Keynesian political economy.[33]

NOTES

1. Ian Gough, "State Expenditure in Advanced Capitalism," *New Left Review,* 92 (July, 1975), 69-70; Leo Panitch, "The Development of Corporatism in Liberal Democracies," *Comparative Political Studies*, 10 (April, 1977), 74-9.

2. Adam Przeworski and Michael Wallerstein, "Democratic Capitalism at the Crossroads," *Democracy*, 2 (July, 1982), 54.

3. John Kenneth Galbraith, "How Keynes Came to America," in Milo Keynes, ed., *Essays on John Maynard Keynes* (Cambridge, 1975), 137.

4. This idea is explored at greater length in David A. Wolfe, "The Delicate Balance: The Changing Economic Role of the State in Canada, 1939-1957" (Ph.D. thesis, University of Toronto, 1980), 369-70.

5. Stewart Bates, *Financial History of Canadian Governments*, study prepared for the Royal Commission on Dominion-Provincial Relations (Ottawa, 1939), 32-103.

6. *Ibid.,* 80; J. Harvey Perry, *Taxes, Tariffs and Subsidies: A History of Canadian Fiscal Development* (Toronto, 1955), I, 257-68; Irving Brecher, *Monetary and Fiscal Thought and Policy, 1919-1939* (Toronto, 1957), 225-35.

7. J.L. Granatstein, *Canada's War: The Politics of the Mackenzie King Government, 1939-45* (Toronto, 1975), 251.

8. J.L. Granatstein, *The Ottawa Men: The Civil Service Mandarins, 1939-1957* (Toronto, 1982), 153-68.

9. House of Commons, *Debates,* 1944, I, 1-3.

10. Department of Reconstruction and Supply, *Employment and Income With Special Reference to the Initial Period of Reconstruction* (Ottawa, 1945). The thinking behind the government's reconstruction planning and the White Paper is discussed in greater detail in Wolfe, "The Delicate Balance," 334-75.

11. Stephen G. Peitchinis, *The Canadian Labour Market* (Toronto, 1975), 308, 316-17; Stuart M. Jamieson, "Trade Unions and Inflation: United States and Canada," in Robert M. Clark, ed., *Canadian Issues: Essays in Honour of Henry F. Angus* (Toronto, 1961), 311, 323.

12. A.F.W. Plumptre, *Three Decades of Decision: Canada and the World Monetary System, 1944-75* (Toronto, 1977), ch. 4; J. Douglas Gibson, ed., *Canada's Economy in a Changing World* (Toronto, 1948), *passim*; R.D. Cuff and J.L. Granatstein, *American Dollars – Canadian Prosperity: Canadian-American Relations, 1945-1950* (Toronto, 1978), chs. 2-4.

13. House of Commons, *Debates,* 1948, I, 135.

14. Cuff and Granatstein, *American Dollars – Canadian Prosperity*, chs. 5, 6.

15. Plumptre, *Three Decades*, ch. 7; J.R. Petrie, "The Credit Squeeze: A Critical Appraisal of Monetary Policy," *Report of the Proceedings of the Eleventh Annual Tax Policy Conference* (Toronto, 1957), 15-18; H. Scott Gordon, *The Economists vs. the Bank of Canada* (Toronto, 1961).

16. Department of Finance, *Economic Overview: A Perspective on the Decade, April, 1980* (Ottawa, 1980), 42 (for the energy trade balance), 101-2 (for the motor vehicle balance); James Laxer and Robert Laxer, *The Liberal Idea of Canada: Pierre Trudeau and the Question of Canada's Survival* (Toronto, 1977), ch. 2.

17. George Haythorne, "Prices and Incomes Policy: The Canadian Experience," *International Labour Review,* 108 (1973), 496: G.A. Berger, *Canada's Experience with Incomes Policy, 1969-1970* (Ottawa, 1973), *passim*.

18. Department of Finance, *Economic Review, April, 1983* (Ottawa, 1983), 224.

19. Reginald S. Letourneau, *Inflation: The Canadian Experience* (Ottawa, 1980), 75-9.

20. Anthony Giles, "The Canadian Labour Congress and Tripartism," *Relations Industrielles/Industrial Relations,* 37 (1982), 98-101.

21. Hon. Donald S. Macdonald, *Budget Speech, May 25, 1976* (Ottawa, 1976), 8-9.

22. The dynamics of this inflationary process are discussed at greater length in Peter Warrian and David Wolfe, *Trade Unions and Inflation* (Ottawa, 1982).

23. Gerald K. Bouey, "Remarks to the 46th Annual Meeting of the Canadian Chamber of Commerce, Saskatoon, Saskatchewan, 22 September 1975" *Bank of Canada Review* (October, 1975), 29.

24. Bank of Canada, *Annual Report of the Governor to the Minister*

of Finance, 1975 (Ottawa 1976), 18; Bank of Canada, *Annual Report of the Governor to the Minister of Finance, 1982* (Ottawa, 1983), 26. A broader discussion of the Bank's monetarist strategy is found in Arthur W. Donner and Douglas D. Peters, *The Monetarist Counter-Revolution: A Critique of Canadian Monetary Policy, 1975-79* (Toronto, 1979), 23-7.

25. Hon. Donald S. Macdonald, *Attack on Inflation*, Policy statement tabled in the House of Commons, 14 October 1975, 4.

26. *Ibid.*. The policy debates leading up to the introduction of the Anti-Inflation Program and the specific nature of the controls program are discussed in more detail in A. Maslove and G. Swimmer, *Wage Controls in Canada, 1975-78* (Montreal, 1980), chs. 2, 3.

27. *Economic Review, April, 1983,* 224; Arthur W. Donner and Douglas D. Peters, "Monetarism: A Costly Experiment," *Canadian Public Policy,* 7 (April, 1981), 233-8; Clarence L. Barber and John C.P. McCallum, "The Failure of Monetarism in Theory and Policy," *Canadian Public Policy*, 7 (April, 1981), 220-32.

28. Clarence L. Barber and John C.P. McCallum, *Inflation and Unemployment: The Canadian Experience* (Toronto, 1980), 72-3.

29. Reginald S. Letourneau, *Inflation and Incomes Policy in Canada,* Executive Bulletin, no. 9, May, 1979 (Ottawa, 1979), 9-13.

30. L.N. Christofides and D.A. Wilton, *Wage Controls in Canada (1975:3-1978:2): A Study of Negotiated Base Wage Rates* (Ottawa, 1979), 88.

31. Social Planning Council of Metropolitan Toronto, "Real Level of Unemployment in Canada – 2,379,000," press release, 18 January 1983.

32. *The National Energy Program, 1980* (Ottawa, 1980); *Economic Development for Canada in the 1980s* (Ottawa, 1981). A good overview of these policy thrusts can be found in G. Bruce Doern, "Energy, Mines and Resources: The Energy Ministry and the National Energy Program," in Doern, ed., *How Ottawa Spends Your Tax Dollars: Federal Priorities, 1981* (Toronto, 1981), 56-89; and Doern, "Liberal Priorities, 1982: The Limits of Scheming Virtuously," in Doern, ed., *How Ottawa Spends Your Tax Dollars, 1982: National Policy and Economic Development* (Toronto, 1982), 1-36.

33. I have discussed the global dimensions of the current economic crisis and its political implications at greater length in "The Crisis in Advanced Capitalism: An Introduction," *Studies in Political Economy*, 11 (Spring, 1983), 7-26.

II
Social Structure

The major changes in Canadian social structure in the last fifty years involve the intensification of trends evident earlier in the century. These trends include the greatly expanded role of the state, the increased bureaucratization of business, and the rise to new prominence of service sectors of the economy. Each of these trends reflects the further development of monopoly capitalism in Canada and each, in turn, as women's employment grew, has affected gender as well as class relations.

The depression greatly increased demands on the state for welfare measures and World War II provided both the necessity and the constitutional means for this massive centralization of power in Ottawa. This rapid growth of state functions and state employment was reflected as well at the provincial and municipal levels. Public-sector employment grew by leaps and bounds and only the growing economic crisis of the 1970's and 1980's has brought into question this development. Yet even with the various freezes and cutbacks, government expenditures and employment continue to rise.

Business, meanwhile, despite rhetorical claims, also saw a huge increase in its bureaucratic employment. The complexities of the multinational enterprise, often with budgets larger than most nation-states, created pools of workers whose functions were often identical to those of their sisters and brothers in the public service. Recent developments in microchip technology and information processing seem to be predicated on just such business concerns, not only the growth of clerical employment but also, of course, the inability to manage and discipline it adequately. Word processors and industrial robots are related phenomena in more ways than just their circuitry.

Finally, the extension of capital into every phase of human life has led to a massive "capitalization" of formerly private and domestic spheres. Thus leisure, sexuality, eating, drinking, playing, relaxing – all preeminently private and domestic in nineteenth-century capitalist society – become "massified" and subject to the concerns and control of corporate capital. All of this in turn means increased employment in the new service-oriented corporate sectors, covering everything from fast food to soft-core pornography to shopping malls.

The places in which Canadians lived also changed significantly with the speeded-up pace of urbanization. Expecially after World War II this process created a new suburban society. In the countryside the farming population fell even more drastically than the urban/rural figures suggest since many people in the so-called rural category were not involved in agriculture.

All these changes in the Canadian social structure led to various responses by Canadians and the period's multifaceted social movements, especially vigorous in the depression and post-war periods and in 1960's, must be partially read in the light of these structural shifts.

FURTHER READING:
On the state, see Leo Panitch, ed., *The Canadian State* (Toronto, 1977). On the world of Canadian business, especially the elite, see: John Porter, *The Vertical Mosaic* (Toronto, 1965); Wallace Clement, *The Canadian Corporate Elite* (Toronto, 1975); and Peter C. Newman, *The Canadian Establishment* (Toronto, 1975). On "consumer" capitalism, Stuart Ewen's *Captains of Consciousness* (New York, 1978), while American in content, is extremely suggestive. On the history of post-war consumerism, classic Canadian sociological accounts can be read with value. See, for example, John Seeley *et al., Crestwood Heights* (Toronto, 1956). A useful account of a particular struggle is James Struthers, *No Fault of Their Own: Unemployment and the Canadian Welfare State, 1914-1941* (Toronto, 1983).

Wallace Clement is a member of the Sociology Department at Carleton University.

Canada's Social Structure: Capital, Labour, and the State, 1930-1980

by Wallace Clement

Canada's past fifty years begin and end with depressions, albeit of significantly different sorts. Between these depressions there was a tremendous industrial expansion during and after World War II, an intensification of resource exploitation, and major changes in the structure of the labour force. The experience of the 1930's and subsequent struggles created a net of social services designed to catch the fall-out of unemployment, although the scale of demand on the state in the early 1980's threatens to burst the net. This paper explores changes in the organization of capital, labour, and the state over the past fifty years in Canada, locating these social structural changes within the context of major social movements, such as nationalism, unionization, and women's struggles. These have been a turbulent fifty years and it will only be possible here to outline some of the most significant trends rather than provide detailed investigations of any specific developments.

Social structures are products of the dynamics of power and resistance; domination and struggle are the motors of history. In other words, the structure of any social formation is the complex outcome of ongoing class and social struggles. It is the expression of institutional formations and practices involving the interaction of the economy and polity in a society's history. Social structures can be defined as sets of enduring relationships among and between key institutions, including the state, capital, and labour. Within these structures are carried out the activities of society as manifest in the nature of the labour market, including levels of employment, demands for skills, occupational differentiation, and gender allocations.

The social structure is social in the sense it is the product of relations between people; it is a structure in the sense of a relatively stable ordering of these relationships into what are often known as institutions. Social structures are as intimate as the family, based on the ideology and practice of patriarchy, or as abstract as the mode of production (the way a society produces and reproduces its material conditions, in Canada's case through capitalism). Such social structures are, of course, subject to change; witness, for example, the movement away from extended families to nuclear families to a growing proportion of single-adult households. Over time even the most central institutions of a society can experience dramatic changes. The decline of the centrality of the church, particularly in Quebec but throughout Canadian society in the past fifty years, has altered the configuration of the social formation. So, too, have the rise of organized labour, the expansion of the state, and the centralization of capital. Since the social structure is a web of relationships connecting such institutions, changes in one part initiate and are influenced by changes to others. Continuing with the example of the church, its decline in Quebec was both precipitated by and stimulated the growth of the state (in health care, welfare, and education) and non-confessional unions.

The relationship between social structures and social movements is difficult to isolate. There has been, for example, an expansion of the women's labour force. This is the result of complex changes in the family, expanded child-care facilities, the need for a women's income for survival, and an expansion of demand within the labour force in areas where women have traditionally been segregated – clerical, sales, and service occupations. The women's movement was an important ideological and political force associated with this increased participation in paid labour but so, too, were the changes in the demand for women workers within the labour force corresponding to changes in the organization of offices, growth of sales occupations, and an expansion of services. Despite pressures by the women's movement, most of the women's labour force remain segregated, low-paid, and dead-end. The social structure has changed but it has carried along with it historical practices and patterns, in part manifesting past ideologies such as patriarchy and in part acting as a structural weakness that can be exploited by employers through the reserve army of labour and occupationally segregated low-wage ghettos. Separating the effects of the women's movement from those of the social structure (including the family, occupational profiles, and labour force demands) is not possible. They are images of one another; each unfolds in the context of the other.

Canada's social structure over the past half century has been characterized by increased concentrations of capital, mobilization of labour, and an expansion of the state. These broad processes are by no means unique to Canada, but particular features make Canada distinctive. Capital has become increasingly concentrated but at the same time fragmented as foreign ownership through branch plants has consolidated control in the productive cornerstones of the economy. While labour has increased in size, there remain important divisions in the movement, especially between national and so-called international unions. Most recent union growth has been in the state sector among clerical and service workers, traditionally regarded as difficult to organize. Their proletarianization and their being the subjects of state restraint have pushed state employees into "the house of labour." Much of Canada's state expansion since World War II (the peak of both state and federal ascendancy in Canada) has occurred at the provincial rather than federal level, leading to greater political fragmentation as manifest in provincialism and separatism. These are some of the major developments to be considered, but first we should examine a few statistics profiling the period.

The most obvious change over the period has been the more than doubling of Canada's population, from 10 million in 1930 to 25 million in 1980.

TABLE 1
Components of Canada's Population Growth, 1931-1976
('000s)

	Total Increase	Natural Increase	Net Migration
1931-1941	1,130	1,222	-92
1941-1951	2,141	1,972	169
1951-1961	4,228	3,148	1,080
1961-1971	3,330	2,608	722
1971-1976	1,424	931	493

SOURCES: Statistics Canada, *Perspective Canada II* (Ottawa, 1977), Table 1.2; F.H. Leacy, ed., *Historical Statistics of Canada,* 2nd ed. (Ottawa, 1983), A339-49.

Table 1 indicates how this growth came about. Net migration during the 1930's was minus 92,000, the result of 242,000 emigrants counteracting only 150,000 immigrants. During the 1940's net migration contributed less than 10 per cent to the population growth, but it represented 26 per cent of the growth in the 1950's, 22 per cent in the 1960's, and 34 per cent during the mid-1970's. The United Kingdom and to a lesser extent the

United States have been the countries of last permanent residence for most modern immigrants to Canada but there were major flows after World War II from Italy (falling off in the late 1960's) and more recently from Asia and the Caribbean (increasing since the late 1960's). Most modern immigrants have located in the major metropolitan centres of Toronto, Montreal, and Vancouver.

Ethnicity is a complex feature of Canada's social structure. At the level of popular culture it has sustained its importance among such groups as Italians, Ukrainians, Scots, and Irish. As a basis for social movements, however, it has been important nationally only for native peoples and Québécois. For these two groups, ethnicity as manifest in nationalism and struggles for self-determination has been of paramount importance over the past fifty years. There has been the formation of a multitude of native organizations, sustained by struggles for aboriginal rights and maintained by concrete actions. In Quebec, quite obviously, the forum of the provincial state has served as the platform to be struggled for and used in the cause of self-determination. Outside these two "nations," ethnicity in Canada has meant the outcome of immigration policies and practices whereby the non-Anglo groups have grown numerically to rival the Anglo majority. Large cities like Montreal and Toronto have become focal points for a variety of groups of mixed ethnic origin while other centres have more homogeneous collectivities (Italians in Hamilton, Ukrainians in Winnipeg, Japanese in Vancouver). Tensions between ethnic groups have certainly fomented since the massive migrations in the post-war era, but they have not come to rival the shameful, systematic racism of World War II when 22,000 Japanese Canadians in British Columbia were interned from 1942 to 1946 even though three-quarters were Canadian citizens and 60 per cent were born in Canada.[1] Contemporary racism in Canada tends to be more individual than systematic, at least for those who manage to penetrate immigration's official barriers.

Tables 2 and 3, using census occupational categories in at least a somewhat meaningful way, map broad labour force changes for men and women over the period 1931 to 1971. They document in a rough way some major structural changes, such as the dramatic increase in the women's labour force: 346 per cent compared to 74 per cent for men. Women's segregation into the commercial proletariat is constant over the period; within this category clerical activities expanded by the greatest rate, followed by sales – which paralleled the overall rate of increase for women – and service, which actually had a lower rate of increase than any of the other major categories. The industrial pro-

TABLE 2
Labour Force Distribution in Canada
by Gender, 1931 and 1971

	Men		Women	
	1931	*1971*	*1931*	*1971*
Managerial	7%	11%	2%	3%
Professional-technical	4	11	18	16
Commercial proletariat[a]	14	21	59	55
Resource proletariat[b]	4	3	0	0
Industrial proletariat[c]	32	34	16	10
Transport/communications	6	7	2	1
Agriculture	34	7	4	3
Total*	101	102	101	100

[a] Commercial proletariat includes clerical, commercial, financial, sales, and service.

[b] Resource proletariat includes fishing, hunting and trapping, logging, mining, and quarrying.

[c] Industrial proletariat includes manufacturing, mechanical, construction, and labourers.

* Total includes 8 per cent of men and 12 per cent of women who were not classified in 1971. Rounding off of percentages has meant that some totals exceed 100 per cent.

SOURCE: Statistics Canada, *Occupations: Historical for Canada and Provinces*, Cat. #94-176, vol. 3, pt. 2 (June, 1978), with calculations.

TABLE 3
Labour Force Changes in Canada
by Gender, 1931 and 1971
('000s)

	Men			Women		
	1931	*1971*	*% Change*	*1931*	*1971*	*% Change*
Managerial	211	594	182	11	86	709
Professional-technical	125	602	382	118	475	304
Commercial proletariat	450	1,171	160	390	1,627	317
Resource proletariat	142	140	–1	—	—	—
Industrial proletariat	1,035	1,911	85	105	289	176
Transport/communications	187	392	110	16	40	148
Agriculture	1,094	400	–63	24	100	318
Not classified	—	439	∞	—	664	∞
Total	3,244	5,649	74	664	2,960	346

SOURCE: see Table 2.

letariat category for women decreased as a proportion over the period but within that the number of labourers grew more rapidly than did that of craft and production workers; for men the opposite was true since the number of labourers actually shrank in absolute terms while craft and production workers grew faster than men's overall growth.

Also revealed in the tables is the rapid decline of agriculture as employment, particularly for men (at least in official statistics, which virtually ignore women's agricultural contribution). In 1930, 30 per cent of the working population was still in agriculture, continuing at 25 per cent in 1940 and falling to 10 per cent by 1960 and below 5 per cent in the 1970's. Parallelling this tendency has been the growing proportion of urban dwellers, rising from 52.5 per cent in 1939 to 76.2 per cent in 1981.

While women in managerial occupations increased at a greater rate over the period, their proportion remains very small (actually less than the number in agriculture). Overall, men tend to be more widely distributed within the occupational structure than women and have become even more dispersed with the decline of agriculture. Over half the women, on the other hand, remain segregated in the commercial proletariat.

TABLE 4
Union Membership in Canada, 1930-1975

	Total Union Membership ('000s)	Non-agricultural Paid Workers in Unions (%)	Union Membership in International Unions (%)
1930	322	13.1	71.7
1935	281	14.5	51.3
1940	362	16.3	62.7
1945	711	24.2	66.2
1949	1,006	29.5	70.9
1955	1,268	33.7	70.5
1960	1,459	32.3	72.1
1965	1,589	29.7	70.8
1970	2,173	33.6	62.5
1975	2,876	36.8	51.4

SOURCE: Leacy, ed., *Historical Statistics of Canada,* 2nd ed., E175-7, with calculations.

A broad indication of unionization, as will be discussed in the body of this paper, is available in Table 4. There has been an unsteady growth in the total number and proportion of unionized workers. The depression took its toll in absolute numbers, if not

proportions, particularly among unions with international affili-
ations. During and immediately following World War II, union
memberships grew steadily, peaking in 1958 at a proportion that
would not be passed again until 1973. During this peak period
industrial unions, particularly internationals, grew most dramatically but appeared to stagnate in the mid-1960's. After this
time unionization of state workers rocketed, especially strengthening national unions at the relative expense of the internationals. The following discussion will reveal some of the factors behind these skeletal figures.

THE DEPRESSION

The 1930's was a period of consolidation, concentration, and retrenchment for the Canadian economy. Ironically, as British
capital withdrew and U.S. direct investment declined, there was
consolidation of the U.S. foothold in Canadian industry. Many
small manufacturers failed and more established firms intensified their hold on core industries. Basing his analysis on the
Royal Commission on Price Spreads, Lloyd G. Reynolds found
that Canadian monopolies fared well during this period, earning
rates of return at 12.2 per cent annually, while competitive industries were folding.[2] Leading the merger movement were
Canadian financial capitalists. The larger firms, especially in
automobiles and related products, gasoline, machinery, tobacco, electrical products, and aluminum, were U.S. branch
plants, many of which had been induced into Canada by a combination of restrictions on exports from the United States in
response to the Hawley-Smoot tariff of 1930 and the introduction of British Imperial Preference in 1932. Resource extraction,
the cornerstone of Canada's exports, was severely curtailed; the
wheat market had collapsed, pulp and paper was slashed to 53
per cent of capacity, and mineral exports dropped by over 60 per
cent.[3]

While resource extraction was located in the hinterland, new
industrial capacity was becoming increasingly concentrated in
central Canada, particularly manufacturing firms controlled in
the United States. Of U.S.-controlled manufacturing plants in
1931, 66 per cent were in Ontario, 16 per cent in Quebec and
only 18 per cent in the other provinces (compared to all manufacturing, which was 42 per cent in Ontario, 31 per cent in
Quebec and 27 per cent elsewhere).[4]

As might be expected, given the economic conditions, the
trade union movement experienced "virtual disintegration" dur-

ing the depression, especially large industrial unions in mining, textiles, clothing, and building trades.[5] There was resistance led mainly by left-wing unions organized through the Workers' Unity League (WUL). By the mid-1930's, the centre of strike activity shifted to Ontario and Quebec, away from the West and British Columbia, as struggles for union recognition followed the development of such heavy industry as steel, automobiles, machinery, chemicals, meatpacking, and clothing and textiles (and away from resource-centred struggles).

The depression radically altered the terrain of Canada's social structure. As Pentland put it, "The Great Depression disposed of the idea that a man seeking employment could always solve his own problem on an agricultural or resource frontier, and demonstrated the superior incomes and stability of industrial employment."[6] Canadian workers were pressed into seeking security through representation in industrial unions, facilitated by the growing concentration of industry into fewer, more centrally located companies in the industrial heartland. The fact that these unions were directed from the United States mirrored the growing presence of U.S. branch plants, and often for similar reasons. The U.S. organizations were more developed than those in Canada, possessing the necessary start-up funds and expertise. Both were welcomed into Canada by their respective constituencies as short-cuts to creating an industrial structure.

THE SECOND WORLD WAR

Although the depression had induced the Canadian state to take a more active role in the economy, such as creating the Canadian Wheat Board in 1935 (only to lapse and have to be reinstated in 1943) and the Bank of Canada in 1935 (effectively nationalized in 1938), it was the Second World War and carry-over to the Korean War that would dramatically alter Canada's social structure. World War II had its main impact on manufacturing; by 1943, 60 per cent of employees in manufacturing were working on war materials.[7] The Korean War's main impact was on resources; the U.S. government's Paley Report (*Resources for Freedom*) identified Canada as the major source for twelve of twenty-two key resources it required for industrial supremacy, thus leading to an intensification of U.S. investment in Canadian resources.[8] By the end of the period, Canada's manufacturing and resource sectors had been dramatically transformed. In 1946, 35 per cent of Canada's manufacturing was foreign-controlled, shifting to 50 per cent by 1953 and by 1957 to 56 per cent; corresponding increases in mining and smelting were from 38 to 57 to 70 per cent.[9]

C.D. Howe, the most powerful minister in the King and St. Laurent administrations, was at the heart of Canada's industrial restructuring. Using broad powers under the War Measures Act, Howe created the War Supply Board and Department of Munitions and Supply, which operated autonomously from Parliament. These agencies would transform the profile of Canada's social structure in a very short period. Twenty-eight Crown corporations were created, and inducements were offered to private capital through special fast write-offs for capital expenditure. Three-quarters of the $700-million government expenditure on plants was for Crown corporations, the rest was private; $500 million in tax credits and depreciation went to private companies, plus expenditures of $800 million on defence construction, aside from purchases of supplies.[10] The War Assets Corporation, created in 1943, transferred facilities to private capital best able to use it. To say it "sold" these assets would be too strong since no "market" as such was cultivated.

Employment in manufacturing had doubled from 1939 to 1943, declining somewhat in 1946 and reaching the 1943 peak of one million again in 1950. Pentland places these developments in context:

> Despite the transfer of several hundred thousand of the most active members of the labour force to the armed forces, Canadians were able to raise the real output of their economy by about two-thirds between 1939 and 1944. A great deal of this output went, of course, to serve war purposes. Nevertheless, the personal consumption of goods and services also rose substantially, by about 30 per cent between 1939 and 1944 and considerably more in 1945 as the war effort slackened.[11]

During the war this restructuring occurred without the benefit of foreign capital.[12] The rapid rise of foreign ownership occurred as these assets were being sold off following the war and during the expansion surrounding the Korean War, as will be discussed in the next section.

In terms of labour, according to Stuart Jamieson, World War II and its immediate aftermath were a "continuation" of forces established in the late 1930's with a series of unionization and recognition strikes.[13] Full employment and labour shortages accompanied unprecedented demand for production while recognition strikes were settled under government pressure, peaking in 1943. These strikes were concentrated in manufacturing (steel, autos, aircraft, and textiles) and mining. The war brought conditions favourable to labour's organizing but it also brought emergency wartime powers, through the War Measures Act of 1939. This made the federal government the centre of labour attention since it had the power to limit wages and restrict the right to strike. These measures were met by intense union opposition, causing the government to pass PC 1003 in 1944, granting "workers' rights to organize, certification of collective bargaining units and compulsory collective bargaining,"[14] thus reducing strike levels, at least temporarily, until controls were finally lifted late in 1947.

One feature of the labour force during the war was the rapid mobilization of women into paid labour. Ruth Pierson has argued that "Canada's war effort, rather than any consideration of women's right to work, determined the recruitment of women."[15] The consequence was, of course, that once the war ended women were expected to return to the home, having served their role as a reserve army of labour. There were few immediate effects in the women's labour force; as Pierson observed, "If women took jobs previously held only by men, they were generally regarded as replacing men temporarily."[16] There were long-term effects, however, as the women's movement in the 1970's was able to point to wartime work by women as demonstrating the capacities of women for "men's work" with considerable success. The political significance of women's work during the war was important ideological ammunition in the struggles of subsequent decades.

POST-WAR RECONSTRUCTION

Following World War II, there was a brief economic slow-down in 1949 and 1950, with expansion accompanying the Korean War and another recession from 1957 through to the early 1960's. C.D. Howe continued to be the prime mover in the federal state. His ongoing initiatives from the Department of Reconstruction and Supply were folded into the Department of Trade and Commerce, which he headed from 1948 to 1957. From these central institutions, Howe actively sought foreign investment; between 1946 and 1960, $1.1 billion was granted in deferred taxes to foreign-controlled companies in Canada.[17] Defence spending increased from less than $400 million in 1949 to over $2 billion in 1952 under Howe's regime. The Massachusetts-born Liberal was instrumental in encouraging the import of

U.S. industry, telling a Boston audience in 1954 that "Canada has welcomed the participation of American, and other foreign capital in its industrial expansion. In Canada, foreign investors are treated the same as domestic investors."[18] In the 1950's, Canada's economy was turned increasingly toward its continental neighbour. Internally the focus was on transportation networks, including the three giant projects of the 1950's: the Trans-Canada Highway (1950), the Trans-Canada Pipeline (1952), and the St. Lawrence Seaway (1954), which featured both shipping and hydro power.

Post-war expansion by the state also included increased social assistance and service activities, such as the Unemployment Insurance Commission, the Department of Health and Welfare, and Central Mortgage and Housing Corporation, as well as a tremendous growth in the Department of Labour. Much of this state expansion was to accommodate demands made by organized labour. From 16 per cent in 1940, the proportion of the non-agricultural labour force organized into unions increased to 29 per cent by 1949 and levelled off at 34 per cent by 1955 (see Table 4). By the mid-1950's, most readily organized manufacturing industries were unionized.

Labour proved willing to strike in the relatively prosperous 1950's. Strikes were common in extractive industries (forest products, fishing, and mining), manufacturing (especially automobiles in Ontario and textiles in Quebec), construction, and particularly transportation. There was a national railway strike of both the Canadian Pacific and Canadian National in 1950 involving 125,000 non-operating employees. This ended when workers were legislated back to work. Again, in 1957 there was a railway strike over technological change by the Brotherhood of Locomotive Firemen and Engineers against the CPR, which ended after nine days when an inquiry was appointed.

In Quebec, as elsewhere in Canada, there was a resource rush following the war, concentrated on cheap hydro power used to stimulate pulp and paper production, aluminum smelting, and the chemical industry. Quebec's Hydro Electric Commission was established in 1944 but complete nationalization was delayed until 1963 (Ontario Hydro had been founded in 1905). Mining was important to rural Quebec: asbestos (Eastern Townships), iron ore (Ungava), plus copper, gold, and zinc (Rouyn-Noranda). In Montreal, manufacture of clothing, textiles, and tobacco was most important.

Unions in Quebec had a particularly difficult struggle. Maurice Duplessis, in power most of the 1936-1960 period, opposed all but the tamest of unions. In 1954 he passed a law to decertify any union that "tolerated Communists" and was the central figure in the now-famous Asbestos Strike of 1949. Duplessis had the Labour Relations Board decertify the asbestos unions and declared the union leaders to be "saboteurs."[19] This strike marked a coming of age for Quebec labour; it was now a force to be reckoned with in Quebec's development. As Gilles Beausoleil observed, "the working class, long neglected, had acquired a freedom of action and an official status."[20] The struggle was difficult: during the Asbestos Strike, 1,973 strikers were arrested, yet support was given by a wide spectrum of society ranging from the church to Quebec public opinion and the labour movement in other provinces.

RISE OF THE PROVINCES

Beginning in 1949, but gaining considerable momentum in the post-OPEC world of the early 1970's, there was a tremendous expansion of energy extraction in Alberta. Controlled by the already dominant multinational oil companies, this expansion was directed from abroad and was highly vulnerable to international forces. It did, nonetheless, create in its wake a rash of construction, exploration, and service activities that served as an accumulation base for smaller, provincially based capitalists[21] who would identify with the Lougheed regime in the 1970's. This tended to be "quick-fix" capital, demanding tremendous labour during construction but being very capital-intensive in its operation. The economy relied on continuous expansion for job creation while the state relied on resource rents to fund its commitments.

The other province undergoing tremendous growth during the 1960's was Quebec. Its growth was mainly in state service activities involving social welfare, health, and education. The Liberal regime ventured into the economy in a limited way through Hydro-Quebec, Société générale de financement (SGF), and Sidérurgie québécoise (SIDBEC), but with limited success. According to K. McRoberts and D. Posgate, "the only instance of outright nationalization was the case of Hydro-Quebec; here Quebec was merely following a precedent long established by other provinces. . . . The autonomy of American and English-Canadian corporations remained intact."[22] While Hydro-Quebec did become the province's largest employer, SGF and SIDBEC were failures in the 1960's, although in the 1970's SGF was somewhat successful in assisting small- and medium-sized Francophone capital.

Quebec and Alberta, joining Ontario's already dominant position among the provinces, represented an unprecedented growth of political power to challenge Ottawa. It was, to quote Pentland, "a decline of national authority and a rise of aggressive provincialism."[23] A combination of provinces seeking out multinational corporations to locate branch plants within their boundaries and intensified resource exploitation caused both interprovincial rivalry and federal-provincial conflict. Provinces were required to meet the increasingly costly demands for social services, and, to satisfy these expenses, they sought to expand their provincial revenue bases.

Growth of state activities had significant implications for the state as an employer. In 1967, federal civil servants gained the right to bargain through the Public Service Staff Relations Act, and provincial government workers, especially in Quebec, also expanded their rights to bargain. While the union movement had stabilized at 1.5 million workers between 1956 and 1964, these new unions added 500,000 members between 1965 and 1968, giving the union movement its first shot in the arm since World War II. The 1960's experienced a wave of "new" strikers: state workers (in hospitals and schools, especially) and newly organized clerical, service, and sales workers (especially in Quebec).

According to Pentland, "the most novel and revealing feature of the labour militancy of the 1960s was the frequent revolt of union membership against their leaders."[24] Members began to question, through their actions, not only their leadership but the state itself: "The propensity of workers to defy legal restrictions which they considered to be unjust was another striking aspect of militancy in the 1960s."[25] An important illustration was the national wildcat strike by postal workers in July and August of 1965 against union leadership's failure to deal with government intransigence on wages, conditions, and technological change.

During the 1960's the first rumblings of concern about the effects of automation were heard and early signs of structural unemployment emerged. Expansion of the state and service sectors was creating new demands for clerical labour as women were pulled into the paid labour force in increasing numbers, laying the groundwork for the development of the women's movement in the next decade.

The late 1960's also began to display two forms of nationalism, one in Quebec and another in English Canada. Nationalism had long been evident in Quebec, primarily of a conservative, defensive nature *(survivance)* to protect the rural people from the non-Catholic, industrial world. In the 1960's an assertive nationalism based on the right to self-determination

(indépendentiste) began to emerge. English-Canadian nationalism was also something that had existed before, primarily in
terms of maintaining loyalty to Mother England, and was most
prominent during the two world wars. The new nationalism was
a response to the perception of domination by the United States
and the loss of Canadian sovereignty. The branch plant was the
primary economic expression of foreign control while dependence upon resource exports at the expense of indigenous manufacturing became a concern for those who feared jobs would be
lost during difficult economic times.

STAGNATION AND CRISIS

By the 1970's the labour movement in Canada had a new shape.
Although still a dominant force in industry, international unions
were no longer the only principals in labour struggles. National
unions had grown with the increase in state workers. The three
largest public-service unions could claim a third of the CLC
membership: CUPE (Canadian Union of Public Employees),
NUPGE (National Union of Provincial Government Employees),
and PSAC (Public Service Alliance of Canada). In Quebec the
FTQ (Fédération des travailleurs du Québec), which represents
industrial workers associated with international unions, is in the
CLC, albeit weakly, tending to concentrate more on relations to
the labour centrals within Quebec. CSN (Confédération des syndicats nationaux) and CEQ (Centrale de l'enseignement du Québec) remain outside the CLC. Over half the CSN's workers are in
the public sector and the CEQ is entirely within the Quebec public
sector.

The labour movement as a whole is under attack in the 1980's.
Public-sector workers, whether federal or provincial, are being
compelled to bear the brunt of state over-expenditure. Industrial
workers are bearing the costs of a distorted economy where
foreign-controlled automobile companies impose massive layoffs and resource firms geared to export do the same.

The economic crisis of the late 1970's revealed fundamental
weaknesses long endemic to the Canadian social structure: resource dependence and branch plant manufacturing. Resource
workers based in such externally dominated activities as mining,
forest products, and fishing have been subject to international
markets and major fluctuations in the demand for the products
of their labour. Aside from these cyclical changes in demand,
there has been a constant tendency to make these activities more
capital-intensive, thus decreasing labour requirements and dis-

placing those traditionally engaged in resource extraction. Herein lies a major source of regional unemployment and unrest in the current period. Detailing layoffs in all resource sectors would be too large a task for this paper (5,000 B.C. forest workers are not expected to be called back and plant closures in the fishing industry on both coasts are legion), so mining will be used to illustrate the point. In 1982, 70,000 of 130,000 Canadian miners were out of work. Workers at the Iron Ore Company of Canada in Schefferville, Quebec, and others in potash, asbestos, and uranium have been affected. In Sudbury, 13,000 nickel workers are unemployed, with the official rate for the community running at 33 per cent. Falconbridge Nickel shut down operations for eight months in 1982 and permanently laid off 1,000 of its 4,000 workers. Inco shut down its labour force for ten months in 1982, with 950 of its hourly workers permanently laid off, leaving its labour force at 8,900 workers in January 1983, compared to 18,000 ten years earlier. The direction of change is expected to remain the same as Inco and Falconbridge estimate an additional 4,400 mining jobs will be lost to Sudbury over the next five years.[26] Mechanization and automation allow mining companies to meet production with dramatically fewer workers.[27]

The implications of job loss extend to the very structure of the labour movement itself, undercutting its ability to represent workers. The United Steel Workers of America, for example, has been particularly hard hit because of its membership in mining and the steel industry; its membership is down to 125,000 from 200,000 only a few years earlier.

In manufacturing the hardest hit has been the automobile industry. This industry is based entirely on branch plants and intimately tied to the United States through the Auto Pact agreement. Automobiles represent about 10 per cent of Canadian manufacturing and 80 per cent of the end-product exports from Canada to the United States. In the eighteen years the Auto Pact has been in place, Canada has accumulated a $41-billion deficit with the United States, including $5 billion in 1982. This means Canadians have been consuming more cars than they have been producing, consequently shifting jobs to the United States. In 1980, 23,200 Canadian auto workers were laid off. Not only have jobs been sacrificed through the Auto Pact, but the quality of the jobs as well. J.J. Shepherd, vice-president of the Science Council of Canada, reports that the U.S. automobile labour force contains 8 per cent skilled workers and 43 per cent semi-skilled (leaving 49 per cent unskilled); in Canada, only 2 per cent are skilled and 23 per cent semi-skilled (leaving 75 per cent unskilled).[28] In 1982 Canadian members of the UAW led their U.S. counterparts in an important strike against concessions, demonstrating that Canadian workers are not going simply to acquiesce to the wishes of capital and are capable of showing leadership in times of crisis.

The most important strike in the 1970's, however, was the 1978-79 battle by Inco workers in Sudbury. Its significance rests not only with the fact that it was the largest strike in Canadian history measured by days lost, lasting eight and a half months and involving 11,700 workers, but it came at a time when capital (reinforced by the state) was attempting to roll back workers' rights. The initial issue was the grievance procedure, won in a 128-day strike in 1969 at a time when nickel was in high demand for the Vietnam War. Inco had a substantial stockpile of nickel, as it always tried to have when it entered negotiations, and using this leverage, it attempted to extend the existing pay rates another year while eroding earlier union gains. Knowing they would be in for a long struggle, the Inco workers rejected the offer and embarked on marshalling support from the labour movement and community. Unlike the disastrous strike of 1958, when community leaders turned against the strikers and the union was left in disarray, the people of Sudbury and the national labour movement gave their support (including Mine-Mill, which had been ousted by the United Steel Workers twenty years earlier). Particularly noteworthy was the formation of the Wives Supporting the Strike Committee, organized by local leadership from the women's movement. This committee fought much of the ideological warfare of the strike and was central to its solidarity. Rather than retreating in their demands, the strikers pushed for a "Thirty and Out" retirement clause, voting down an offer seven and a half months into the strike when it failed to include this demand. Finally, after 261 days, the settlement represented a victory for Inco workers and was symbolic of the general resolve of Canadian workers not to retreat.[29]

White-collar workers have not been immune from the crisis. In 1982, General Motors cut 500 salaried jobs, as did MacMillan Bloedel and Eaton's; also, Gulf cut 400 and Inco 320, to list but a few examples.[30] Cuts such as these have induced white-collar workers to unionize, even outside the state sector. The largest white-collar union in the private sector, with 25,000 members in 300 bargaining units, is the Office and Professional Employees International.[31] As clerical work becomes increasingly automated and routinized, the potential for unionization expands, particularly for women. The proletarianization of white-collar work makes possible greater working-class solidarity, but the struggle will be difficult because of legislative barriers, employer resistance, and various unions competing for the same workers.

By the end of the 1970's the labour movement had reached 40 per cent of all non-agricultural workers, a significant increase from the 34 per cent it had at the beginning of the decade or the 30 per cent it appeared to have stagnated at in the 1960's. As the labour movement expanded its power, however fragmented in terms of national direction, the state responded with policies designed to moderate that power. Both the federal and provincial governments frequently used back-to-work legislation throughout the 1970's to force government workers, who had only gained the right to strike in the late sixties, to end their strikes. The Anti-Inflation Program of 1975-78 empowered the Anti-Inflation Board to roll back collective agreements to conform to wage guidelines in both the public and private sectors. In 1982 the Public Sector Compensation Restraint Act imposed mandatory "6 and 5" per cent increases, for the following two years suspending the right of federal workers to bargain or strike. The largest provinces followed suit for their employees with Quebec imposing the most severe cutbacks.

DIRECTIONS OF CHANGE

Labour shortages during World War II reinforced the power of the working class, which in turn permitted some working-class demands to be accomplished in the 1950's and 1960's. These had the effect of expanding the welfare role of government and creating a dynamic new category of workers, themselves placing demands on government revenues as they insisted on and received recognition. Both federal and provincial governments became important employers and purveyors of increasingly expensive services.[32] During the current economic crisis government revenues have declined and expenses increased; particularly heavy were payments on foreign debt, which reached 18 per cent of the Gross National Product in 1980. Foreign interest payments were $4.3 billion and dividend payments $2.9 billion in 1980 alone. In its rush to stimulate investment the federal government presses for megaprojects in energy and the provinces press for intensified resource extraction. These are inherently unstable answers. The construction these policies induce (when they work at all) provides a "quick fix," but there are few long-term jobs in these capital-intensive activities and the concessions offered to entice foreign capital depreciate the value of the resource rents. The spiral is one of increasing dependence and insecurity of employment.

Like the union movement, the other major social movements

of the 1970's have been less than successful. Regionalism as a social, political, and economic phenomenon continues to reflect the uneven development of the country. Provincialism has increased as the provinces continue to struggle with the federal government over scarce resource rents and over-extended financial responsibilities. Even the Department of Regional Economic Expansion, which failed by any reasonable standards, has been dissolved into the Ottawa bureaucracy. English-Canadian nationalism has made limited gains: there is a watered-down Foreign Investment Review Agency and Petro Canada is now a major actor in the petroleum field (but foreign ownership still stands at 75 per cent). There can be little pleasure for nationalists that foreign control of manufacturing slipped back to 48 per cent since the major reason has been deindustrialization, the very fear that prompted nationalists in the first place. Branch plants are leaving behind empty shells, not a vibrant industrial base. All levels of government are once again courting foreign investors. In Quebec the nationalist Parti Québécois was elected, but even its diluted sovereignty-association referendum failed and its labour practices as an employer have been more severe than could dare be imagined.

The impact of the women's movement may well have been the most subtle and far-reaching of all. Out of economic necessity women are entering the labour force at a rapidly increasing rate. By 1980, over 50 per cent of women were in the labour force, accounting for 40 per cent of the entire employed labour force. Women, nevertheless, continue to experience higher rates of unemployment, greater part-time work, and lower incomes than men.[33] The proletarianization of clerical, sales, and service work has had its greatest impact on women who were recruited in large numbers into these activities during the 1960's and 1970's. Increasingly, teachers, nurses, and insurance and bank workers are turning to unionization as the pay levels and content of their work fail to correspond to the privileged image of white-collar work. Labour force segmentation means, however, that there tend to be gender-segregated unions. Through newer unions, like CUPE, such women's issues as paid maternity leave, child care, and equal pay for work of equal value are placed on the agenda. Patriarchial attitudes and practices, however, persist among many male unionists, and calls can still be heard for women to "return to the home so men can have a job." Not only has the women's movement provided a counter-ideology to such calls, but the material conditions that would allow them to occur no longer exist. Traditional families are no longer the norm and two income-earners have become a necessity, especially for younger members of the working class. Women in the 1980's will not and cannot serve as a reserve army of labour to absorb the shocks of labour shortages and surpluses as they did during and after the wars. Unemployment is not quite so invisible when the traditional home is no longer a refuge.

The upper echelons of the Canadian economy have been immune to most of the major social forces of the post-war era. Neither the women's movement nor Québécois nationalism has gained ground in the economic elite, nor has regional representation changed greatly. The one consequential force has been foreign ownership, although its penetration has not served to dislodge the cornerstones of corporate power. Large Canadian capitalists, rather, have entered into an unequal alliance with foreign capital, thus reinforcing the strength of each.[34]

Throughout the past half-century capital has engaged in a multitude of control practices, often working hand-in-hand with government policies designed to facilitate capital accumulation "in the national interest." During the 1930's repression was the order of the day – work camps and the Regina Riot. During World War II there was heavy reliance on an ideology of unity in the face of adversity (spiced with a heavy dose of long overdue concessions to labour). The immediate post-war period relied on practices of conciliation and liberalized labour legislation designed to bring labour into a national partnership, on the condition that labour keep its own house in order and eliminate "extreme" elements, leading to massive purges (such as the CLC's expulsions of the United Electrical Workers', Mine-Mill, and the United Fishermen and Allied Workers' Union). In the boom of the sixties, prosperity and immigration reigned until the crisis of the seventies forced the state to both cut immigration and place wages under controls. Like the 1930's, coercion has once again become the order of the day, but this time less physical and more legislative. Unemployment, wage controls, and regressive labour laws discipline the labour force. Each province seems in a race with the federal government to cut back wages more severely and reduce workers' rights even more. First Nova Scotia seemed to be in front, then Quebec pulled ahead, only to be overtaken by Saskatchewan, and then by British Columbia. Under these conditions the labour movement is directly challenged, even its most wage-conscious sectors. More unified than ever, labour has never been more directly challenged. Its response will be the key to charting the 1980's.

Canadian society remains a fractured, distorted formation.

There is a dynamic tension between capital and labour, with the state becoming an increasingly direct actor in the relationship – mediating on behalf of capital and itself as an employer.

NOTES

1. See Rolf Knight and Maya Koizumi, *A Man of Our Times: The Life of a Japanese-Canadian Fisherman* (Vancouver, 1976).
2. See Lloyd G. Reynolds, *The Control of Competition in Canada* (Cambridge, 1975), 60-1.
3. See Donald Creighton, *Canada's First Century* (Toronto, 1970), 200-1.
4. See Herbert Marshall, Frank A. Southard, and Kenneth W. Taylor, *Canadian-American Industry: A Study of International Investments* (New Haven, 1936), 222.
5. See Stuart Jamieson, *Times of Trouble: Labour Unrest and Industrial Conflict in Canada, 1900-1966,* Study #22, Task Force on Labour Relations (Ottawa, 1968), 214.
6. H. Clare Pentland, *A Study of the Changing Social, Economic and Political Background of the Canadian System of Industrial Relations,* Task Force on Labour Relations (Ottawa, 1968), 251.
7. See O.J. Firestone, *Canada's Economic Development, 1867-1953* (London, 1958), 214.
8. See Melissa Clark, "The Canadian State and Staples: An Ear to Washington" (Ph.D. thesis, McMaster University, 1979), 90-101.
9. See Gideon Rosenbluth, "Concentration and Monopoly in the Canadian Economy," in Michael Oliver, ed., *Social Purpose for Canada* (Toronto, 1961), 206.
10. See Department of Reconstruction and Supply, *Encouragement to Industrial Expansion in Canada* (Ottawa, 1949), 13.
11. Pentland, *Changing,* 196.
12. See *ibid.*, 197.
13. See Jamieson, *Times of Trouble,* 276.
14. *Ibid.*, 294.
15. Ruth Pierson, "Women's Emancipation and the Recruitment of Women into the Labour Force in World War II," in Susan Mann Trofimenkoff and Alison Prentice, eds, *The Neglected Majority: Essays in Canadian Women's History* (Toronto, 1977), 125.
16. *Ibid.*, 145.
17. See Robert Bothwell and William Kilbourn, *C.D. Howe, A Biography* (Toronto, 1979), 238.
18. Quoted in David Wolfe, "Political Culture, Economic Policy and the Growth of Foreign Investment in Canada" (Master's thesis, Carleton University, 1973), 120.
19. See Gilles Beausoleil, "History of the Strike at Asbestos," in Pierre Elliott Trudeau, ed., *The Asbestos Strike* (Toronto, 1964), 152-3.

20. *Ibid.,* 179.
21. See John Richards and Larry Pratt, *Prairie Capitalism: Power and Influence in the New West* (Toronto, 1979).
22. Kenneth McRoberts and Dale Posgate, *Quebec: Social Change and Political Crisis* (Toronto, 1980), 111.
23. Pentland, *Changing*, 259.
24. *Ibid.*, 382.
25. *Ibid.*, 383.
26. See *The Globe and Mail*, 19 October 1982, p. 4.
27. See Wallace Clement, *Hardrock Mining: Industrial Relations and Technological Change at Inco* (Toronto, 1981). For a similar pattern in the forests, see Ian Radforth, "Woodsworkers and the Mechanization of the Pulpwood Logging Industry in Northern Ontario, 1959-1970," *Historical Papers* (1982); Pat Marchak, "Labour in a Staples Economy," *Studies in Political Economy*, 2 (Autumn, 1979).
28. J.J. Shepherd, "Slam the brakes on auto pact's vicious circle?" *The Globe and Mail,* 21 November 1978, p. 7.
29. See Clement, *Hardrock Mining*, 322-31.
30. See *The Globe and Mail*, 1 May 1982, p. 11.
31. See *The Financial Post*, 5 March 1983, p. S3.
32. See Hugh Armstrong, "The Labour Force and State Workers in Canada," in Leo Panitch, ed., *The Canadian State: Political Economy and Political Power* (Toronto, 1977).
33. See Pat and Hugh Armstrong, *A Working Majority: What Women Must Do for Pay* (Ottawa, 1983).
34. See Wallace Clement, *Continental Corporate Power: Economic Elite Linkages Between Canada and the United States* (Toronto, 1977).

III
The Working Class

The half-century from the onslaught of the Great Depression to the tensions of the Anti-Inflation Board and "6 and 5" has seen massive changes in the composition of the Canadian working class, in the nature of the Canadian labour movement, and in the state system of industrial relations which attempt to set the parameters of class conflict in Canada.

The Canadian working class has been transformed in terms of both its composition and its function. Massive post-war immigration has dramatically reconstituted the ranks of the working class, bringing to Canada masses of southern Europeans and later East Indians and West Indians. The complexity of Canadian ethnic and racial relations has grown by leaps and bounds as previous informal racist immigration restrictions were dropped. In addition, the growth of monopoly capital brought a huge increase in state employment and in office work, both of which brought into the labour market increasing numbers of women. This growth of service and public-sector employment also redefined the nature of the working class, moving it away from the resource sector and heavy industry to various forms of office work, food processing, and light, albeit intensive, assembly work.

The Canadian labour movement has also changed. Initially it fought the great struggles of the late depression and World War II years for industrial unionism and to win the right to legally enforced collective bargaining. The triumph of the Congress of Industrial Organizations and the rise to prominence of the Congress of Canadian Labour eventually forced a reluctant American Federation of Labour-Trades and Labour Congress craft union hierarchy to recognize a new world; in 1956 the creation of the Canadian Labour Congress symbolized this new unity. More recently, the rise to prominence of public-sector unionism and the rapid growth of the Canadian Union of Public Employees, the National Union of Provincial Government Employees, the Public Service Alliance of Canada, and their Quebec equivalents have led to considerable tensions within organized labour between public- and private-sector unions, conflicts which governmental public-sector wage restraint programs and cutbacks are aimed at intensifying.

The triumph of industrial unionism in the 1940's brought with it also the legal entrenchment of trade-union rights, which were enshrined in the Canadian Industrial Relations and Disputes Investigation Act of 1948. This Act, following on the heels of the great struggles in Windsor and in Hamilton, continued the Canadian tradition of mediation and arbitration. Windsor had also brought the Rand Formula, a sophisticated device to provide union security while demanding in return that the union function to police the sanctity of the contract, thus aiming to prevent strikes during the life of a collective agreement. All these innovations and those that followed in the 1950's created an immensely complex legal network of labour relations boards and ever more costly arbitration procedures. The growing trade-union bureaucracy shifted more and more of its attention to such legal complexity and less and less to the immediate shop-floor complaints of their members.

In the 1970's and especially in the 1980's this complicated system appears increasingly to be on the verge of breakdown. A wave of labour militancy in the late 1960's led to extended discussions about voluntary wage restraints and tripartism. When these talks broke down the government imposed wage and price controls and set up an Anti-Inflation Board to administer the controls. This agency and its legislative mandate proved, as labour had feared and predicted, to be far more effective at controlling wages than prices. Labour protests culminated in a day-long general strike in October 1976, which saw 1,000,000 Canadian workers protest against the legislation. This program has subsequently been followed by more selective restraint programs aimed only at public-sector workers. These various governmental attacks on the carefully constructed consensus of the post-war period have placed the Canadian industrial relations system in considerable jeopardy. The direction for the future is now being battled out between capital and the state, on one side, and labour on the other.

FURTHER READING:
The development of the Canadian industrial relations system is outlined in Laurel Sefton MacDowell, "The Formation of the Canadian Industrial Relations System During World War II," *Labour/Le Travailleur*, 3 (1978), 175-96, and is covered in more detail in her *"Remember Kirkland Lake": The Gold Miners' Strike of 1941-42* (Toronto, 1982), and "The 1943 Steel Strike Against Wartime Wage Controls," *Labour/Le Travailleur*, 10 (1982), 65-85. A useful critique is Leo Panitch and Donald Swartz, "From Free Collective Bargaining to Permanent Exceptionalism: The Economic Crisis Bargaining in Canada," *Labour/Le Travailleur*, 13 (1984). Some major strikes of the period are covered in Irving Abella, ed., *On Strike* (Toronto, 1974). Interesting biographical accounts of key struggles are given in Gloria Montero, *We Stood Together* (Toronto, 1979). Irving Abella surveys from a nationalist viewpoint the development of the CIO in *Nationalism, Communism and Canadian Labour* (Toronto, 1973). Interesting memoirs and accounts of working-class leaders include: Tom McEwen, *The Forge Glows Red* (Toronto, 1974); Joe Davidson and John Deverell, *Joe Davidson* (Toronto, 1978); Rick Salutin, *Kent Rowley* (Toronto, 1980); Tim Buck, *Yours in the Struggle* (Toronto, 1977); and Silver Donald Cameron, *The Education of Everett Richardson: The Nova Scotia Fishermen's Strike of 1970-71* (Toronto, 1977).

Wayne Roberts is a free-lance labour historian in Toronto. **John Bullen** teaches labour history at Erindale College, University of Toronto. Both have also taught for a number of years at the Labour College of Canada.

A Heritage of Hope and Struggle: Workers, Unions, and Politics in Canada, 1930-1982

by Wayne Roberts and John Bullen

By now, Canadians have become accustomed to hearing phrases such as "the worst since the depression" or "the most severe since the 1930's" to describe current social conditions. Such comparisons make it difficult to view the 1930's as a "low dishonest decade" apart, a dramatic backdrop to the prosperity and planning of our times. Rising unemployment, the surge in welfare recipients, government inaction, the drive of business to exact concessions, the hopelessness of youth, the rise of right-wing populism, the apparent political listlessness of the working population – change a few place names, faces, and figures and the early 1980's sound like the Great Depression revisited.

But working Canadians have made tremendous advances over the last half-century. Most laid-off workers receive a year's unemployment insurance before being forced to apply for welfare. A wide range of social services from medicare to pensions is available to citizens without submission to humiliating means tests. Most working-class families live above the poverty line. Unions look out for the interests of approximately one-third of the labour force. These gains, threatened though they are, represent the legacy of the labour movement over the past fifty years.

Such advances have not resulted from simple and gradual social evolution. Each step forward required the collective effort of working people to combat the hostile interests of business and the calculated indifference of government. In the political arena, on the shop floor, and in the streets, workers have withstood determined and sometimes violent resistance to their efforts to guarantee themselves and their children a more just and secure place in society. Some obstacles to progress, however, have been internal to the labour movement. Although collective action has succeeded in the past, sustained worker solidarity has remained an elusive goal. Conflicting ideologies among workers and their leaders have been an additional impediment to political and social gains. From all perspectives, the history of the labour movement in Canada is a story of struggle.

The following overview cannot do justice to the last fifty years of development, let alone pay tribute to the varied and anonymous contributions that made advancement possible. But some of the major episodes that captured the spirit of a moment and established important trends in the work force will be examined. Standard sources have been consulted in most cases, but many first-hand accounts inject a personal perspective into the story. Most of these events centre on conflict. There are two reasons for this, one academic, the other real. Conflicts are the easiest events to document and present. Also, they form the essence of labour history.

THE DIRTY THIRTIES

"It was hell on wheels," Harry Pomeroy winced, looking back on the early days of the 1930's. A plumber from northern Ontario, Pomeroy spent the early depression years hustling odd jobs until he found full-time work at Stelco in Hamilton. "It was hot and heavy work, but it was a dream," he sighed. "You were an aristocrat if you had a job, even if it only paid twenty-eight cents an hour."[1]

Mass unemployment defined the contours of working-class life during the 1930's. With 30 per cent of workers jobless and 20 per cent of the population on relief, it could not be otherwise. Foremen acquired near-tyrannical power as they paced the lines of desperate faces every morning at mine and factory gates to choose the huskiest candidates for a day's work. And if any worker dared complain about conditions, there was a standard ritual. "They treated you like their disposables," recalled Johnny Shipperbottom. "'If you don't like it you know what to do.' That was the regular thing with the foreman. 'There's the gate'."[2]

Working conditions became a national scandal six years into the depression when the Royal Commission on Price Spreads exposed horror story after horror story. "Low wages and high profits" were the rule in the tobacco industry, the Commissioners found. Conditions in the garment trade, they insisted, "merit the most emphatic condemnation. They should not be tolerated in any state that claims to call itself civilized."[3] The litany went on and on.

Despite overpowering odds, working people who were thrown back on their own resources established some of the practices that would later allow a mass insurgent movement to settle accounts for ten lost years. The early 1930's was a time of sporadic struggles. There were few significant breakthroughs, but many people came to terms with basics and took the first steps toward their own protection. Harvey Ladd, who later played critical roles in a series of strikes from British Columbia to Newfoundland, is not overly romantic in his remembrance of the 1930's. "People during the years of the depression were very compassionate. It was the great leveller. There was no keeping up with the Joneses, because Jones was on welfare, too," he said. "You look back and you say they were very, very tough times. But you know, there was also something you can't buy with prosperity, and that is a feeling of good will toward your neighbour. And it was real. It was just real."[4] One should only note that conditions did not allow that compassion to translate itself into solidarity for another decade.

The most notable labour struggles of the early 1930's broke out in small towns and backwaters, areas where a strong sense of community could fuse with workers' grievances and provide some chance of victory. Thus it was community, not communism, that gave the Communist Party-backed Workers' Unity League (WUL) the opportunity to break through the barriers of economic collapse and launch some kind of counter-offensive.

The WUL came into existence in 1929 as a branch of the Communist Party's Red International of Labour Unions. The WUL represented a new strategy for the Communist Party of Canada, whose trade-union activity throughout the 1920's had confined itself to "boring from within" the Trades and Labour Congress (TLC) and the All-Canadian Congress of Labour. In the absence of any motion from the moribund, craft-dominated TLC, the WUL provided leadership and a national campaign network for sporadic outbreaks of strike action. In 1933, the League sponsored eleven industrial unions and claimed responsibility for three-quarters of the strikes in Canada.

Although they left little in the way of an institutional legacy, these strikes count among the most dramatic in Canadian history. In isolated resource areas, in particular, authorities gave no quarter and treatment of workers was harsh. In Souris, Saskatchewan, for instance, coal miners went on strike against a wage cut in 1931. The town council in nearby Estevan banned a strike demonstration and created conditions for a bloody clash with the RCMP. Three workers were killed, several others jailed or fined.[5]

The next year, in Crowsnest Pass, Alberta, mine owners threatened workers with layoffs and then joined the local chapter of the Ku Klux Klan in accusing immigrant strikers of foreign and subversive activity. In the next local election, however, several Communists won positions on town council.[6]

The WUL saw action in Ontario as well. In 1933, 700 furniture workers in Stratford walked out on strike for higher wages, shorter hours, and union recognition. When violence flared on the picket line following one company's attempt to ship out goods, Stratford's nervous mayor tried his hand at overkill and appealed for military aid. Four machine-gun carriers and 120 soldiers descended on the "war zone," sparking a support rally for the strikers that attracted 3,000 indignant citizens. Two months later, a settlement was reached granting wage hikes, shorter hours, and recognition of shop committees. This victory inspired another strike, of women chicken-pluckers. The impact of these strikes was revealed in the next municipal election, which catapulted one of the strike leaders to the mayor's chair and six labour candidates to the town council of ten.[7]

Despite its record of energetic and reasonably capable organizing, the WUL was short-lived. In 1935, the Communist International ordered it to disband and direct its affiliates back into what had previously been described as the "social fascist" TLC. This abrupt turn was only partially due to changing circumstances in Canada. Of greater importance was the Comintern's sudden interest in world-wide unity against fascism in Europe. The League had defied common sense and tried to organize workers in the depth of a depression. It broke new ground among previously unorganized workers and it showed that large numbers of common folk would accept militant and even revolutionary leadership if it would lead to better working conditions. But the huge factories in more impersonal industrial and resource centres remained untouched. A more systematic and sustained drive in more favourable circumstances would be required before these workers would accept the challenge of unionism.

The unemployed had less to lose and more to gain from organization, and associations of the unemployed mushroomed across the country. The overwhelming majority of these focused their attention on municipal governments because this was where relief was issued and where political pressure could be most effective. They drew support from particular constituencies, such as veterans' and ethnic groups, and introduced tens of thousands of Canadians to collective organization and established such basic civil liberties as the right to petition and demonstrate.

Founded in 1931 in a working-class suburb of Toronto, the East York Workers' Association (EYWA) fought for the needs of the 45 per cent of the borough's population that was on relief. By 1934, the EYWA had 1,600 members and attracted up to 500 people to weekly meetings. The EYWA forced a switch from a complicated and humiliating voucher system of relief payments to a straight distribution of cash. Relief recipients were required to work for the dole so that governments could be assured that payments were not subsidizing idleness. This forced-work program created a workplace collectivity for the unemployed. In 1935, the EYWA initiated a strike of relief workers to oppose pay cuts. Parades, demonstrations, occupation of the council chambers, and a support rally of 1,200 at Massey Hall defeated the move. Later that year, the Association's president was elected reeve.[8]

The militancy of Calgary's unemployed won that city the highest standards of relief in the country. In one strike of relief workers, 4,000 ex-servicemen surrounded police and scabs and came at them, future public-sector union leader Pat Linehan remembers, "roaring like Indians. It was like one of those movie pictures."[9] The strikers won their case but authorities sought their revenge by sentencing the leaders to six months at hard labour.

In 1935, the single unemployed working in military-run relief camps in the boondocks of British Columbia took action against their barren future and launched a protest of national momentum. British Columbia's climate worked like a magnet for homeless unemployed youth – you might still starve there, but at least you wouldn't freeze to death, it was said. When desperate, the "boys" worked in relief camps for board, twenty cents a day, and a pouch of tobacco. By 1935, the WUL-affiliated Relief Camp Workers' Union succeeded in organizing a cross-province walkout from the camps. The strikers descended on Vancouver, where they occupied the city museum and tin-canned and snake-marched their way through the city in a bid for funds. Despite massive public sympathy – on Mother's Day, for instance, women marched in heart formation in support of "their boys" – the protest soon snagged on constitutional squabbles designed to pass the buck. Fearing exhaustion of their own and their supporters' patience, the relief strikers decided to take their cause directly to Ottawa. Some 1,500 men illegally scrambled onto freight cars and started rolling east. Trekkers were warmly welcomed and fed during overnight stays in most towns. As the trek picked up speed, Prime Minister Bennett saw red and prepared for a confrontation. That confrontation came in Regina when city police, firemen, train guards, and RCMP broke up a peaceful rally in a police riot of unprecedented proportions. The trek was over, and the trekkers were sent back home at public expense. Those who returned to British Columbia found improved conditions and rates of pay in the relief camps. [10]

Memories of the WUL and the Regina Riot were still fresh when a new labour organization surfaced in the United States that would change the face of unionism. At a rowdy convention of the American Federation of Labor (AFL) in 1935, John L. Lewis of the United Mine Workers sent "Big Bill" Hutcheson of the Carpenters' union sprawling on the floor after a heated debate on craft versus industrial unionism. Lewis dusted himself off, walked out of the convention, and spearheaded the Congress for Industrial Organizations (CIO) to organize the unorganized in mass production industries. The CIO in the United States, backed by federal legislation guaranteeing the right to organize and bargain collectively, steamrollered from victory to dramatic victory in anti-union strongholds across the country.

The slight let-up in the depression, along with the inspiration of flash successes south of the border, led to similar efforts in Canada. Unions drew first blood at the General Motors plant in Oshawa, Ontario. In 1936, GM workers suffered their fifth wage cut in as many years despite the company's announcement that it had surpassed all previous profit levels. The workers soon made the connection. In February 1937, CIO organizer Hugh Thompson arrived from Detroit and helped establish Local 222 of the United Auto Workers. But just as GM was prepared to sign a union contract, Ontario Premier Mitch Hepburn stepped in.

Hepburn's business friends alerted him that a CIO victory in Oshawa would unleash a flood of union organizing that could swamp Ontario's mining and industrial concerns. Determined that CIO agitators would not capture Ontario, he convinced GM to break off negotiations, and Local 222 declared a strike on April 8. Claiming that violence was expected at any moment, the Premier put law enforcement agencies on alert and recruited a special police force that won acclaim among the strikers as "Hepburn's Hussars" and "Sons of Mitch's." But the conduct of the Oshawa strikers, and overwhelming support from the community, denied Hepburn any excuse to smash the strike with force. Both the mayor and the chief of police praised the strikers. One striker took advantage of the relaxed and friendly mood and celebrated his marriage on the picket line. Hepburn's histrionics could not delay a settlement indefinitely. GM had its own fish to fry and needed a settlement to resume production. On April 23, a contract provided better hours, higher wages, and limited local union recognition.[11]

Union success in Oshawa relied on enormous worker and community solidarity, a recipe difficult to duplicate for the rest of the 1930's. In the midst of the turmoil at Oshawa, for instance, eighty eastern European immigrants at the Holmes Foundry in Sarnia sat down on the job in imitation of the famous organizing tactic of the CIO in the United States. Shortly, upright citizens of Anglo-Saxon descent saw an opportunity for employment and descended on the factory with baseball bats, hospitalizing several of the workers. This style of Anglo-Saxon law and order bothered no one in authority. Hepburn used the incident to issue a stiff warning: "My sympathies are with those who fought the strikers," he declared. "There will be no sit-down strikes in Ontario. This government is going to maintain law and order at all costs."[12]

The union drive stalled across the country. In June 1938, the recently formed International Woodworkers of America in Blubber Bay, British Columbia, struck the Pacific Lime Company following management's refusal to adhere to an arbitration board's order to improve working conditions and to reinstate twenty-three employees dismissed for union activity. Despite substantial support, the union's soup kitchen could not hold body and soul together for more than fourteen months and the strike collapsed.[13]

If Canadian workers did not inherit the successes of the CIO in the United States, they inherited the split in the labour movement when craft and industrial unionists bitterly parted ways. By 1938, when the CIO severed all ties with the craft-based AFL, the factionalism spilled over into Canada. Industrial union organizers in Canada, who had maintained a relationship with the craft-dominated TLC, were shown the door on orders from the AFL in the United States. The TLC could not stand up to the AFL's threat to withhold dues of Canadian craft unionists and expelled the CIO forces in 1939. Canada's fledgling industrial unions merged with the nationalist All-Canadian Congress of Labour in 1940 to form the Canadian Congress of Labour (CCL).

Although the dirty thirties ended with a bang when war was declared in 1939, the union movement saw out the decade with a whimper. Industrial unions were leaders without a following, as were the political parties oriented to labour. The Co-operative

Commonwealth Federation (CCF), a coalition of agrarian, academic, and labour radicals, had developed a following among emergent union leaders. Charlie Millard, president of Local 222 during the Oshawa strike, saw to it that CCF stalwarts were appointed to key positions in the CIO organizing committees he commanded. But there was no substantial, let alone structural, support for the CCF in labour areas, with the exception of Cape Breton. The Communist Party was as well-positioned in the lower levels of union activists and as marginal in the work force at large. In general, the seeds of the future fell on barren soil during the 1930's and did not sprout until the rains of war fell in the 1940's. But the thirties were crucial years. They provided memories which many workers would never forget, and which, they were determined, they would never live through again.

THE FIGHTING FORTIES

It was not the welfare state, but the warfare state, that finally gave working people the opportunity to even the score for a decade of humiliation. There is nothing like a war to break down old-fashioned opposition to public works expenditures, so money was no object as long as it financed destruction, not construction.

The vagrant youth who were treated like pariahs and bullied from town to town throughout the 1930's received a heroes' send-off when they signed up for three square meals per day and a pair of boots in the army. Resource and mass-production industries geared up for war production and hired anyone with a body temperature of 98.6°. By 1941, full employment made it possible for the federal government to introduce unemployment insurance, contributions to which provided a nice nest egg for the costs of war. One year later, the "manpower" shortage was so severe that major companies scoured the country for female recruits and the government set up child-care facilities and introduced special tax concessions for working women.[14] By 1943, the labour market was so tight that government denied workers and employers in essential industries the right to quit or fire at will. This guaranteed employers a stable work force and presented unionists with a chance to come out of the closet with organizing drives. The government wage freeze of 1940 barely held the line to keep wage standards at 1926-29 levels as unscrupulous employers outbid each other for workers and pleaded for loopholes and exemptions in the legislation. As the dread and discipline of unemployment receded, the imagination of working people was at last freed. They expressed their hopes and fears by flocking to unions and radical parties in unprecedented numbers. In 1943, a public opinion poll placed the CCF one percentage point ahead of both the Tories and Liberals. By 1945, unions had doubled in size over 1939 and expressed the exuberant impulses of close to 400,000 new members.

Although employers and governments found themselves on the defensive as a result of their need for new workers and stable industrial relations, they acted as though the best defence was a strong offence. Workers and unions had to fight for every concession. Early wartime legislation referring to workers' rights to collective bargaining proved to be a dead letter. At best, it expressed the opinion of government that essential industry employers "should" recognize unions backed by a majority of their work force. At worst, government evasion and double talk covered up for employer resistance to unionization. But with the federal government in the constitutional driver's seat for the duration of the war, this negligence laid the basis for a national labour movement with a set of concentrated campaigns and symbols of justice and injustice.

In 1941, the steelworkers' union spearheaded a campaign for uniform national wages across the industry but was stonewalled by the War Labour Board. According to the Board's decision in the Montreal Peck Rolling Mill case, wage patterns should honour the substandards of depressed regions as set in the late 1920's. Union lawyer J.L. Cohen denounced the decision for its implication that some "are mere stepchildren in the Canadian social order" who should expect "to be satisfied with a lower standard of living." [15]

In the same year, government-appointed controllers took over the troubled National Steel Car plant in Hamilton. Despite three wildcat walkouts over piece rates and union recognition, the government officer refused to recognize the union voted in by the workers and actually set up a counter employees' association subject to management domination. The vote in favour of an independent union had been 1,740 to 542, a mere point of baseball trivia to officiating cabinet minister C.D. Howe, who called it "a case of three strikes and out." [16]

Government leaders defended their refusal to enforce laws supporting collective bargaining as a sincere effort to avoid compulsion in industrial relations. Labour historian L.S. MacDowell has judged the government's sudden distaste for compulsion as hypocritical. "While the government was prepared to impose compulsory wage controls, and compulsory re-allocation of labour," she writes, "it continued to maintain that its opposition to 'compulsion' precluded the introduction of collective bargaining legislation."[17]

Conflict over this issue came to a head during the 1941-42 strike of gold miners in Kirkland Lake, Ontario. After months of delay imposed by government conciliators, who recognized the justice of the miners' demand for union recognition but pressured the miners to compromise on an organization of their employers' choice, some 3,000 miners voted to strike in the dead of winter. Union recognition was the only issue, and miners and their wives huddled on picket lines in –40° weather became a symbol of how labour was left out in the cold by government indifference and opposition.

The federal government was unwilling to lay down its own laws on collective bargaining, even after the owners unilaterally walked out of conciliation hearings. The provincial government was not so squeamish about compulsion and Ontario Premier Hepburn announced that Ontario jails were "just yawning" for CIO organizers. He mobilized an occupying force of provincial police that marched through downtown Kirkland Lake every day before taking up rounds of picket-breaking duty. From the employers' point of view, anti-strike tactics were a textbook case of the notorious anti-union "Mohawk Valley formula" – discredit union leaders as agitators and subversives; raise a hue and cry about law and order; intimidate strikers with an overpowering police presence; demoralize strikers by staging a highly publicized "back-to-work" movement.

The Kirkland Lake miners had no such formula or power, but by sheer commitment and determination they kept their strike alive until unionists across the country responded with financial and moral displays of solidarity. "Remember Kirkland Lake" headlined the miners' union leaflet, acknowledging that they had been starved into submission: "A skirmish lost – a battle yet to be won. And won it will be, for these men held out long enough to educate a great deal of Canada."[18] The defeat may have educated Canadians, but the labour movement is not built on heroic defeats. The hands of governments and employers were forced by a militant wave of political and industrial insurgence that continued to crest despite the defeat at Kirkland Lake. In this respect, it was not the defeated Kirkland Lake strike itself but the undefeated militance following in its wake that led to eventual concessions.

One day after the collapse of the strike, an unknown CCF candidate stopped a comeback by Conservative leader Arthur Meighen in its tracks. The 1942 upset by-election victory in

York-South, a Toronto Tory stronghold, was closely linked to the issues raised by Kirkland Lake. The CCF had campaigned hard for the beleaguered miners and issued joint fund appeals for the strike and election campaign. CCF trade union committees gained new vitality and in 1943 the CCL endorsed the CCF as the political arm of labour. In the same year, thirty-four CCFers, including nineteen unionists, formed the official opposition in Ontario.

Eager to present a new image before an aroused electorate, old-line politicians changed their spots. Ontario's Liberal Labour Minister, Peter Heenan, promised legislation to "force those employers who are still living in the past" to face reality.[19] Not to be outdone, Tories contradicted themselves by adopting the tag "Progressive Conservative" and unveiled a twenty-two-point platform of reforms. Still, opinion polls in 1943 showed the CCF capable of a national victory. The axis of Canadian politics had tilted permanently to the left and the welfare state was set in place.

This deep-seated leftward move was buttressed by the uncanny ways working people justified new social aspirations by declaring their own agenda of war aims. A populist bias to war propaganda reflected the national consensus in English Canada and prevented the country's leaders from using war fever to enforce conformity and discredit dissent. On the contrary, unionism and social reform were unified and sanctified by popular definitions of the war's purpose.

People took their own propaganda, not the government's, to heart. Working women, who entered the mass production factories in the midst of all this turmoil, found their own way of redefining new openings made legitimate by the war. Governments could harangue women to do their bit for the menfolk and "back them up to bring them back." But the women of all ages and backgrounds who donned bandanas and dungarees often relished the opportunities, wages, and independence of industrial work. "Most of the women enjoyed it thoroughly – it was a nice change from cleaning up," reminisced Saskatchewan-born Vida Richards. Another woman war worker commented: "I wanted to work at Stelco because it meant I could live on my own in a city and I could afford to have some fun before I got married."[20]

Wartime talk of democracy evidently highlighted some of the abuses people experienced at work. Bob Miner, a Communist unionist who dutifully campaigned to bring experienced Timmins gold miners to the Sudbury nickelbelt where they could make a significant contribution to war production, kicked off a mass refusal to work overtime for straight pay at Inco. "You think you're pretty goddamned smart," his foreman snarled. "Someday this war's over and we'll fix you bastards then." To which Miner replied: "Partner, on the contrary, Hitler's not going to win this war." Miner believed that the war "started a lot of people thinking. They heard about a war for the four freedoms, and all this sort of crap, and they knew bloody well that the mine managers didn't believe in that. Of necessity, they were going to have to organize to even force these people to admit that we'd won a war."[21]

Fear of the prospects of a post-war world also fuelled the process of identifying union victory with military victory. Alf Ready, key in-plant organizer at Hamilton's giant Westinghouse plant, recalled how memories of the depression haunted war workers concerned about post-war unemployment: "That made you want to secure the union. You had a fear that you had during the depression, that you didn't want to face it again. It's a horrible feeling when you and your wife have got nothing. . . . My own people lost their home, my wife's people lost their home. And who got them? After a while, these were the reasons why political parties like the CCF took off."[22] In 1943, this style of political and social questioning, buoyed by the confidence that accompanied full employment, fused to produce massive unrest. One unionist in three hit the bricks that year, leading to over a million days in time lost to strikes.

The threat of a general strike in steel loomed high. Everyone felt the pressure of unionized Sault Ste. Marie and Sydney workers pressing for parity with the steelworkers of Hamilton. "The membership is utterly disgusted," stewed Sault union leader Bill Mahoney, "and if we are not careful, that feeling will be as strong towards us as it is towards the government and company." Prime Minister Mackenzie King pressed his cabinet colleagues to make concessions before a strike brought publicity to the workers' cause. "Once actual living conditions begin to be exposed, the government will be terribly on the defensive," he cried. "The government would have to make concessions and it had better be at once or larger concessions will have to come later." King succeeded in leading the steelworkers on a wild goose chase through government inquiries and promises of further government investigations into reform of collective bargaining legislation. But he had to congratulate himself in private. His short-sighted Bourbon cabinet mates showed no appreciation for King's wiliness: "none of them see what has been prevented, which is always greater than anything that is accomplished."[23] This would become the measuring stick of successful government sleight-of-hand in the years ahead.

The prospect of aggressive strikes persuaded governments to concede to the labour movement. Here, King needed to plumb the bottom line of union leaders. He could see that many more might pursue the same course unless legislation could turn the inevitable into an orderly process. Could King take one step forward and dangle out the carrot of a stable recognition process in return for one step backward to his fundamental aim of industrial peace? A vital clue was sent out during a conciliatory meeting between King and a CCL delegation on February 11, 1944. Union leaders stressed their desire for good relations and called for collective bargaining legislation and compulsory arbitration to prevent strikes and lockouts between contracts.

PC 1003, the so-called Magna Charta of Canadian labour law, offered just that on February 17, 1944. For the first time, federal legislation guaranteed automatic recognition once a union gained majority support through a government-supervised vote. For the first time, too, all workers were denied the right to strike between contracts. Thus, the legislation that supposedly guaranteed the right to unionize also restricted the right to strike. King had discovered the minimum demand of the union leadership, and it did not include a rank-and-file movement with the ability to press shop-floor conflicts to a direct conclusion. Significantly, no labour leader of stature mentioned, let alone protested, this legal innovation. The blind eye of that generation of union figures suggests something of the dovetailing link between King's genius as a prevaricator and the critical commitments of union leaders.

PC 1003 brought relative calm to the labour front in 1944, but in 1945 the end of wartime hostilities pushed domestic problems to the fore. Unions had won formal recognition in major industrial and resource locations across the country. Many unionists wondered if the reality behind recognition would prevail in the post-war era when high unemployment was forecast and concessions were no longer required for industrial peace. Some feared that the reconversion to peacetime industry would lead to a reconversion of workers to the standards of the 1930's. This fear was well-placed in the case of women workers who, having brought their men back, returned to their homes as governments closed daycare centres and cancelled tax concessions.[24] The issues of union security in the post-war world were posed most sharply in the landmark Ford Windsor strike of 1945. The union of the 17,000 plant workers insisted on a closed shop that guaranteed stability of union membership and finances. Ford's Canadian management refused and the issue was joined. The strikers sealed off the plant, refused admission to administration and production workers alike, and even shut down the plant powerhouse, threatening permanent damage to critical equipment. When government officials threatened to use police to break the picket lines, defiant strikers and citizens jammed 2,000 cars, trucks, and buses at the plant entrance and closed all avenues to police advance.

Rank-and-file workers and Ford managers refused to give an inch, but politicians and union leaders tried to find a way out short of massive confrontation. While they searched for a formula, union locals and labour councils across the country began calling for a general strike in support of the Ford workers. In this, they encountered the opposition of top CCL and CIO leaders, who feared that the showdown was sponsored by Communists and untutored militants who could not walk the tightrope between controlled protest and all-out confrontation. The international UAW and Canadian union leaders fretted that general strike action would divert attention from union security, terrify the public, and open the door to massive reprisals and repression. The rank and file had to be convinced of this ominous possibility, and it took two votes before the strikers accepted their leaders' urgings to return to work and await an arbitrated settlement. The government had gained the breathing space to launch an inquiry under Justice Ivan Rand. Rand's arbitration judgement was breathtaking in its frankness and shrewdness. Unions were part and parcel of modern-day industrial government, he insisted. The tide could not be turned back. The only question that remained was: would a jungle-style war for survival force unions to resort to tooth and claw, or could stable administration tame the beast in industrial relations and promote a civilized evolution?

As for the immediate issues at hand, Rand proposed a formula whereby unions received an automatic check-off of dues from all workers' paycheques in a unionized establishment, thus granting the union the means to finance its many activities. In return, the union agreed to allow individuals to opt out of formal union membership and to forfeit its dues if it sanctioned illegal strikes between contracts. [25]

The Ford strike and Rand settlement revealed the critical ingredients of the industrial order that emerged after World War II. Popular attitudes of the period cut both ways. Workers who feared a return to the 1930's could be very defiant; they could also be very cautious. Thus, caution and militance were close on the continuum. Union leaders had many reasons to err on the side of caution, especially when it came to speculations about the outcome of proposed general strike actions for a clean-cut victory. What if these calls were based more on bluster and bombast than brains and actual ability to deliver? But err on the side of caution they did, and quelled an upstart and rash movement bustling with rebellion and solidarity, attuned to confrontations and breakthroughs. In short, from union leaders' point of view, an immature movement that dared to struggle, dared to lose. Instead, they built a labour movement oriented to piecemeal, slow but steady advances based on chipping away concessions in successive rounds of collective bargaining. They won a place in industrial responsible government, but had to keep order in the colonies if they were to hold their seat at the head table.

By 1950, 90 per cent of unions had the Rand Formula and had transformed the steward system. Stewards no longer harassed rank-and-file workers for union dues. In the new streamlined system, workers paid their union dues alongside other payroll deductions, stewards filed their grievances, and unions offered formal education programs with funds provided courtesy of the automatic check-off.

Much was gained. Unions were able to turn their sights to problems above and beyond survival; the shop-floor tyranny of foremen was severely restricted by a web of impersonal rules honoured in good times and bad. Much was lost. Employers could shut down, lay off, suspend, and fire. Unions would have to be content with the check-off and the right to seek redress through the machinery of industrial government – a four-step, one-year, one-hundred-dollar-a-word arbitration procedure. This was the trade-off that union, government, and business leaders bargained in the first post-war settlement, elements of which were embodied in provincial labour codes passed later in the decade. As it turned out, they all got more than they bargained for.

The acceptance of the Rand Formula at Ford carried no guarantees, and the dust from the old system of industrial relations did not settle until post-war labour militance peaked and declined between 1946 and 1949. By 1946, the army was being demobilized, and 45,000 veterans brought their traditions and aspirations to the next round of industrial confrontation. Although veterans were eager to pick up the threads of broken lives and became best-known for the baby boom of the mid-1940's, "make love not war" was not a slogan that would have captivated them. They were prepared for both.

It was clear from the outset that veterans were ready for a fight on the homefront. Overseas soldiers had overwhelmingly voted CCF in 1945. Many who returned to Canada that year had left it in 1939, the last year of the dirty thirties. They looked back in anger and forward with determination. Mike Carson, a Cape Bretoner who had joined the navy at sixteen, insisted that a parade was not enough to welcome the boys back. They had gained confidence during the war "that there could be something better than what they had left," he remembered, "and no one was going to stop them. They weren't going back on the streets, to be without work and without dignity again."[26] Veterans enjoyed unbounded optimism based on what they had seen during the war, according to decorated veteran, radical, and future history professor Joe Levitt. "The propaganda of the thirties had always been that the government had no money, couldn't do anything about it, and that's the way things were," he recalled. "But the war taught people a lot. It was a matter of common sense and simple to understand that if the government could find money for war, then they could find it for peace."[27]

But veterans returned home only to find that there were no houses. Face to face with the worst housing crisis in the country's history, the veterans took action. When rent controls were lifted after the war, they formed picket lines to block evictions of soldiers' widows. Homeless Veterans' Leagues surfaced in cities across the country and organized take-overs of unoccupied buildings. In Vancouver, one group used military tactics to commandeer a hotel slated for demolition. The action was cheered from coast to coast. One Liberal MP saluted their enthusiasm: after taking so many towns in Europe, he said, they deserved at least one hotel in Canada.

In Mimico, Ontario, veteran Sam Colberry led a group of homeless families in an occupation of city hall. When police moved in to evict them, Colberry mobilized fans from a nearby lacrosse match to man the barricades. Veterans, he said, were not the same vagrant youth who had been bullied from town to town in the 1930's. "I can remember my brothers being hit on the head with billies and thrown in jail when they pulled into a town," he snapped. "After the war, it got to the point where they couldn't do that to these fellows anymore. They were trained soldiers. Any cop try to take a billy to one of them, he'd take it and hit the cop on the head with it."[28]

In industry, the vets were not about to be treated as buck privates. The post-war years witnessed the biggest strike wave in the country's history as battlelines were drawn on the labour front. Tony Gervasio, fresh from a stint in the navy, said vets were not prepared to take marching orders from the captains of industry. "We servicemen all had the same idea. We've been off to war and when we go back we're going back to fight the war for a better country. A better Canada, a free Canada – they kept giving you all these slogans. So a lot of servicemen came back a little bit militant." This spirit soon expressed itself in the union movement.[29]

In 1946, a nationwide steel strike defied government wage controls left over from the war. In Sault Ste. Marie and Cape Breton, the steel mills were shut down. In Hamilton, government trustees, armed with decrees declaring the strike illegal, tried to keep Stelco in operation. It was a trial of strength, between unions and government, unions and employers. The strikers immediately placed the plant under siege. A strikers' navy kept supplies from reaching shore. Planes, operated by war aces from the union ranks, conducted mock dogfights with company planes trying to bring in supplies. And at the plant gates, an army of picketers prevented trucks, trains, and scabs from entering or leaving.

Veterans were also in the frontlines of the battle for public opinion. Budding unionist Bill Scandlon worked with his former army buddies to build a massive support demonstration that turned the tide of public opinion in the union's favour. Stelco strikers joined in with whatever battledress they could muster. The parade passed by an army trades school and was joined by 700 servicemen in full uniform proclaiming "We're in the union army now."

The conduct of the Stelco strike revealed another post-war trend – the development of unions as family and community institutions. Local market gardeners and merchants donated food and supplies. The Italian community sponsored a spaghetti dinner for the strikers. Amateur and professional entertainers helped pass the hours away. Several weddings made use of the ready-made receiving line at the Stelco gates. And the women's auxiliary figured prominently on the picket line, where sandwiches and coffee were always available. But the women had to fight for recognition as well. "There's an awful lot of men who don't like women's organizations in their clubs. It's a man's club and they want to keep it a man's club," women's auxiliary leader Betty Shipperbottom recalled. "Only the men couldn't make the sandwiches and coffee and go on like we did, so they had to call on us. So there's another case of how they couldn't do without women."[30]

The Stelco strikers broke the government wage guidelines to net a modest wage increase, the Rand Formula, and, most importantly, real recognition of their union as a battle-worthy organization over and above the government certification process. Many strikers later recalled it as a strike for recognition, although this was not formally the case. The strike set the pattern for settlements across the country, many of which occurred within days of the Stelco agreement. The wage gains were modest. Most unionized workers still lived below the poverty line, and most settlements failed to meet the pre-strike objectives of minimum decency as set by welfare councils.

Like other strikes of the period, the Stelco conflict expressed workers' defiance of particular employer and government policies without defying the economic system as a whole. This limitation of union militancy carried no implication that bargaining positions of management and labour were mere quibbles over pennies. A frankly adversarial system was established. Both employers and workers understood the state of industrial relations in post-war Canada. The political level of confrontation remained relatively low. The CCF began its rapid decline and labour declared its own Cold War against Communism during this period of peaking militance. The economic system absorbed the conflict. But it did so only at the price of a series of concessions among which the tidbits of 1946 marked only the beginning.

The development of mass-based labour movements in Quebec and British Columbia also illustrate the dynamism of this period. In 1946, the International Woodworkers of America (IWA) led a province-wide strike to protest the government's intention to continue wage controls. The thirty-seven-day strike received near-unanimous support from other unions in British Columbia. An arbitrated settlement granted the loggers a fifteen-cent increase, a forty-hour week, and improved union security. The labour movement had come out of the woods. Ten thousand new members signed up during the strike, bringing the IWA's membership to 27,000 and making it the largest union in the province.[31]

Our understanding of Quebec has reached far beyond the stage when the Asbestos Strike of 1949 could be presented as a singular event that brought Quebec kicking and screaming into the twentieth century. Fifteen out of twenty leading industries in Montreal were unionized by 1945, a very reputable ratio by national standards. The militant textile strikes of the immediate post-war period were typical of the time. The Asbestos Strike was "unlike the others" only in that it climaxed two decades of development.

In 1949, 5,000 asbestos miners struck for four and a half months to gain a healthier work environment, better pay, and union check-off. They defied incredibly harsh and even illegal anti-labour injunctions and took their case to the public. In response, the provincial government decertified the union for refusing to wait out the prolonged arbitration process. The police-company axis was dubbed a lendlease program, and strikers took comfort from Father Jacques Cousineau's urgings to "value social justice more highly than legality." The Canadian and Catholic Confederation of Labour, which led the strike, was subject to clerical influence: parish halls were used as strike headquarters; strikers' wives faced tear gas from police and recited rosaries as they stood their ground; supportive church officials called for donations to the strikers in the name of mercy and pity for the masses. But there was no meekness in Monsignor Joseph Charbonneau's May Day sermon: "The working class is a victim of a conspiracy which seeks to crush it. . . . We want to have peace in our society, but we do not want to see the working class crushed. We are more attracted to man than capital."[32] Catholic nationalist unionism would no longer submit to the dictates of Caesar.

The Asbestos Strike ended in July 1949, having exposed all levels of Quebec society to the winds of change. In early 1950, a collective agreement was signed. Quebec labour, like its counterpart elsewhere in the country, had passed through a stormy adolescence. Its identity, however, had not yet been fully moulded.

THE FEISTY FIFTIES

In the 1950's, the president and vice-president of the Stelco union during the 1946 strike dropped their activity in the labour movement. In 1946, vice-president George Martin barnstormed the country in search of support and played a role in several picket-line confrontations. He was charged with throwing rocks at scabs during the "Battle of Wellington Bay." He was acquitted after pleading: "It's coming to a pretty thing when a man, free, white and twenty-one can't stand on the beach and skip a few stones without being treated like a common crook."[33] In the 1950's, he noted that the briefcases of union negotiators kept growing bigger and bigger, and he felt out of place.[34] Former union president Reg Gardiner, an active CCFer inspired by Christian socialism, dropped out of union activity in a huff when he could no longer take the flow of booze at union conventions. He decided to turn his efforts to the co-operative movement rather than stay with a self-seeking labour movement.[35] The heroic self-denying age of unionism seemed to be over.

But the fifties were not as flat as they seemed. Cold War ideology dominated the decade. Radicalism was in retreat. Collective bargaining generally became more routine and gentlemanly. Yet it was also a decade when the work force was fundamentally reshaped by immigration, technology, and structural change. It was a decade when unions made major bargaining advances and innovations. And these brought their share of dramatic confrontations. Overall, it was not the complacent time caricatured by one trio of complacent historians: "The economic order no longer demanded fundamental reform, and virtually no one was asking for it any more," claim authors Bothwell, Drummond, and English. "Progress and prosperity seemed to have obliterated discontent almost everywhere, leaving only a few isolated pockets of misery and malcontents. In the fullness of time these too would join the past where, so it seemed, they already belonged."[36]

Radical or anti-capitalist ideas previously associated with the labour movement did decline during the decade. The Communist Party of Canada was reduced to a sect with a minor toehold in the unions. The CCF hurried into liberalism and discarded the socialist phrases of the Regina Manifesto in favour of a shopping list of welfare-state reforms. The TLC and CCL, formerly divided by politics and inspiration, took a major step toward labour unity by amalgamating into the Canadian Labour Congress (CLC) in 1956. These indicators of labour accommodation, however, were not as one-sided as they appear.

The elimination of the CPC as a factor in Canadian labour was the product of a long-standing factional fight, carried on long before right-wing extremists claimed a monopoly on anti-Communism. The decision of the CCL in 1943 to endorse the CCF signalled the beginning of the end for the Communists. The wartime feud between the CCF and the CPC usually saw the CCF on the left, because it promoted independent industrial and political action in opposition to the CPC's front of national unity. The CPC overcorrected its right-wing policies as soon as Russia was out of danger and called for militant action at Ford and Stelco while refraining from following its own advice in locals it led. But this burst of energy could not eliminate the stain of a record that revealed beyond all doubt that CPC union policies were designed primarily to suit the twists and turns of Russian foreign policy, not the needs and moods of Canadian workers.

By 1950, the TLC and CCL had steamrollered over unions alleged to be Communist-dominated. Sometimes this was done on the flimsiest of organizational charges. The International Union of Mine, Mill and Smelter Workers (Mine-Mill), for instance, was expelled from the CCL when the union's publication insulted a top CCL leader; the United Electrical, Radio and Machine

Workers (UE) were expelled for late payment of dues. Sometimes the expulsions were executed under orders from American labour leaders. The Canadian Seamen's Union, for example, was sunk in favour of the gangster-ridden Seafarers' International Union. Other times expulsions were not necessary, as when the CPC leaders of the IWA, feeling the pressure of a vicious anti-Communist campaign spearheaded by CCL officials, mistook themselves for the members and bolted from their own union in 1948.[37]

But the housecleaning of Communists paled in importance compared to the general housebreaking of the labour movement as a whole. Communists were as much a part of this process as they were its victims. Unions led by the CPC posted unexceptional records in terms of collective bargaining breakthroughs, membership involvement, or – save for the ceremonial statements and press releases that deceive labour historians – anything more than radical posturing. UE, which was subject to the brunt of anti-Communist raiding, held its own when it came to baiting opponents. UE slammed would-be raiders of a Brockville local with a smear attack on their subversive political aims. "Don't give up your political freedom!" the UE leaflet proclaimed. "Don't let your union become a political tool! Don't be a milch cow for the CCF. Vote UE and remain free."[38]

Communist expulsions were hardly critical in themselves. They were critical insofar as they turned the labour movement into a snakepit of witch-hunting, name-calling, and mindless factionalism in which truth and integrity were the first casualties, and serious political thinking the second. They were critical inasmuch as labour leaders simultaneously enlisted as yes-men for American foreign policy when the need for political consensus was crucial for the Cold War. In this way, labour indicated its respectability, responsibility, and willingness to work within the system. But working within the system did not mean acceptance by the system, let alone accepting the system as it was – and these distinctions left enough room for continuing struggle.

Once unions followed up formal recognition with real recognition in the post-war years, they set their sights on significant collective bargaining gains. In the late 1940's, most unionized workers still earned wages that the National Welfare Council designated as insufficient to maintain a family above the poverty level. This situation dramatically changed during the 1950's. The work week was reduced to forty hours following a trend set by a railway strike in 1950. Real wages rose significantly. Paid holidays, pensions, and medical benefits became standard features of union contracts. These "fringe benefits" were far from marginal: they eliminated many of the arbitrary distinctions between white- and blue-collar workers' wages and conditions; they broke the power of employers to intimidate older workers with threats to withhold company-controlled voluntary pension plans; they established the basis for extending the welfare state. This came about partially because employers decided to transfer the costs of fringe benefits to the public welfare system, and partially because "fringes" touched on issues of an alternative vision of social organization. In 1959 at Sault Ste. Marie, for example, steelworkers set up their own community health clinic with salaried doctors and an emphasis on preventive medicine as an alternative to the rising costs of private medical schemes.

As with earlier demands for union recognition, the capitalist system was able to absorb these labour advances and even turn them to advantage. In the absence of decent government-legislated social security, negotiated benefit packages became "golden handcuffs" tying workers to a particular employer. Thus, employers secured a more permanent work force, which was increasingly important as industry moved to a "process" style of production that required a stable stock of semi-skilled employees.

Union demands for strict job classifications, designed to protect skill levels and ensure equal pay for equal work, laid the groundwork for a thorough rationalization of the division of labour along the lines of scientific management, if only because management was at last informed of the precise jobs that were done in a plant. Likewise, strict seniority requirements, demanded by unions mindful of the damaging role played by favouritism and "apple-polishing" in the non-union era, encouraged employers to de-skill as many positions as possible. Like most generals, labour leaders followed the lessons of the last war, and were not very pro-active in terms of new trends in the economy and work force.

These qualifications to union successes, however, do not minimize the significance of the struggles to achieve them. During the recession of the late 1950's, a government-business offensive against unions put the labour movement on alert. In Murdochville, Quebec, copper miners, goaded by an employer who fired leading unionists after refusing to recognize certification vote victories over a five-year period, faced harsh company-government reprisals when they struck in March 1957. Provincial and company police held strikers at bay for half a year. Not only was the strike defeated, but the United Steelworkers encountered court costs of over $2.5 million for its role in the spontaneous and illegal strike. As a result of this conflict, Murdochville

earned the title Murderville, while the newborn Quebec Federation of Labour set out to marshall its forces in bitter opposition
to the reactionary regime of Maurice Duplessis.[39]

In Sudbury, a strike of Mine-Mill workers in 1958 ended in
disaster. A depressed nickel market, hostile public opinion, including church opposition to the "Communist-dominated"
union, and finally a mobilization of miners' wives forced the
union back to the bargaining table where a three-year settlement
with a 1, 2, and 3 per cent wage increase was imposed.[40] At
Stelco in Hamilton, a three-month strike the same year led to
similar results, although in this case the loss shook up the union
local and propelled a left-wing slate into office.[41]

In Newfoundland, the full fury of the anti-union assault was
borne by hapless loggers fighting for a first contract and an end
to the pitifully primitive conditions in the lumber camps.
Church, press, and government mobilized against the IWA strike
and hysteria reached a climax when Premier Joey Smallwood exploited the death of an RCMP officer who was struck over the
head while his fellow officers brutalized a picket line. Hepburn's
attacks against the CIO in Ontario faded into insignificance
beside this show of opposition to independent organization of
the work force, and the IWA was sent packing.[42]

This breakup in the march of slow and steady progress threw
labour into political turmoil. In Sudbury, Mine-Mill was sufficiently discredited to allow the Steelworkers to launch a final assault on the last stronghold of the isolated union. In 1962, following a bitter campaign in which smear attacks were the order
of the day, Inco's work force narrowly voted to join the Steelworkers.[43] Despite the alignment of forces during the campaign,
the switch-over only confirmed that Inco, not Mine-Mill, had
been responsible for the militance and radicalism of the area.
The Steelworkers' victory ushered in an era of increased political
and strike action.

Across the country, the defeats of the era, including the near-
obliteration of the CCF caucus in the federal election of 1958,
put fire under the feet of labour leaders, who talked of a new
party of labour. The CLC and CCF combined their talents and set
up "New Party" clubs to promote a wide-ranging coalition of
progressive elements. In 1961, these clubs, together with union
and CCF delegates, launched the New Democratic Party (NDP).
From the CCF side of the fence, party architects stared hopefully
at the green fields of an unaligned progressive vote, but this was
not to materialize. The events of the late 1950's had hardened
old class lines, but they had not loosened the voting patterns of
most workers. In this sense, the formation of the NDP properly

brought the decade to a close. Its aspirations for an alliance with the middle class and its endorsement of the Cold War – Tommy Douglas threatened to resign as party leader unless the convention reversed its anti-NATO stance – had a fretful existence within a party rooted in a labour movement that still had to struggle for its most elementary goals.

THE SOARING SIXTIES

The 1960's are known for the Quiet Revolution in Quebec. To an extent, this was like the labour movement: neither was quiet nor revolutionary. In the 1960's, the face of the labour movement changed as forcefully as did Quebec and, indeed, all of Canadian society.

New trends in the work force, based on demographic and structural changes dating from the 1950's, set the labour movement twirling on a new set of axes. These shifts were most visible in the rise in industrial conflict and in the extension of unionism to new groups, such as public-sector workers and women. Equally important, though less visible, was a shift in the thrust of union demands that expressed a new set of universally common standards among all working people. As the peculiar traditions of regions and industries receded before the homogenizing forces of modern mass society, the working class lost many of its ancient strengths and ancient weaknesses. It also gained some new ones.

Labour's new frontier in the 1960's was found among white-collar and public-sector workers. In the past, government workers had tolerated relatively low wages and patronizing relationships in return for job security and possible advancement. By the 1960's, these advantages did not count for much, if only because stable employment and advancement seemed to be enjoyed by a majority of workers. Rather than counting themselves lucky to have a steady job, public-sector workers began counting the ways they were slipping behind their unionized private-sector counterparts.

The most militant public-sector union to emerge in these years was the Canadian Union of Postal Workers (CUPW). Far from public view, inside postal workers experienced unhealthy and stressful working conditions and bristled under orders from military-type supervisors and would-be postmaster "generals." Once government made it clear that their wages would continue to slip far behind firemen and policemen, who were seen as pace-setters by those delivering mail in Her Majesty's Service, the mailmen launched a spontaneous strike in 1965 in defiance of government and their own employee association leaders.[44]

This action placed the government in a quandary. The government had been planning to introduce some kind of collective bargaining for its employees for some time. If it did not soon establish machinery for legal bargaining it would find itself bargaining in jail cells with a new generation of impatient union leaders. Preferring a more comfortable atmosphere for labour relations, the government legislated reality and passed the Public Service Staff Relations Act in 1967. Of course, there was a *quid pro quo* for the concession of bargaining rights. Union jurisdiction lines were defined by government in such a way as to create bureaucratic monstrosities removed from the levers or pressure of rank-and-file action. Severe restrictions were placed on the right to negotiate and strike, both for occupations considered essential and for unions generally. For instance, unions were required at the outset of bargaining to choose between a strike or arbitrated settlement. The arbitration route was the more popular in the early years until union negotiators realized that their own denial of a strike threat eliminated their only bargaining power. As well, job classifications could not be negotiated. Despite these inadequacies, the government gave while the giving was good and subdued most militance in the work force by ceding on bargaining rights and even wages while holding tight to the reins of power. Nonetheless, a new source of power emerged in the labour movement as large Canadian-controlled unions, such as the Public Service Alliance of Canada and the Canadian Union of Public Employees (CUPE), took their place alongside the traditional blue-collar pillars of the CLC.

The most spectacular action to develop in this milieu took place in Quebec in 1972. There a common front of public-sector workers – including teachers, whose leaders espoused a neo-Marxist analysis of the wrongs of the educational system – coordinated their bargaining and refused to accept any settlement that denied a major wage hike to the most lowly paid workers. A massive strike was launched, it was declared illegal, and the major leaders were jailed, sparking a spontaneous Quebec-wide walkout of thousands of private-sector workers.[45] Quebec workers were rediscovering the type of solidarity and tactics that had not been practised on the continent since 1919.

Women workers also began to come into their own during the 1960's and figured prominently in a series of strikes against employers in the low-wage manufacturing sector. In Picton, Ontario, a small town with a strong sense of its pioneer loyalist heritage, women strikers, fighting for a slight advance on the minimum wage, were joined by a community rally of 1,000 supporters. Decked out in old-fashioned dresses, the women asked: "Our dresses went up. Why not our wages?" The five-month International Union of Electrical Workers strike featured picket-line clashes as police and managers dodged tomatoes and eggs. One striker claimed that the violence was exaggerated: "We can't help it if the company's truck tips over when somebody leans against it. Those trucks are pretty top-heavy, you know." [46]

Picket-line confrontations underlined the general worker discontent of the era. The rise in strike rates – 17 per cent of unionists went on strike in the late 1960's as compared to 6.5 per cent during the early years of the decade – suggested a rebellion against employers. The increase in illegal wildcats – about 25 per cent of the strikes of the late sixties – suggested a rebellion against union leaders. Both trends pressured the government to appoint a Privy Council investigatory committee on the state of Canadian industrial relations.

Most union unrest, together with such other indicators as rising absenteeism and job turnovers, was attributable to a new generation that knew little about the depression but a lot about Benjamin Spock and Elvis Presley. For reasons that remained a mystery to Royal Commissioners, these spoiled brats appeared to be dissatisfied with the way they were treated at work. In 1968, British Columbia telephone workers voted to strike and appealed to the community for support. Their multinational employer, it was said, "treated an employee as a machine rather than a human being," and morale "had deteriorated to the point that the employee's respect for his employer no longer exists." The next year, strikers tried to shut down telephone operations with militant "flying squads," but supervisors were able to carry on. This held the promise of some benefit since managers learned how boring the jobs were and vowed to do something about it. That commitment vanished once the regular work force returned to the job. [47]

Despite these new trends in the work force, unions remained largely reactive organizations, while business introduced the real innovations. Printers, the proudest of artisanal tradesmen, were humiliated by technological innovation in 1965 when the three Toronto dailies introduced automated equipment and broke the power of the typographers' union. "The union, with 700 men aboard, drifted to disaster," one report concluded. [48] A test case of traditional craft unionism against new technology saw the work force divided into fourteen unions, thirteen of which heartily scabbed on the printers. It was a traumatic incident in labour history, but one that few unions took to heart. Despite the relative prosperity of those years, only a small minority of unions – the Canadian Union of Postal Workers was the most notable exception – bargained for meaningful technological-change clauses in that decade or the decade after. In the years ahead, inflation, not technology or concern for more humane working conditions, defined the tasks of most unions. For that reason, the influence of the 1960's has not yet ended. It remains a decade with an uncompleted agenda.

THE SOURING SEVENTIES

Double-digit inflation was the story of the 1970's just as double-digit unemployment would be the story of the 1980's. Inflation brought new legions of workers into unions or union-like activity. It revitalized the importance of unions to their members as only the need for cash will do. It pressed union leaders into action on familiar issues, however unfamiliar the consequences. It provoked an atmosphere of economic and political crisis that required all parties to industrial relations to examine fundamentals. Thus, the restlessness that began brewing in the late 1960's came to a head in a turbulent environment that gave full play to new forces in the labour movement.

The statistics on strikes, rising wages, and the cost of living are somewhat contradictory, but this much seems clear. Most unions were stuck in long-term contracts – a legacy of the more stable 1950's – and negotiated new contracts itching for major gains that would allow them to "catch up and keep up." Any given contract generally kept pace with inflation to that date. But many workers fell behind as a result of conservative estimates of future inflation and were thus forced to catch up again. This pattern accounts in large part for the "leap-frog" phenomenon noted by many observers of the contemporary labour scene.

A second pattern was equally important. As money lost its traditional value at a mind-boggling rate, workers lost their sense of place. The idea of universal standards that had gained widespread acceptance in the 1960's led teachers, hydro-workers, nurses, orderlies, doctors, police, and factory workers to look at each others' pay packets and raise the ante. Hourly workers were no longer willing to take their place in the pecking order. They wanted the same as everyone else. In a society based on inequality, that caused a crisis. One-quarter of all work stoppages since 1900 occurred between 1971 and 1975. These figures are not prejudiced by a few outstanding strikes. Rather, as the *Financial Post* of August 27, 1983, noted: "the time lost in these epic struggles has been submerged in a general wave of bargaining breakdowns occurring across the country one year after another."

Individual companies could no longer hold the line on prices or workers' desires to stay on top of inflation. That led the Liberal government to pass labour legislation in 1975 that imposed severe limitations on collective bargaining. The legislation also created an Anti-Inflation Board (AIB) with the power to roll back illegal increases. Prime Minister Trudeau laid the blame on a worldwide revolution of rising expectations. We expect high living standards "as a matter of right," he complained. "In this struggle, we must accomplish nothing less than a wrenching adjustment of our expectations – an adjustment of our national life style to our means." A group of prominent economists jumped on the bandwagon and outlined the problem: "The struggle over who should get what share of the pie undoubtedly complicates the problem of containing inflation in Canada," the economists noted. "Indeed, it may be the heart of the problem. The legitimacy of the whole social-political economic system is now in question."[49]

As union members passed through the AIB gauntlet, labour leaders became more militant in their rhetoric. At first, they pledged obedience to the law regardless of their objections. The ostensibly Communist-run UE was one of the first unions to come under controls, but Westinghouse workers were told to accept controls and save their fight for the next election. Then Ontario Federation of Labour (OFL) leaders such as David Archer felt the pulse of union activists and proclaimed that any labour leader worth his salt had better be prepared to defy the law and go to jail. Militant rhetoric became more inflated than the economy. Once labour leaders warmed to the joys of grandstanding, they discovered that nothing was as powerful as a bluff whose time had come. Talk of general strike went the rounds. At the CLC convention of 1976, plans were set in motion for cross-country job walkouts. Following a massive mobilization of the membership, in which top leaders joined with lower-echelon militants, the first nationwide one-day general strike, dubbed a Day of Protest to avoid legal recriminations, took place on the anniversary of controls.

The AIB had succeeded in creating a national labour movement with a national focus for the first time since World War II. Furthermore, it created a highly charged movement alive to the realities and possibilities of politics. Even the labour-backed NDP fell victim to this process as unions lambasted NDP governments in Manitoba and Saskatchewan for accepting controls.

Union leaders developed the habit of thinking in terms of social systems. The OFL called for a socialist economy. The CLC entertained the idea of tripartism, and in 1976 adopted a contradictory manifesto calling for a labour-business-government coalition to govern the economy.[50] The coalition, the document insisted, would need to grant labour a decisive say; otherwise, unions would become mere disciplining agents for their members. The manifesto became a hot potato within the labour movement and was heavily criticized by the left. But it did not provide any serious guidelines for a new approach to industrial relations. In retrospect, it was not any particular proposal that was significant; it was the realization that labour leaders were energetically pursuing big answers to big questions.

The AIB dragged out its days after the giant protest but no systematic campaign can take credit for dismantling it. By the time it passed away in 1978, having accomplished few of its goals, unemployment was sufficiently high to control wages. "Free-market" forces could become dominant again. No government planning strategies based on more than whim or electoral opportunism have since been developed, the controls on public-sector wages introduced in 1982 being no exception. There has been daydreaming about European-style mechanisms for incorporating labour leaders into a network of national decision-making and there have been well-financed government departments to promote "quality of working life" through joint decision-making and redesign of social-technical systems of work. But the basic structure of industrial relations remains adversarial and, aside from approximately twenty highly publicized experiments, shop and office floors remain bastions of exclusive management power, limited only by collective bargaining.

Once controls were dropped, the labour movement was free to address some of its own compelling internal problems. Of these, the most important centred on the rules and conduct governing international unions. The issue was not a new one. American-based internationals had been calling the shots for their Canadian affiliates since at least 1902. Some industrial unions had gained a reasonable degree of autonomy by the 1960's, but this was quite tentative. In the early 1970's, then-UAW leader Dennis McDermott quashed a Brampton aircraft local that had held out for a settlement beyond President Nixon's voluntary wage guidelines accepted by American unions. The Steelworkers' paper was still published and vetted in Pittsburgh. Both unions' leaders balked at any talk of nationalism or anti-Americanism. Labour leaders were also in the forefront of the moves to hound the NDP's nationalist Waffle wing out of the party in the early 1970's.

A new alignment of forces, however, brought nationalist sentiments to the fore. Public-sector unions were almost uniformly Canadian and were not tolerant of union practices set in the United States. In Quebec, where CLC unions faced serious competition from the nationalist Confederation of National Trade Unions, there was also a major drive for autonomy. Over and above these institutional factors, nationalism, or at least anti-American sentiment, was widespread in union ranks. Several unions, such as the Canadian Paperworkers' Union, broke away from their American parents and established independence. Some unions joined a new nationalist labour central, the Confederation of Canadian Unions. The CLC accommodated these pressures, first in 1971 and more comprehensively in 1974, by adopting strict guidelines on Canadian autonomy. Canadian members of international unions would now have adequate research and support staff and major officers would be directly elected by Canadian locals.[51]

In the building trades, international union officers refused to tolerate this kind of interference in an individual union's affairs. Ken Rose of the electricians adamantly declared that he would not be told what to do by a bunch of garbagemen – an obvious slur on the members of CUPE. Moreover, the building trades officers, all of whom were appointed from Washington, objected to the way the CLC operated. The CLC system of representation by locals, they charged, gave undue weight to public-sector unions that had large numbers of small locals. Efforts by the international skilled trades bodies, backed by the CLC executive, to replace the system of locally elected delegates with a system that would give more weight to roadmen and business agents failed to pass the 1974 convention.

The international building trades unions not only refused to Canadianize their operations but withheld dues in an effort to blackmail the financially troubled CLC. The building trades found allies in several sectors of the labour movement, most notably in provincial federations where leaders feared that defection of the building trades would eliminate a major block of well-disciplined conservative voters. But pressure from the other direction was even more compelling. Canadian-based unions were enjoying some success in raiding internationals, especially in the West. Many other unions were gaining autonomy. The Quebec wing of the CLC was threatened with oblivion if autonomy was not guaranteed. Finally, in 1981 CLC president McDermott took the decisive step and suspended the building trades. The following year the building trades set up their own labour central, the Canadian Federation of Labour, and have maintained control over most of their Canadian locals.

The drive for women's equality also received forceful expression within the labour movement in the 1970's. Many unions established women's caucuses and sponsored special conferences on women's issues. Most unions pronounced themselves in favour of key demands, such as daycare, maternity pay, and equal pay for work of equal value. Affirmative action programs also found their way onto the agenda, although union insistence on seniority has made implementation of such measures difficult.

Women have also established themselves on the plane of action. Throughout the 1970's, women unionized at three times the rate of men and counted for 30 per cent of union members by 1980. Small groups of women, ghettoized in low-wage manufacturing and warehousing operations, have taken on companies, strikebreakers, and police to win first contracts. In Exeter, Ontario, seventy-eight women from the Fleck auto-parts plant, many of them sole-support mothers, stood up to provincial police to win a highly publicized first contract. The same strike produced a public bill of $1 million to pay for the police escort of strikebreakers.[52] Within larger organizations as well, women have played prominent roles in strike activity. The dramatic actions of wives' support committees are widely credited for the success of striking miners in Baie Verte, Newfoundland, in 1974 and in Sudbury in 1978. In 1980, women clerks employed by the federal government, traditionally viewed as marginal workers who would accept any offer, took the country and their union by surprise by launching spontaneous strike action that won substantial contract gains. That strike, and the failure of the Public Service Alliance of Canada to provide proper co-ordination, is generally seen as a turning point in PSAC's history, which led to the election of Pierre Samson as national president in 1981.

THE EERIE EIGHTIES

So far, the 1980's have earned more of a reputation for what has been done to labour rather than what has been done by labour. Companies have executed wholesale layoffs. Governments have eliminated collective bargaining in the public sector. Yet the labour movement has shown no signs of readjusting its structures or policies to deal with these enormous challenges.

On the collective bargaining front, unions resisted the down-ward trend in real wages against overwhelming odds from 1978 until the end of 1982. An eight-month strike by Sudbury nickel miners beat back concessions in 1978 by coupling work-force determination with a nationwide publicity campaign – under-taken, it should be noted, without much support or aid from established union leaders. In British Columbia, striking tele-phone workers made their point in a dramatic occupation of key company installations, reviving a tactic associated with early industrial unions. In 1981, Hamilton steelworkers, under the leadership of militant former Waffle member Cec Taylor, broke from their district leadership and took on Stelco in a four-month strike that netted major advances. In 1982, Chrysler workers broke ranks with their international union and refused further concessions to the ailing auto giant. The only strike defeat of major importance in this period occurred in Ontario in 1981 when hospital workers became the whipping boys of a vindictive government. Even that strike was lost in large part due to leader-ship abdication within CUPE and the lack of co-ordinating struc-tures. Unlike American labour leaders, no Canadian unionist of stature endorses the concept that concessions are necessary to re-vive the economy. Nevertheless, real wages have deteriorated slightly since 1975.

The period since 1978 has also witnessed increased union activity in the area of health and safety. Most provinces have legislated workers' rights to refuse unsafe work and education programs have created an aggressive new group of shop-floor activists attuned to a wide range of health and safety concerns. Nevertheless, unions have been hamstrung by government un-willingness to enforce health and safety legislation. Govern-ments prefer to restrict themselves to an informational and con-ciliating role. Thus, health and safety issues have given birth to a new breed of union activists, familiar with the realities of the shop floor and oriented to a combination of direct and political action.

Despite its respectable showing in these areas, the labour movement has been paralysed by the large-scale issues that de-mand centralized and co-ordinated action. Federal and provin-cial governments tore up contracts and outlawed collective bar-gaining for public-sector workers in 1982, but have so far faced little resistance. For labour leaders, it was a case of the mouth that roared, although they stopped threatening general strike ac-tion as soon as the legislation was passed.

Microtechnology will drastically alter the workplace and the number of workers throughout the 1980's, yet only a small minority of unions have contracts that provide protection against layoffs or other changes brought about by new technology. Moreover, unions have virtually no presence in the private-sector offices where this brave new world will be pioneered. Although unions showed themselves capable of mounting an unprecedented 100,000-strong protest in Ottawa against runaway interest rates in 1981, they have done virtually nothing to organize the unemployed or even to advance demands for a shorter work week to provide employment.

The labour movement faces absolutely breathtaking problems. But few of its structures are geared to mounting an aggressive campaign on current issues. Even fewer leaders are talking about the structures and policies that might be necessary. (CUPW's Jean-Claude Parrot and UAW's Robert White, who have both called for moves in the direction of amalgamation and co-ordination, are exceptions.) If this trend continues, the relationship of the structures and leaders of today to any upsurge in the future may well be as negligible as the relationship between the leaders and structures of the 1930's to the upsurge of the 1940's.

Present and future challenges aside, it is indisputable that the efforts of organized labour over the past fifty years have led to a decent standard of living and improved working conditions for millions of Canadian workers. The road to labour's just society, however, has been strewn with obstacles and temptations. Disagreements among unionists over goals and tactics, and battles for political allegiance, have often squandered limited resources. On occasion, union negotiators have accepted business and government compromises rather than test their own strength and ideals. Despite their mass-based structure, most unions have only been able to attract a small minority of their members to ongoing local activity. Several union leaders, such as Sean O'Flynn of the Ontario Public Service Employees' Union, Grace Hartman of CUPE, and Jean-Claude Parrot of CUPW, have served time in prison for upholding the collective will of their members, while many businessmen have received lesser sentences for fraud, influence-peddling, and illegal investments.[53] And finally, all union gains have done nothing to alter the fundamental political and economic structure of Canadian society. Private corporations and business-oriented governments have maintained basic control of the economy, workplace, and social system while unions are forced to engage in a continuous battle to keep up. In fact, the gap between rich and poor in Canada today is wider than in 1945. As in the past, unions will need to adjust their goals and tactics as new challenges arise. To cite a popular CUPW slogan – "the struggle continues." Only working people can determine the extent and direction of that battle.

NOTES

1. Wayne Roberts, ed., *Baptism of a Union: the Stelco Strike of 1946* (Hamilton, 1980).
2. *Ibid.*
3. Royal Commission on Price Spreads (H.H. Stevens, Chairman), *Report* (Ottawa, 1935).
4. Interview with Harvey Ladd by Wayne Roberts.
5. S.D. Hanson, "Estevan 1931," in Irving Abella, ed., *On Strike: Six Key Labour Struggles in Canada, 1919-1949* (Toronto, 1974).
6. Warren Caragata, *Alberta Labour: A Heritage Untold* (Toronto, 1979).
7. Paul Craven, "When Stratford Workers Went on Strike: A Forgotten Chapter of Canada's Labour History," *Ontario Report* (January-February, 1975); James D. Leach, "The Workers' Unity League and the Stratford Furniture Workers: The Anatomy of a Strike," *Ontario History*, 59, 2 (June, 1967); Desmond Morton, "Aid to the Civil Power: The Stratford Strike of 1933," in Abella, *On Strike.*
8. Patricia V. Schulz, *The East York Workers' Association: A Response to the Great Depression* (Toronto, 1975).
9. Interview with Pat Linehan by Gil Levine (PAC).
10. Michiel Horn, ed., *The Dirty Thirties: Canadians in the Great Depression* (Toronto, 1972); R. Liversedge, *Recollections of the On-to-Ottawa Trek* (Toronto, 1973); Gloria Montero, *We Stood Together: First-Hand Accounts of Dramatic Events in Canada's Labour Past* (Toronto, 1979).
11. Irving Abella, "Oshawa 1937," in Abella, *On Strike.*
12. Duart Snow, "The Holmes Foundry Strike of March 1937: 'We'll Give Their Jobs to White Men,'" *Ontario History*, 69, 1 (March, 1977).
13. Myrtle Bergren, *Tough Timber: The Loggers of British Columbia, Their Story* (Toronto, 1966).
14. Ruth Pierson, "Women's Emancipation and the Recruitment of Women into the Labour Force in World War II," in S.M. Trofimenkoff and Alison Prentice, eds., *The Neglected Majority: Essays in Canadian Women's History* (Toronto, 1975).
15. L.S. MacDowell, "The 1943 Steel Strike Against Wartime Wage Controls," *Labour/Le Travailleur*, 10 (Autumn, 1982).
16. Craig Heron *et al.*, *All That Our Hands Have Done: A Pictorial History of the Hamilton Workers* (Oakville, 1981).
17. L.S. MacDowell, "The Formation of the Canadian Industrial Relations System during World War Two," *Labour/Le Travailleur*, 3 (1978).
18. L.S. MacDowell, *"Remember Kirkland Lake": The Gold Miners' Strike of 1941-42* (Toronto, 1983).

19. *Ibid.*
20. Heron *et al.*, *All That Our Hands Have Done.*
21. Wayne Roberts, ed., *Miner's Life: Bob Miner and Union Organizing in Timmins, Kirkland Lake and Sudbury* (Hamilton, 1978).
22. Wayne Roberts, *Organizing Westinghouse: Alf Ready's Story* (Hamilton, 1978).
23. MacDowell, "The 1943 Steel Strike."
24. Pierson, "Women's Emancipation."
25. David Moulton, "Ford Windsor 1945," in Abella, *On Strike*; S.C. Cako, "Labour's Struggle for Union Security: the Ford of Canada Strike, Windsor 1945" (M.A. thesis, University of Guelph, 1971).
26. Wayne Roberts with Karen Levine, "Lest We Forget: Veterans and the Labour Movement," CBC Radio, 11 November 1982.
27. *Ibid.*
28. *Ibid.*
29. *Ibid.*
30. Roberts, *Baptism of a Union.*
31. J. Lembcke, "The International Woodworkers of America in British Columbia 1942-1951," *Labour/Le Travailleur*, 6 (Autumn, 1980).
32. Fraser Isbester, "Asbestos 1949," in Abella, *On Strike*; Pierre Trudeau, ed., *The Asbestos Strike* (Toronto, 1974).
33. Roberts, *Baptism of a Union.*
34. Interview with George Martin by Wayne Roberts.
35. Interview with Reg Gardiner by Wayne Roberts.
36. Robert Bothwell, Ian Drummond, and John English, *Canada Since 1945: Power, Politics and Provincialism* (Toronto, 1981), 164.
37. Irving Abella, *Nationalism, Communism and Canadian Labour: The CIO, the Communist Party and the Canadian Congress of Labour 1935-56* (Toronto, 1973); Arnold Bennett, "Red-Baiting – Trade Union Style: Cold War Factionalism in the Canadian Trade Union Movement," *Our Generation*, 13, 2 (Spring, 1979); Jack Scott, *Canadian Workers, American Unions* (Vancouver, 1978); John Stanton, *Life and Death of the Canadian Seamen's Union* (Toronto, 1979).
38. Terry Copp, *The IUE in Canada* (Elora, Ont., 1980).
39. Desmond Morton with Terry Copp, *Working People: An Illustrated History of Canadian Labour* (Ottawa, 1980); Bryan Palmer, *Working-Class Experience: The Rise and Reconstitution of Canadian Labour 1800-1980* (Vancouver, 1983); Stuart Jamieson, *Times of Trouble: Labour Unrest and Industrial Conflict in Canada, 1900-1966* (Ottawa, 1968).
40. John Deverell and the Latin American Working Group, *Falconbridge: Portrait of a Canadian Mining Multinational* (Toronto, 1975); Jamie Swift and the Development Education Centre, *The Big Nickel: INCO at Home and Abroad* (Kitchener, 1977).
41. Bill Freeman, *1055: Political Life in a Union Local* (Toronto, 1982).

42. Jack Williams, "Notes on a Lecture on Newfoundland Loggers' Strike 1959," Labour College of Canada (Ottawa, 1980).
43. Swift, *The Big Nickel*.
44. Joe Davidson and John Deverell, *Joe Davidson* (Toronto, 1978).
45. Robert Laxer, *Canada's Unions* (Toronto, 1976).
46. Copp, *The IUE in Canada*.
47. Elaine Bernard, *The Long Distance Feeling: A History of the Telecommunications Workers Union* (Vancouver, 1982).
48. Students' Administrative Council, *The Study Commission of the Toronto Newspapers Strike February 1965* (University of Toronto, 1965).
49. H.D. Woods and P. Kumar, *Canadian Perspectives on Wage/Price Guidelines* (Kingston, 1976).
50. Canadian Labour Congress, *Labour's Manifesto for Canada* (Ottawa, 1976).
51. R. Adams, "Canada-U.S. Labour Link Under Stress," *Relations Industrielles/Industrial Relations*, 15, 2 (October, 1976); M. Thompson and A. Blum, "International Unionism in Canada: The Move to Local Control," *Relations Industrielles/Industrial Relations*, 22, 1 (Winter, 1983).
52. Ellen Tolmie, "Fleck: Profile of a Strike, The OPP and the Fleck Strike," *This Magazine*, 12, 4 (October, 1978).
53. See Allan Fotheringham, "For this is the Law – and the Profits," *Maclean's*, 7 April 1980.

IV
Violence and Protest

In the years from the depression to 1980, from Maurice Duplessis to René Lévesque, Quebec has figured prominently in the national polity. While regionalism has coloured all of Canadian history, and although its Maritime and western Canadian variants have enjoyed considerable vibrancy in the last two decades, the national question in Quebec forces itself on Canadian history in ways that do not lend themselves simply to regional analysis. As a people with their own history, language, and culture, and as a conquered group, Québécois distinguish themselves from other Canadian regional or ethnic populations. (Although one should note that the Canadian native peoples and Newfoundlanders demand separate consideration as well.)

While not discussed here explicitly, the major Canadian postwar political confrontation – the October Crisis of 1970 – was one violent manifestation of the rising tensions in Quebec. The kidnapping of Quebec cabinet minister Pierre Laporte and British diplomat James Cross, and the eventual execution of the former, represented the height of separatist political violence. The Trudeau government's massive military response under the War Measures Act again alarmed many Canadians and Québécois about the fragile nature of civil liberties in this country.

Regionalism in the Canadian East and West was a major phenomenon of the period. This controversy, of course, underlay the mounting tide of political violence that culminated in October 1970. Western discontent seethed in the depression, quieted in the 1950's, and swept forward again in the later Trudeau years. The East, meanwhile, existed in quiet despair, although recent developments, such as offshore oil and gas, have led to a renewal of regional sentiment. In Ontario, of course, regionalism has always hidden its identity by disguising itself as Canadian nationalism. This least discussed of the Canadian regions also was discovering its "regional" heritage as the economy worsened in the 1970's.

Quebec, because of its cultural insulation from Canada, experienced industrialization differently than other Canadian regions. While the economic process was much the same, the cultural and ideological effects appear to have been muted by the conservative nationalism of the clergy and the traditional professions. In the 1940's and especially the 1950's, this old conservative nationalism was fragmented by the rise of new class forces in Quebec. With the ascendancy of Jean Lesage's Liberals the first stage in this transformation was accomplished, and the torrent of reform instituted during the Quiet Revolution swept away the remaining conservative dams, leading to the ultimate succession of the separatist and social democratic forces of the Péquistes.

Michael Behiel's essay focuses on the ideological debates among the emerging social groups that stepped forward in the years after World War II to challenge and to defeat Duplessis and the remnants of clerical nationalism. The recent fracturing of the PQ's alliance with labour and with its own civil service raises interesting questions about the ongoing political viability of the nationalist movement. The general economic contradictions faced by the Canadian nation-state are only exaggerated by provincial intransigence within the federal system, as both the Quebec case and, more recently, the Newfoundland experience suggest. These economic crises imply, of course, that control of the provincial state brings political power too limited to achieve any significant social change. This powerlessness, ironically, forces the Lévesque government to attack its own supporters virulently through public-sector and social-service cutbacks, yet also reinforces, for those in power at least, the necessity of separation. The ongoing economic crisis and the class conflicts it engenders may well realign the Quebec ideological map in the next decade. If so, events in Quebec may prove as central to the Canadian polity in the 1980's as they did in the 1960's and 1970's.

FURTHER READING:
A useful historical overview of Quebec, which stops short of our period, is Paul-André Linteau, René Durocher, and Jean-Claude Robert, *Quebec: A History, 1867-1929* (Toronto, 1982). On the role of the Quebec intellectuals, see Pierre Elliot Tru-

deau, *The Asbestos Strike* (Toronto, 1974). For general overviews of the Quebec scene, good accounts are Kenneth McRoberts and Dale Posgate, *Quebec: Social Change and Political Crisis* (Toronto, 1980); Sheilagh and Henry Milner, *The Decolonization of Quebec* (Toronto, 1973); and Henry Milner, *Politics in the New Quebec* (Toronto, 1978). Also on Quebec nationalism, Timothy Reid's *The Shouting Signpainters* (New York, 1972) is helpful, as is the powerful autobiography, Pierre Vallières, *White Niggers of America* (New York, 1971). The October Crisis of 1970 is covered by John Saywell, *Quebec 70* (Toronto, 1971); Ron Haggart and Aubrey Golden, *Rumours of War* (Toronto, 1971); and Marcel Rioux, *Quebec in Question* (Toronto, 1971), while RCMP repression is well-covered in John Sawatsky, *Men in the Shadows* (Toronto, 1980); and Jeff Salott, *Nobody Said No* (Toronto, 1979).

Michael D. Behiels teaches history at Acadia University in Wolfville, N.S.

Quebec:
Social Transformation and Ideological Renewal, 1940-1976

by Michael D. Behiels

Despite the steady migration of rural French Canadians to the towns and cities of Quebec, New England, and Ontario since the 1870's, the myth of French Canada being an agrarian society remained prevalent until World War II. Many outside observers retained the outmoded impression of a pleasantly quaint and stable community steeped in the values of Catholicism and a rural life cycle that had remained in their essentials unchanged for over two centuries. Few could foresee the fundamental changes this society would experience as a result of a new round of industrialization and urbanization initiated by the war and prolonged by post-war economic expansion. The emergence of the social welfare state in Ottawa, coupled with the creation of a consumer-oriented society, was to have profound social, economic, ideological, and political implications for all classes of the French-Canadian society, in particular the established clerical and secular elites.

Just what were the major socio-economic changes experienced by the Francophone society of Quebec in the three decades following the outbreak of the war in 1939? These changes will be examined along with the critical responses of a growing number of individuals, groups, and associations. In the first stage these individuals and groups articulated a critique of the prevalent ideology of conservative, clerical nationalism. They then proceeded to propose alternate ideologies based on welfare-state liberalism, social democracy, and eventually, democratic socialism. The Francophone intelligentsia was to become increasingly divided on the question of whether or not their respective liberal, social democratic, or socialist visions of society should be structured according to neo-nationalist imperatives, that is, oriented pri-

marily toward the development of a dynamic and powerful Québécois nation-state. The neo-nationalists were divided over
whether or not the achievement of their nationalist-imbued objectives could be attained within a renewed Canadian federal
system or via the acquisition of full political independence.

DEMOGRAPHIC, ECONOMIC, AND SOCIAL TRANSFORMATION

Since 1940 Quebec has experienced social change on an unprecedented scale. In the mid-1950's this upheaval prompted the director of *Le Devoir*, Gérard Filion, to remark that the province
of Quebec was undergoing a degree of socio-economic change
unparalleled in any other Western industrialized country.[1] A
great deal of the pressure for change was prompted by a considerable increase in Quebec's population. Most of the growth was
due to natural increase but this was supplemented by the influx
of immigrants in the post-war years. Furthermore, immigration
to the United States had remained difficult for most Quebecers,
thereby forcing them to seek employment at home or in other
parts of Canada. As a result of this pattern, Quebec witnessed a
22-per-cent increase in its population in the 1940's, a 30-per-cent
increase in the 1950's, and another 15 per cent in the 1960's. In
1971 over 6 million people lived in "la belle Province"compared
with 3.3 million three decades earlier.[2]

The renewal of industrial and urban expansion brought about
a precipitous decline of agriculture both as an economic activity
and as a way of life for what remained of the rural society.
Widespread rural depopulation, caused by a sharp decline in agricultural commodity prices, became one of the dominant features of post-war Quebec. Not only were one out of every two
sons leaving the ancestral home as in the past, but entire families
were abandoning farming in pursuit of employment in the factories in and around metropolitan Montreal or in the towns associated with such resource industries as mining and pulp and
paper. Within a generation the number of French Canadians on
farms declined from 1.1 million to 285,000, that is, from 41 per
cent of the Francophone community in 1941 to 6 per cent in
1971. The number of French Canadians living in urban centres
rose from 1.5 million in 1941 to over 3.7 million or 78 per cent of
the Francophone population by 1971. Metropolitan Montreal,
with 40 per cent of Quebec's population by 1961, dominated the
economic and cultural life of the province. Montreal became the
new home for two-thirds of those French Canadians leaving

their farms as well as for virtually all the post-war immigrants. Because Montreal's Anglo-Scottish financial, commercial, and industrial elite dominated the Canadian and Quebec economies, the language of work and, to a degree, social intercourse inevitably was English. It was just as predictable perhaps that Montreal, the point of contact between Francophone and Anglophone communities, would emerge as the centre of contemporary French-Canadian neo-nationalism in the 1950's.[3]

Quebec was able to absorb the vast majority of its native-born sons and daughters as well as thousands of immigrants largely because of the rapid growth in the provincial economy. Between 1946 and 1956 the gross provincial product grew by 45 per cent in constant dollars. The traditional manufacturing sectors, such as food, textiles, clothing, tobacco, rubber, leather, and wood, all increased their production. But the newly created or expanded high-technology and capital-intensive industries, such as non-ferrous metals, non-metallic minerals, iron, transportation, electrical appliances, and chemical and petrochemical products, experienced the strongest growth in production and employment. Quebec entered the 1950's with a bullish and diversified economy.[4] The vibrant domestic and American demand for Quebec's mineral resources and forest products and relatively cheap hydroelectricity spurred the rapid development of these resources. The spin-offs for the industrial and service sectors were tremendous.

One of the most significant social aspects of the expansion and diversification of Quebec's economy has been the dramatic shift in employment from the primary sector to the tertiary or service sector. The dramatic decline of agriculture and the ever-increasing mechanization of the resource sector explain the drop in proportion of employment in the primary sector from 32.4 per cent in 1941 to 7.5 per cent in 1971. Employment in the manufacturing sector grew only slightly in this period, but the proportion of Quebecers employed in the service sector – utilities, transportation, public services, commerce, and professions – rose from 41 per cent to 62.9 per cent of the labour force.

This shift to jobs in some cases requiring a higher degree of education, and therefore providing higher economic remuneration, has not been as extensive for French Canadians as for Quebec's other ethnic groups. While French Canadians are now slightly overrepresented in manufacturing jobs and have made significant gains in the clerical and sales category, in 1971 they remained significantly underrepresented in managerial and administrative positions.[5] Because the growth in prosperity has not been distributed very evenly, with managerial, administrative and highly skilled unionized employees reaping the highest rewards, French Canadians as a collectivity were found by the Royal Commission on Bilingualism and Biculturalism to rank near the bottom of the income scale in 1961.[6] This situation has improved to some extent during the past two decades.[7] Nevertheless, the growing awareness of this ethnic cleavage during the 1950's and 1960's undermined the perception of growing class distinctions in contemporary Quebec. More importantly, this ethnic cleavage contributed to the re-emergence of strong neo-nationalist sentiments among well-educated, middle-class French Canadians whose aspirations for upward mobility were being thwarted.

Perhaps the most significant ideological and political development emanating from this rapid process of socio-economic change was the emergence of an expanded and diversified middle class in French Canada. The traditional French-Canadian professional petty bourgeoisie of doctors, lawyers, notaries, journalists, clerics, and small entrepreneurial businessmen was expanded to incorporate social scientists, scientists, engineers, technicians, and private and public managers and administrators. This was due in large measure to the partial modernization of French Canada's educational institutions.[8]

Deeply concerned with the serious problems facing the French-Canadian *petite et moyenne bourgeoisies* in competing with the Anglo-Canadian and American financiers and industrialists, the Liberal government of Lomer Gouin created in 1907 the *Ecoles des hautes études commerciales* in Montreal as well as encouraged the expansion of several commercial academies at the secondary level. Nearly half of the Francophone economic elite by the 1940's had been educated in these or similar institutions in order to maintain and hopefully extend their role in the development of the Quebec economy. Concerns with overcrowding and serious competition from other ethnic groups prompted the Francophone professional petty bourgeoisie to advocate the creation of faculties of science at Laval and the Université de Montréal in the 1920's.[9] Similar concerns, coupled with the emergence of a liberal interpretation of Catholic social doctrine and social action, led to the creation of faculties of social science at both Francophone universities in the 1930's and 1940's.[10] Hampered by the unwillingness and, often, the inability of classical college graduates to pursue careers in these new faculties, as well as by the non-existence of a Francophone public secondary system providing its successful graduates with automatic access to university faculties, the growth of the new faculties of pure and applied sciences was slow and the social sciences even slower.

This situation changed dramatically during and after World

War II. By the academic year 1952-53, the number of Laval and Montréal students enrolled in the faculties of science and commerce was almost on par with those enrolled in medicine, law, and dentistry. Furthermore, nearly 40 per cent of these students did not have a classical college degree but had been recruited from the *écoles primaire supérieur* or the commercial academies.[11] As a result of this expansion considerable numbers of graduates from these non-traditional faculties were on the job market by the 1950's. Most of them faced two difficult choices. French-Canadian scientists, engineers, and business managers had to seek employment primarily in the private sector, which was largely dominated by Anglo-Canadian and American companies. These French Canadians found the competition with Anglophones particularly tough, and when they were hired it was usually "in sales, public relations, and personnel work rather than in production and general administration."[12] French-Canadian social scientists, administrators, and educators sought employment in the health, social welfare, and educational institutions, but this meant they had to work under the direction of religious personnel since the Catholic church owned and operated the vast majority of these institutions. Indeed, this process of co-opting members of French Canada's new middle class strengthened momentarily the position of the traditional political and clerical elites.[13]

With the arrival in 1960 of the Liberal Party led by Jean Lesage and the beginning of the process of political modernization, this new middle class became the most vociferous advocate of the ideology of neo-nationalism. It would use effectively a rejuvenated and modernized Quebec state to wrestle control from the Catholic church over all health, social welfare, and educational institutions, as well as to begin to challenge the Anglophone elite's control over Quebec's economy.[14]

IDEOLOGICAL RENEWAL

Quebec's "quiet revolution" originated during the depression, gained momentum in the 1940's and 1950's, and eventually found political expression in the 1960's and 1970's. In retrospect, it was primarily an ideological revolution. It was initiated by a renewed and reinvigorated Francophone intelligentsia intent on instituting a social revolution that would install it as the dominant ruling class in contemporary Quebec. Prior to 1940, ideological pluralism existed in Quebec, but the Francophone intelligentsia was committed pretty exclusively to the ideology of traditional French-Canadian nationalism. With the exception of a small handful of outspoken individuals, such as the journalist Jean-Charles Harvey and Senator T.D. Bouchard, economic and social liberalism did not find favour with French Canada's clerical or professional petty-bourgeois elites. Liberalism found a forum only in the ranks of international unions, the commercial and industrial *petite et moyenne bourgeoisies*, and the Quebec Liberal Party of Premier Alexandre Taschereau.[15]

During the 1940's and 1950's the Francophone intelligentsia became quite diversified, thereby ending its long-standing monolithic outlook. This occurred in the face of a Catholic church intent on preserving the only rural and Catholic nationality in North America as well as in the climate of the socially regressive political regime of Maurice Duplessis. His Union Nationale administration, while co-operating with the traditional clerical and petty-bourgeois elites, encouraged the rapid exploitation of Quebec's natural resources by American capital for American needs. Neither Duplessis nor his clerical and secular supporters showed much insight into or sympathy for the problems of the burgeoning proletariat created by the economic boom.

Cité libre Liberalism

Since the late 1930's the Francophone Catholic labour movement of Quebec, faced with the threat of being undermined by the American industrial unions, became increasingly militant and aggressive in its demands and collective bargaining tactics. This process culminated in the famous 1949 Asbestos Strike. In the aftermath of this turbulent strike during which over 5,000 French-Canadian workers courageously defied an anti-labour coalition of the Duplessis government and American mining interests, a young, dynamic group of Francophone liberals, social democrats, and democratic socialists came together in June 1950 to found a new periodical entitled appropriately *Cité libre* or "open society." Co-edited by Pierre Elliott Trudeau and Gérard Pelletier, *Cité libre* served as a focal point for labour advisers and militants, such as Charles Lussier, Réginald Boisvert, and Pierre Vadeboncoeur, and such literary critics and journalists as Maurice Blain, Guy Cormier, and Jean Le Moyne, as well as a number of social scientists, namely Marcel Rioux, Fernand Dumont, Jean-Charles Falardeau, and Léon Dion. *Citélibristes*, as they came to be called, undertook a wide-ranging, in-depth analysis of Quebec's socio-economic and political institutions and of the ideology of traditional French-Canadian nationalism they saw being used by the established clerical and professional petty-bourgeois intelligentsia to retain its control over the

Francophone society. *Citélibristes* were ardent French Canadians and practising Catholics who wanted to modernize and democratize Quebec's Francophone and Catholic institutions at all levels and in all areas of activity.

The first prominent institution to be challenged by *Cité libre* was the Catholic church in Quebec. Many of *Cité libre's* members had participated actively in the anti-nationalist and social-oriented Catholic action movements established in Quebec during the 1930's. Most members had also absorbed the "liberating" and inspiring personalist philosophy of France's left-wing Catholicism as articulated by Jacques Maritain, author of *Humanism intégrale*, and Emmanuel Mounier, editor of *Esprit*.[16]

As a result of these influences and their own experience with growing up in Catholic institutions, *Citélibristes* called for three reforms. First, the church had to democratize its internal operations by allowing lay participation in its councils. This step would help rid it of its excessive authoritarianism, dogmatism, and social conservatism.[17] Second, there had to be a separation of church and state. The administrative clericalism that stemmed from the church's control over health, social welfare, and educational institutions threatened to compromise severely the church's spiritual mission. Only a complete separation of church and state in these areas would enable the French-Canadian society to modernize and expand these essential services without jeopardizing the Catholic church's autonomy and its spiritual role.[18] This reform would also undermine the more insidious form of social clericalism whereby church officials and priests used the power and the influence they garnered in the spiritual realm to impose their views on social and political issues. The church, *Citélibristes* contended, had no right to determine the nature and extent of social and political debate in Quebec society. French Canada was no longer a "sacralized" society. It had become a secular society in which the relationships between human beings were considered just as important as those between an individual and his Creator. For democracy and pluralism to flourish in Quebec, French Canadians had to realize that they, not some distant providential power, were responsible for the development of the temporal City.[19] Third, the Catholic church in Quebec had to end its long-standing practice of censuring public debate on important secular issues, such as education and political morality. It must also end its historic intolerance of other religious groups and allow French Canadians freedom of choice. Freedom of thought and expression coupled with an acceptance of religious pluralism were essential if the

French-Canadian society were to become genuinely open, pluralistic, and democratic.[20]

The second major impediment to the political and social modernization of Quebec was the prevalence of the ideology of traditional French-Canadian nationalism. "What had nationalism and the nationalists given Quebec?" was the rhetorical question posed by Trudeau in his celebrated introduction to a monograph on the Asbestos Strike. By the 1950's French Canadians faced an anti-social, anti-democratic, anti-labour, and excessively pro-capitalist regime. Premier Maurice Duplessis spoke the rhetoric of traditional French-Canadian nationalism and never failed to denounce the federal government for its "centralist" social welfare policies. Yet in the same breath Duplessis would deny the need to reform Quebec's anachronistic health, social welfare, and educational institutions on the grounds that they were uniquely French and Catholic. He would then go on to extol the virtues of selling off Quebec's natural resources at ridiculously low prices without thinking that this policy might well be against the best interests of French Canadians.[21]

Trudeau and several of his colleagues, Blain, Vadeboncoeur, Dumont, and Rioux, advanced the thesis that an ever-growing credibility gap had developed between the realities of modern French Canada and the dominant clerical and petty-bourgeois vision of nationalism that had prevailed since the mid-nineteenth century. Traditional French-Canadian nationalists had, out of their desire to create a distinct society, construed an ideal society that was totally unprogressive, anti-modern, and destructive of the individual. In a post-war Quebec deeply transformed by successive waves of industrialization and urbanization, this vision of a homogeneous rural society no longer corresponded to the new realities.[22]

Citélibristes, led by Trudeau, argued effectively that traditional French-Canadian nationalism had prevented French-Canadian intellectuals from drawing on new developments in the modern social sciences and had led to a reactionary interpretation of the social thought of the Catholic church. The pervasiveness of this nationalism on the political level had made it impossible to implement solutions to socio-economic problems proven successful for the Protestant and "materialistic" Anglo-Saxons. The traditional nationalists' equation of state intervention with communism and socialism had made the implementation of a meaningful provincial autonomy impossible and impeded the growth of a democratic concept of authority and the role of the state. The solutions proposed by nationalists since the early part of the century, such as return to the land, small businesses, co-operatives, Catholic labour unions, and Christian corporatism, were all, in Trudeau's estimation, conservative and even reactionary programs intended to impede the necessary secularization and democratization of French Canada's values and institutions. Unfortunately, many of French Canada's most important institutions – the Société Saint-Jean Baptiste, the *Ecole sociale populaire*, the classical colleges, the universities, the church, and the Catholic unions – had been imbued so thoroughly with traditional French-Canadian nationalism that it was virtually impossible for them to make the transition to the modern secular world. [23]

Since nationalism had served the French-Canadian society so poorly, *Cité libre* proposed that only a widespread and genuine commitment to the ideology of liberal democracy would bring about the urgently required regeneration and modernization of French Canada. *Citélibristes* were convinced that the persistence of an authoritarian, conformist, and patronage-ridden political regime led by Duplessis was largely because French Canadians were anti-democratic. Out of historical necessity and a devotion to national survival, French Canadians had learned early on to use democracy rather than adhere to it as political philosophy to be fought for and cherished in its own right. [24] Hence the rallying cry for *Citélibristes* became "democracy first."

They set out, after the notorious dirty-tricks provincial election of 1956, to create a political movement, called *le Rassemblement*, to help establish genuine parliamentary democracy in Quebec. [25] In doing so, *Citélibristes* were opting for a society that placed its priority on the defence and development of individual rights and freedoms via liberal democratic institutions. *Cité libre* called for the creation of a ministry of education as soon as possible, for the creation of a modern educational system would allow the full and effective realization of every individual's potential. The ministry should undertake the building of a Francophone public secondary system administered by new regional school boards. This system would replace the elitist church-controlled classical college system and the truncated *Ecole primaire supèrieur* system, thereby providing all Francophones with equal access to all levels of post-secondary education. [26] *Citélibristes* also supported the eventual secularization of Quebec's Catholic universities and colleges and strongly opposed the church's plans to allow the Jesuit order to build a new university in Montreal. [27]

The revenues for necessary reforms could be obtained, according to *Cité libre*, from a more rational development of Quebec's vast natural resources. The modern neo-liberal state had a clear responsibility to intervene in the economy to ensure high employment, orderly and planned development, and a reasonable return for the treasury from the exploitation of publicly owned resources.[28] The wholesale sell-out of iron-ore deposits in Ungava for one cent per ton was considered a violation of the public's right to equitable resource rents and detrimental to the overall development of Quebec's economy. Natural resources had to be processed within the province to increase the quantity and quality of jobs in the manufacturing sector. A more productive and diversified economy would enhance the revenues accruing to the treasury, making more funds available for social programs and education reforms.[29]

Finally, *Cité libre's* perception of federalism and federal-provincial relations was determined by its strong advocacy of liberal and social democratic policies and practices. *Cité libre* vigorously opposed not the social objectives but the fiscal and monetary goals of the "new federalism" that emerged in the federal bureaucracy during and after the war. Following Trudeau's assessments of post-war economic developments in Ottawa, *Cité libre* rejected Maurice Lamontagne's plea that French Canada accept the imperatives of the modern world and participate in a lucid integration of Quebec into the new federalism.[30]

As a result of this line of thinking, Trudeau on behalf of *Cité libre* objected strongly to the federal government's decision in 1951 to grant subsidies to Canadian universities as recommended in the Massey Commission Report. Trudeau maintained that federal grants to universities violated the spirit and the law of the constitution. Agreeing with neo-nationalists at *Le Devoir*, he was adamant in his belief that the federal government should not use its general taxing powers to encroach on provincial responsibilities. It was up to Quebec voters to pressure their provincial government to provide a better financial deal for post-secondary education because this area was a provincial, not a federal, responsibility. It was only logical, given this conception of federalism, that Trudeau and his colleagues supported the imposition of a provincial income tax by the Duplessis government in 1954. Most of the revenue was slated for education and the legislation was a perfect example of the government responding to public pressure.[31]

The provincial income tax created quite a row with Prime Minister St. Laurent and the federal bureaucrats. Following several months of verbal bombast Ottawa consented, albeit reluctantly, to share in a minor way the personal income tax field. While *Citélibristes* rejected the nationalists' claim that the provinces had an exclusive or priority right in the area of direct taxation, they supported their proposal that Quebec taxpayers be allowed to deduct, to a certain level, provincial income tax from their federal taxes. In short, there should be a sharing of the taxing resource base to serve both levels of government in proportion to their respective constitutional responsibilities. Among Ottawa's responsibilities Trudeau included financial equalization between the have and have-not provinces, economic stabilization, and full employment programs. Canada, *Citélibristes* firmly believed, could have strong autonomous provinces financing their own responsibilities as well as a strong federal government capable of directing and regulating a rapidly expanding industrial and technological society.[32] *Citélibristes* did not believe that constitutional changes pertaining to the division of powers between both levels of government were necessary or advisable. French Canadians had all the provincial powers they required to build an open, democratic, and pluralistic society under their control. Given this perspective, it was only natural that *Cité libre* would characterize the re-emergence of separatism in the early 1960's as the new treason of the intellectuals and would denounce the separatists as political counter-revolutionaries.[33]

The Birth of Neo-nationalism

Indeed, the neo-nationalism formulated by a small contingent of French Canada's intelligentsia during the 1940's and 1950's could easily be given a separatist orientation by disgruntled and ambitious members of French Canada's rapidly expanding new middle class. In fact, neo-nationalist historians at the Université de Montréal – Michel Brunet, Maurice Séguin, and Guy Frégault – were developing a secular nationalist interpretation of Quebec's past that weighed heavily in favour of political independence as the only viable guarantee of the survival of the French-Canadian nationality in North America. In the 1950's most neo-nationalists were not yet willing to accept this interpretation. Yet in 1952, to his rhetorical question "Is there a crisis of Nationalism?" André Laurendeau responded with a categorical yes. In the wake of the demise of the *Bloc populaire canadien* in 1947, the creation of Ottawa's welfare state, and the growing identification of nationalism with the regressive policies and practices of the Duplessis administration, nationalists had become terribly confused. In fact, as Laurendeau was quickly discovering, much to his chagrin, many were indifferent and some were hostile to nationalism.[34]

French Canadians generally, but in particular the rural professional petty-bourgeoisie and the clerical leaders, rejected an abrupt departure from past practice. Consequently the Union Nationale, with its vigorous defence of the rural way of life, of the strong presence of the Catholic church in education, health, and welfare, and of the constitutional prerogatives of the province against an ever-encroaching Ottawa bureaucracy, was able to regain and retain power with relative ease for a decade and a half following its defeat of the Liberal and *Bloc* parties in the 1944 election.[35]

If French-Canadian nationalism, argued André Laurendeau and Gérard Filion, were to become once again an effective ideological force in contemporary Quebec, capable of influencing the direction of government policies and programs, it would have to be reformulated to reflect the needs and aspirations of an urban/industrial society. The neo-nationalist leaders, Filion and Laurendeau, were well placed to undertake this task. In April 1947 Filion had become director of *Le Devoir*, French Canada's most influential nationalist daily. He then hired Laurendeau as editor-in-chief. This was an inspired move because Laurendeau had impeccable nationalist credentials and, despite his liberal-reformist leanings, was generally acceptable to the more traditional nationalists. In 1948 Laurendeau was also reappointed for a second five-year term as director of French Canada's leading nationalist periodical, *l'Action nationale*. During the 1950's *Le Devoir's* editorial staff included Paul Sauriol, Pierre Vigeant, Pierre Laporte, and Jean-Marc Léger. *Le Devoir* quickly became the centre of the debate about the future of the Francophone society and its role in Canada.

At the very heart of the political and ideological crisis facing French-Canadian nationalism was its inability to win over the hearts and minds of French Canada's dominant social class, the urban working class.[36] There were a number of divergent reasons for this: the homogenizing nature of the industrialization process; the lack of an urban French-Canadian culture and institutions; the foreign domination of Quebec's economy.[37] But the most important reason, according to neo-nationalists, was that the traditional nationalists had simply lost touch with the people by failing to elaborate a realistic and meaningful doctrine and program of action. A group of Université de Montréal students, who had created the *Equipe de recherches sociales* in 1947 to inculcate a social conscience in their fellow students, contended that the traditional nationalist elite of petty-bourgeois professionals and clerics was more concerned with defending its own particular class interests than with advancing the collective interests of the French-Canadian nation.[38] Somewhat surprisingly, the students found immediate support for their interpretation from abbé Gérard Dion and Joseph Pelchat of the Department of Industrial Relations at Laval, as well as from Claude Ryan, an organizer in the Catholic action movement, and Jean-Paul Robillard, a former *Bloc* militant. André Laurendeau gave the interpretation qualified support while encouraging the group to pursue its activities.[39]

The solution to the crisis was not, as the *Citélibristes* proposed, to abandon nationalism but rather to reorient and redefine it to meet the needs of contemporary Quebec. French-Canadian neo-nationalists accepted the fact that their society was no longer rural and agricultural but urban and industrial. The challenge confronting the French-Canadian people was to assimilate the new urban/industrial order and turn it to the advantage of a revitalized French-Canadian nation.[40] Neo-nationalists set out with considerable determination to break the identification of nationalism with anti-social, anti-labour, xenophobic, and petty-bourgeois values and interests. Nationalism, for them, was to become an ideology of socio-economic reforms, an ideology that would help undermine the dehumanizing and depersonalizing aspects of the urban/industrial social order. With the revitalization of such institutions as the family and the community and the acquisition of greater autonomy for the individual, perhaps nationalism might well become a valued ideology among French Canada's working-class majority.[41]

The neo-nationalists' concern with the integration of the French-Canadian working class into the nationalist mainstream was reinforced by a growing awareness that the social, political, and economic interests of the French-Canadian middle class, old and new, were in serious jeopardy. This predicament was the natural outgrowth of the ever-increasing economic inferiority of French Canadians as individuals and as a collectivity. This issue was at the very centre of the neo-nationalists' concerns throughout the 1950's. It contributed directly to their decision to look toward the Quebec state as the key to the creation of a modern, secular society under the leadership of a new Francophone middle class.

Neo-nationalists observed the post-war economic boom with considerable trepidation. While Duplessis's laissez-faire economic policies and strong encouragement of foreign investment certainly created plenty of jobs and profit in the resource sector of the economy, they also accelerated the economic inferiority of French Canada's financial, commercial, and industrial *petite et moyenne* bourgeoisies. It was painfully apparent that French Canada lacked a financial and industrial *haute* bourgeoisie to compete with Montreal's Anglo-Canadian and American capitalists who dominated the most crucial sectors of Quebec's economy.[42] French Canadians, who constituted 30 per cent of Canada's population, could lay claim to only 8 per cent of the country's wealth. In Quebec, where they formed 80 per cent of the population, they could lay claim to merely 25 per cent of the wealth. Little wonder that only 5 per cent (400) of the 8,000 company directorships listed in the 1954 *Directory of Directories* were French Canadians and only a small proportion of these held sizable stock portfolios.[43]

In general, neo-nationalists accepted the standard explanations for the absence of a French-Canadian bourgeoisie. While it remained true that French-Canadian family-based businesses feared the risks of going to the open market for expansion funds, it was no longer true that French Canada lacked internal capital resources. The real challenge was how to marshal those resources in an effective and efficient manner to enable the emergence of a Francophone *haute* bourgeoisie.[44] Laurendeau, Filion, Léger, and Laporte all had been convinced for some time that the Francophone majority's only effective method of achieving control over the provincial economy was to create a dynamic, interventionist, and secular nation-state. Consequently, they were very receptive to a reinterpretation of French Canada's past proffered by the Université de Montréal's neo-nationalist historians. Michel Brunet, Guy Frégault, and Maurice Séguin were contending that the Conquest of 1760 was the single most important event explaining the absence of a modern secular bourgeoisie in French Canada.[45] In short, their political explanation for French Canada's position of economic subservience encouraged other neo-nationalists to believe that a political solution was an important element in the attempt to redress an untenable situation.

Extensive government intervention, it was believed, was needed in the planning and development of the economy. To become economic masters in their own house, French Canadians must start by regaining control over their vast natural resources – hydroelectricity, pulp and paper, and mining. If private companies refused to allow French Canadians to become the majority stockholders and managers of the resource corporations or to provide the citizens of Quebec an equitable share of the economic rents of their resources, the Quebec state had no alternative but to nationalize the companies.[46] Neo-nationalists were particularly incensed at the Duplessis government's decision in 1946 to grant the Iron Ore Company, a consortium of several American steel companies, the right to develop the iron ore de-

posits in northern Quebec for a fixed annual royalty of
$100,000. This amounted to little more than one cent per ton of
ore! Certainly jobs were created but the public's share was
meagre indeed. They might also have added that Francophones
were conspicuous by their absence in the upper echelons of the
corporation. Duplessis's resource policy appeared particularly
galling when he proclaimed time and time again that his government lacked the revenue to improve educational and social services. It was also imperative, argued neo-nationalists, for the
government to create, as soon as possible, a state-controlled
steel corporation to mine and process Quebec's iron ore.[47]

After initially resisting the call for increased provincial activity in the social welfare and health fields for fear of alienating
the church, neo-nationalists by the late 1950's supported organized labour's pleas for provincial medicare and hospitalization
programs. Neo-nationalists perceived the reform of Quebec's
anachronistic and unco-ordinated education institutions as the
central element in their drive to create a modern, secular,
French-Canadian nation-state.[48] Indeed, the pressures for educational reform were quite widespread by the 1950's, a fact that
was clearly demonstrated by the 140 briefs on education presented to the Tremblay Commission on Quebec's constitutional
problems (1953-55). Over fifty organizations also participated in
a highly publicized provincial conference on educational reform
in June 1958 to deal with such urgent problems as the low participation rate of Francophones at the secondary and post-
secondary levels, the abysmal lack of funding at all levels, the
persistence of undemocratic structures and procedures, poorly
qualified and underpaid teachers, and finally, the total lack of
co-ordination between the various levels.[49]

Neo-nationalists, led by the work of Arthur Tremblay, a
Laval education specialist and the moving force behind the 1958
conference, supported raising the compulsory age of attendance
from fourteen to sixteen to ensure that French Canadians were
better prepared to face the demands of the work world and to
pursue, if qualified, further education at the post-secondary
level.[50] Neo-nationalists also wanted school boards and the *Con-
seil de l'Instruction publique* to become fully secularized and
democratized – all lay members were to be elected by universal
suffrage.[51] They also came to realize that French Canada's private secondary and post-secondary system of classical colleges
was totally inadequate to serve the needs of a modern society.
Unlike the *Citélibristes* who wanted to scrap the system in its en-
tirety, the neo-nationalists wanted to make the classical Latin-
science curriculum available to all qualified students through a

network of secular, state-supported regional high schools. This would democratize access to secondary education and provide the universities with well-prepared recruits for the science and social science faculties and the professional schools. Only in this manner could French Canada provide itself with a modern, secular middle class capable of managing the apparatus of an interventionist state and thereby gain control over Quebec's foreign-dominated economy.[52]

Much of the reform at the primary and secondary levels was dependent on the modernization of Quebec's three French-language universities run by the church. Well-funded, dynamic, secular Francophone universities were seen by neo-nationalists as a *sine qua non* for the flourishing of an autonomous Québécois nationality.[53] Neo-nationalists in the late 1950's still remained cautious about demanding the reinstatement of a ministry of education for fear of arousing the wrath of the church, thereby endangering the growing consensus for reform at the other levels. Laurendeau recommended in 1960 that the newly elected Liberal government of Jean Lesage establish a Royal Commission to investigate all aspects of education and prepare the groundwork for long overdue reforms.[54] Lesage agreed and created the Parent Commission, named after its neo-nationalist chairman, Monsignor Alphonse-Marie Parent, former rector of Laval. With Filion and Arthur Tremblay appointed to the Commission, neo-nationalists were in an excellent position to influence the direction of education reform in contemporary Quebec.

Inevitably, the neo-nationalists' campaign for a dynamic, interventionist nation-state was to have serious implications for their perception of Quebec's role within the Canadian federal system. Their initial reaction was to demand that Ottawa respect the provincial and cultural compacts nationalists argued were inherent in the British North America Act of 1867. In due course they came to feel that fundamental constitutional revisions to entrench the equality of the French-Canadian nation and to accommodate the urgent requirements of the "new" Quebec were imperative.

This shift was consolidated by two full-scale battles between Ottawa and Quebec over taxing powers and education. The first struggle entailed the Duplessis government's rejection of the tax-rental scheme Premier Godbout had signed in 1942, which expired in 1947. While Duplessis refused to sign a new agreement his government also refused to take any decisive action to counter this fiscal centralization. The neo-nationalists campaigned aggressively for the province to exercise its taxing powers by imposing a personal income tax. This action would produce one of two effects. The federal government might conceivably allow Quebec citizens to deduct their provincial tax from their federal tax or Ottawa could choose to reduce its personal tax level by an amount equivalent to the provincial tax. If Ottawa refused to budge, Quebec's politicians could effectively blame it for imposing double taxation.

Thanks to the co-ordinated efforts of the neo-nationalists, the *Chambre de Commerce de la Province de Québec*, and the *Chambre de Commerce de Montréal*, the Tremblay Commission was able to persuade a very reluctant Duplessis to implement a provincial income tax in 1954. When the federal government agreed after several months of turmoil to share in a very small way the personal income tax field the neo-nationalists were elated.[55] As subsequent events demonstrated, Ottawa's decision marked the effective demise of the tax-rental system and the beginning of a new era of fiscal sharing. While Duplessis refused to press his hard-won advantage, the neo-nationalists, having seen their strategy of aggressive provincial autonomy reinforced by success, expressed the view that this was merely the beginning. Just think, they wondered out loud, what the province could accomplish if its political leaders subscribed wholeheartedly to a policy of state-building!

The second issue to arouse the ire of nationalists, old and new, was the federal government's decision to provide direct grants to universities as recommended by the Report of the Royal Commission on National Development in the Arts, Letters and Sciences (1951). The scheme was a direct challenge to the neo-nationalists' campaign to develop a dynamic Quebec state because it involved the federal government in an area of provincial jurisdiction. That area, education, was considered sacred to the survival and development of a distinct French-Canadian nationality. No national minority could allow central government bureaucrats and politicians, who mostly represented the values and aspirations of Canada's English-speaking majority, to control its educational institutions. In the words of the *Ligue d'Action Nationale* and Michel Brunet, Quebec City, not Ottawa, was the capital of the French-Canadian nation.[56] The Duplessis government accepted the federal grants for 1951-52 but the vociferous reaction of all nationalists forced it to reject all future subsidy proposals of the federal government. Neo-nationalists kept pressuring the Duplessis administration to put its money where its mouth was and start providing the necessary financial support to Quebec's hard-pressed universities, especially the Francophone universities, which were facing rapidly increasing enrolments and enduring antiquated and totally inadequate facilities. They proposed that Ottawa, as an alternative, provide Quebec with a larger slice of direct taxes, personal or corporate, or increase the province's equalization grant by two million dollars. Pressure could then be put on Duplessis to spend this money on post-secondary education.[57] In fact, after several years of wrangling and continued poverty for Quebec's Francophone universities, the first proposal was precisely the solution that Ottawa and Quebec adopted after lengthy negotiations between Premiers Paul Sauvé and Jean Lesage and the Diefenbaker government.

The significance of these federal-provincial disputes was that they prompted neo-nationalists to consider seriously the need to revise the constitution. Two constitutional options emerged. The *Ligue d'Action Nationale* in its brief to the Tremblay Commission, authored by Jean-Marc Léger, proposed the creation of a highly decentralized confederal system in which the provinces had expanded prerogatives, including all residual powers, while the central government retained only limited and specific economic, military, and political responsibilities. Maximum decentralization was imperative if the French-Canadian nation, which had its homeland in Quebec, was going to survive and achieve equality with the English-Canadian nation.[58] The second option was proposed by the *Société Saint-Jean-Baptiste de Montréal* in its brief, authored by Michel Brunet, to the Tremblay Commission. Since it appeared that English Canadians considered Ottawa to be their national government it was not likely that they would support a highly decentralized system. If the French-Canadian nation, in its view, was to survive and achieve equality, it required its own highly autonomous nation-state. That state could be none other than Quebec. A revised constitution had to recognize the "special role" of Quebec by granting it greater taxing powers than other Canadian provinces as well as complete control over all social security, health, education, and cultural responsibilities. In short, Quebec required a constitutionally entrenched "special status."[59] The Tremblay Report sanctioned both of these proposals while suggesting a couple of practical methods of moving toward greater fiscal decentralization and provincial control over all social programs. To facilitate intergovernmental relations the commissioners proposed the creation of a Federal-Provincial Relations Secretariat and a Permanent Council of the Provinces.[60]

Laurendeau and Filion strongly favoured the special-status option and *Le Devoir* would become, in the 1960's, one of the most strident voices for a renewed constitution entrenching this special status. The emergence of a bureaucratic middle class intent on establishing its control over the urban/industrial French-Canadian society had focused considerable attention on the powers and prerogatives of the Quebec state. It was only a matter of time before some members of this new middle class would begin to question the serious constraints of federalism and North American monopoly capitalism.

Parti pris: **Quest for a Socialist and Independent Quebec**

The Quiet Revolution of the 1960's symbolized more than a political changing of the guard from the conservative, rural notables of the Union Nationale to the progressive, urban technocrats of the Liberal team of Jean Lesage. For many young French Canadians it marked the end of the *ancien régime* and the beginning of a cultural and ideological revolution whereby a new intelligentsia, with the support of a progressive middle class, would bring about a wholesale social revolution. Just as the *Cité libre* and neo-nationalist movements had developed, in part, as response to the policies and practices of the Duplessis régime, the various movements for an independent and socialist Quebec were, to a large degree, a response to the perceived shortcomings of liberal neo-nationalism and its proponents, the Liberal Party. The *Rassemblement pour l'indépendance nationale* (RIN), created in September 1960 as a political movement, became a centre-left political party in March 1963 under the leadership of Pierre Bourgault. While right-wing separatist groups also flourished – the *Alliance Laurentienne* (1957), the *Parti Républicain du Québec* (1962), and the *Ralliement Nationale* (1964) – it was the combination of secessionist nationalism and socialism that provided the most innovative and politically challenging ideological development of the 1960's.

In 1963-64 three periodicals, *Parti pris*, *Socialisme*, and *Révolution québécoise*, appeared on the scene to articulate and disseminate the ideology of socialist nationalism. *Parti pris* proved to be the most dynamic and influential of the three because of the composition of its editorial team and its strong neo-nationalist orientation. The five founders of *Parti pris*, Pierre Maheu, Jean-Marc Piotte, Paul Chamberland, André Brochu, and André Major, were all in their early twenties. All except Major, the poet, were university-educated and were heavily influenced by the socialist-nationalist theories pertaining to the decolonization movement of Third World countries, such as Frantz Fanon's *Les damnés de la terre* (1961), Albert Memmi's *Portrait du Colonisé* (1957), and Jacques Bergue's work on Arab countries.[61]

Parti pris militants and ideologues set themselves the challenge of creating an independent, secular, and socialist Quebec.[62] The tremendous difficulties of reconciling the "class" imperatives of their socialism with the "nationalist" imperatives of their commitment to independence for the Québécois nation plagued *Parti pris* throughout the entire five-year period of its existence. *Parti pris* members were caught in a dilemma not entirely of their own making. A genuine working-class consciousness did not, as of the mid-1960's, exist among the vast majority of French-Canadian workers, as was clearly demonstrated by the total lack of political success of the *Parti socialiste du Québec* or the Quebec wing of the New Democratic Party. Quebec's labour leaders were simply unable or unwilling to ensure that unionists would vote for a working-class party devoted to a socialist and independent Quebec. Socialism had been anathema to the French-Canadian society for several generations. Nationalism, on the other hand, had been part of the ideological and political landscape since the early nineteenth century. In the 1960's and 1970's, neo-nationalism dominated the political, cultural, and social environment even to the point of becoming, perhaps for the first time, a genuine mass, as opposed to a middle-class, ideology. This historical development helps to explain, in part, why nationalism prevailed so easily over socialism in the *Parti pris* elaboration of its ideas and its strategy of political action.[63]

The commitment to political independence for Quebec was paramount. Relying on the revisionist work of the neo-nationalist historians at the Université de Montréal, *Parti pris* members argued that the Québécois nation had become, since the Conquest of 1760, a colonized nation, first by Great Britain and then by English Canada. This imperialism had debilitating and destructive effects on the French-Canadian people, such as creating a deep sense of inferiority and alienation.[64] Only complete political independence would destroy the persistent colonial subordination of the French-Canadian nation by the English-Canadian nation.[65] It was imperative, given the Marxist view of society elaborated by *Parti pris*, that the national revolution not be controlled and monopolized by the neo-bourgeoisie to create a powerful national bourgeoisie that would merely perpetuate the exploitation of the working class under new political structures. French-Canadian workers could achieve complete decolonization of themselves and their society only if the political revolution was followed by an economic and social revolution.[66]

The *Parti pris* assessment of the nature and extent of the social reforms required in Quebec was based on a neo-nationalist rather than a socialist interpretation of the crisis facing their society. Following the theory of several Quebec sociologists, *Parti pris* viewed the French-Canadian society essentially as a proletarian nation – an ethnic class – because the exploited and dominated French-Canadian working class constituted the vast majority of the French-Canadian nation.[67] The French-Canadian bourgeoisie, old and new, was weak and ineffectual and, largely, beholden to the dominant Anglophone community for its minor political, social, and economic privileges. Given this reality it was only natural that French-Canadian workers, in attempting to come to grips with their sense of alienation and inferiority, did so in ethnic rather than class terms.[68] The struggle for the survival of the French-Canadian national culture – essentially a working-class culture – entailed, according to the *Parti pris* manifesto of 1965-66, an overthrow of the Anglo-Canadian and American colonial and capitalist dominations, which had brought a foreign "mass culture" to Quebec.[69] In an independent Quebec, the working class could secularize all institutions and end the negative effects of an authoritarian Catholicism on the family and the individual. It could also ensure that education at all levels served the needs of the working people rather than the interest of the bourgeoisies. Finally, the working class could create the institutions needed to develop a genuine and humanistic Québécois culture, one allowing for the achievement of an individual's full potential within the framework of the nation.[70]

The *Parti pris* assessments of industrial capitalism and the role of the state were also influenced by its neo-nationalist outlook rather than by a genuine socialist analysis. Quebec had a neo-capitalist industrialized economy that exploited and alienated workers, but this had not created a class reaction. Instead, it had fostered a sense of greater ethnic cleavage, especially among ambitious middle-class professionals, managers, industrialists, and businessmen because the development of the province's natural resources and a large part of the manufacturing sector were controlled by foreigners. Quebec's economy was underdeveloped because it relied on the export of primary products and the importation of manufactured goods, thus ensuring that the standard of living was considerably lower for French Canadians than for Canadians in general.[71] Finally, the existing system of neo-capitalism fostered a petty-bourgeois business unionism that concentrated on economic gains while refusing to develop a working-class consciousness and a working-class party. Hence, the unions were not in position to lead either the national or the social revolutions.[72] The Quebec state, argued *Parti pris*, was controlled by a ruling class comprising a foreign bourgeoisie and a subservient French-Canadian neo-bourgeoisie. The increased role of the Quebec state in the 1960's, such as the nationalization of hydroelectricity and the modernization of the education system, served primarily the interests of the foreign bourgeoisie by creating better-educated workers. The process also enhanced the political power of, and job opportunities for, the French-Canadian neo-bourgeoisie, which controlled the state apparatus.[73]

Parti pris, nevertheless, rejected the logic of its fairly crude Marxian analysis of Quebec society. Instead, its neo-nationalism brought it to argue that its priority was to achieve independence because, with the use of the modern state being established in Quebec by the bureaucratic middle class, it would be possible to create a new society. Chamberland contended that the French-Canadian petty bourgeoisie lacked internal cohesion. This would enable the working class to gain control eventually of the state and use it as a tool for its own liberation.[74] This meant, of course, that *Parti pris* would, for what it argued were tactical and strategic reasons, support all reformist elements of the new petty bourgeoisie that supported the cause of independence. The acquisition of an independent, democratic, and bourgeois state was a great gain because it allowed the working class to conquer "selon le mot de Marx, *le terrain de la lutte*."[75]

By the summer of 1965 it appeared that the thrust had gone out of the Quiet Revolution as the conservative forces within the Liberal government were gaining the upper hand. It also appeared to some members of *Parti pris* that organized labour was finally becoming militant and even showing signs of political action. They formed the *Mouvement de Libération populaire*, developed a "minimum" program that would appeal to the working class, and joined forces in March 1966 with the *Parti Socialiste du Québec* (PSQ) to contest unsuccessfully a handful of seats in the 1966 provincial election. The PSQ was lukewarm at best on the issue of independence and the projected ties with organized labour never materialized.[76] *Parti pris* quickly abandoned its support for the PSQ. Piotte, in the fall of 1966, called for a return to the former strategy of revolution by stages, that is, a tactical support for the progressive wing of the French-Canadian petty bourgeoisie.[77] Other members, including Gabriel Gagnon, Luc Racine, and Gilles Bourque, disagreed strongly with this strategy. Any attempt to consolidate the power of the French-Canadian petty bourgeoisie would, they maintained, be suicidal for all socialist groups and would undermine any chance of building a genuine socialist labour party.[78]

The "independence first" faction, led by Piotte, retained the upper hand in this ideological dispute. Since the Liberal Party was out of office and its progressive wing had abandoned it, *Parti pris* decided to support the RIN, a petty-bourgeois party devoted to an independent, socialist Quebec.[79] In the fall of 1968, the RIN was swallowed up in the vortex of the newly created Parti Québécois and this reopened the ideological crisis within *Parti pris*. The socialist faction led by Bourque and Racine rejected the concept of sovereignty-association because it denied both the socialist and nationalist revolutions and they decided to quit *Parti pris* in the summer of 1968.[80] The neo-nationalist faction defended the strategy of "independence first" and joined forces with the emerging Parti Québécois. *Parti pris* disappeared from the scene, a victim of the ideological struggle between left-wing neo-nationalists who gave their priority to independence and the ardent socialists who wanted to achieve their revolution through a working-class party founded on a militant organized labour movement.

THE IMPACT OF IDEOLOGICAL RENEWAL

By the mid-1960's the ideological landscape of Quebec was certainly a lot more pluralistic and complex than had been the case some thirty years earlier. This was largely a reflection of the expansion and diversification of the Francophone middle class. Each sector of this new middle class – public- and private-sector middle managers and administrators, unionized professionals and semi-professionals, and organized labour leaders – developed its own particular ideological outlook to attain control over the levers of power represented by the recently expanded state. The three groups represented the neo-liberal, the social-democratic, and the socialist wings of the new middle class. Nevertheless, these three groups overlapped considerably depending on what issues were being debated.

The ideological evolution of the Catholic labour movement demonstrates well the impact of changing socio-economic and political structures. Thanks to *Cité libre*, welfare-state liberalism found a small but vocal intelligentsia willing and able to articulate and disseminate a societal model based on neo-liberal assumptions and tenets. Under the influence of liberal social Catholicism and encouraged by *Cité libre* activists, the Catholic labour movement abandoned its long-standing commitment to social corporatism and campaigned for the establishment of industrial democracy in Quebec through a system of co-management, profit-sharing, and co-ownership of industry. The emphasis was placed on the democratization and humanization of the workplace as a prelude to the democratization and humanization of contemporary society.[81] This step was particularly important because it encouraged the Catholic labour movement, led by Gérard Picard and Jean Marchand, to come to terms with the welfare state and, by 1958, to support the creation of national hospitalization and medicare systems administered concurrently by Ottawa and the provinces.[82]

The Catholic labour movement's commitment to neo-liberalism was also symbolized by the gradual secularization of its outlook and its operations during the 1940's and 1950's. This process culminated by 1960 in the adoption of a new set of principles and a new name, *Confédération des syndicats nationaux* (CSN). During the first half of the 1960's, the CSN actively supported the Liberal administration's reforms of the social service systems, the provincial bureaucracy, the political institutions and process, and the labour code, as well as its attempts to gain control over the Quebec economy through government planning, regional economic development, and direct intervention, such as nationalization of the private hydroelectric companies after the 1962 election.[83]

While the Lesage government was no doubt motivated by its commitment to the creation of a liberal democratic society, the most pervasive and influential ideological force behind the Quiet Revolution proved to be neo-nationalism because the various sectors of the new middle class quickly perceived that if the modernization of Quebec society was accomplished by the state under the aegis of nationalist goals and aspirations it was imperative to gain firm control over the levers of power. Only then would the new middle class, or at least one segment of it, emerge as the dominant social class, displacing the traditional Francophone petty bourgeoisie, the church, and, it might be hoped, the Anglo-Canadian and American bourgeoisies who controlled the economy. Neo-nationalism was a perfect ideology to appeal to the masses for the political support essential in a system of parliamentary democracy. Moreover, the emergence of a powerful new class (and the internal struggle between its various elements) was camouflaged by the rhetoric of collective rights and aspirations.

By the mid-1960's disenchantment set in over the limitations of the Quiet Revolution. The three groups of the new middle class parted ways. The public-sector managers and administrators and the unionized professionals whose power was based on knowledge and the private-sector petty bourgeoisie and emerging Francophone bourgeoisie clashed over the issue of political sovereignty for Quebec as well as over the question of the kind of society that should be created in Quebec – a neo-capitalist welfare state or a decentralized social-democratic society with a high degree of public ownership of important sectors of the economy. After the Liberal defeat in 1966, René Lévesque led a small radical wing out of the party and created the *Mouvement Souveraineté-Association* which several months later became the Parti Québécois. The Parti Québécois articulated the national and social vision of the middle-class technocrats, bureaucrats, and professionals – the men of knowledge, such as Arthur Tremblay, Deputy Minister of Education, Claude Morin, Deputy Minister of Intergovernmental Relations, and Jacques Parizeau, an economist. These state managers and professionals formed part of a bureaucracy that expanded dramatically in the 1960's, from 2,103 professionals in 1964 to 4,646 in 1971. The vast majority were committed to using the powers of a politically independent Quebec state to create a modern Québécois society controlled increasingly by them.[84]

After considerable wrangling, the Quebec Liberal Party of Jean Lesage, who was replaced by Robert Bourassa in 1970, rejected both the special-status and sovereignty-association options and argued for a strong Quebec within a renewed federal system. The various Anglophone and Francophone private-sector bourgeoisies that supported the Liberal Party wanted no further economic expansion of the Quebec state. Bourassa agreed and put the emphasis on encouraging the private sector to create urgently needed jobs for the fastest growing labour force in the western world. Increasingly under pressure from neo-nationalists in all quarters, Bourassa introduced language legislation, known as Bill 22, which made French the official language of the province, limited the choice of schooling for new Quebecers, and encouraged the use of French in the work world. These measures, it was felt, would help stem the integration of immigrants into the Anglophone community and would in time open the English-dominated sectors of the economy to newly educated Francophones. Bourassa, encouraged by his party's landslide victory in 1973, pursued these policies until his government was defeated by the Parti Québécois on November 15, 1976.[85]

Organized labour also became increasingly disenchanted with what it considered to be the petty-bourgeois limitations of the Quiet Revolution. The recently expanded public and para-public unions, most of them affiliated with the CSN, found the bourgeois-dominated governments, be they Union Nationale or Liberal, to be extremely hard-nosed, even provocative, in negotiations. After 1968 organized labour found itself confronting what some authors have called the coercive or disciplinary state.[86] Of course, the emergence of a socialist-imbued, neo-nationalist intelligentsia, albeit fractious and immature, helped to create an ideological and psychological climate conducive to the radicalization of the labour movement.

Both Quebec centrals, the CSN and the FTQ, responded to these circumstances by adopting a neo-Marxist interpretation of the working class's continued exploitation and subordination. The CSN, in its 1971 pamphlet *Ne comptons que sur nos propres moyens*, denounced the powerful American economic elite – supported by its Anglo- and French-Canadian compradors – that controlled the federal and provincial governments. The CSN and its fiery president, Marcel Pépin, called upon the workers to carry out a program of co-ordinated direct action to overthrow the existing neo-capitalist system and establish a democratic socialist society in Quebec. The FTQ, not wanting to be left behind in the struggle for new members and under the leadership of the dynamic Louis Laberge, followed the road to democratic socialism after 1965. In its 1971 pamphlet *L'Etat, rouage de notre exploitation*, the FTQ denounced the bourgeois liberal states, federal and provincial, for serving primarily the interests of American economic imperialists and of the English- and French-speaking bourgeoisies. The bourgeois liberal state confiscated public capital and transformed it into private capital, thus reinforcing all forms of exploitive capitalism. In 1971 Laberge called for a Common Front *(Un seul front)* of all progressive forces to liberate Quebec society from the bondage of neo-capitalism and the bourgeois liberal state and to create a democratic socialist society.[87]

The CSN and the FTQ leaders organized a general strike of over 200,000 public and para-public workers in the spring of 1972. The Common Front campaigned for an expansion of the collective bargaining parameters – the right to negotiate at a central table the amount of the government budget to be devoted to salaries. In particular, the Common Front wanted a minimum wage of $100 per week for all public employees. The Bourassa government stonewalled the labour leaders with delays, court injunctions, and, finally, Bill 19, which forced all public-sector employees back to work. The leaders, Pépin, Laberge, and Charbonneau, advocated civil disobedience of the Bill – for which they were later charged and jailed – but the Common Front disintegrated as the majority of strikers returned to work. While the CSN lost some members over the strike, the general outcome was the further radicalization of labour's ideological outlook and a toughening of its resolve to gain greater powers.[88]

Public-sector bargaining became the central focus of conflict between competing elements of the new Francophone middle class. By the mid-1970's organized labour leaders and militants felt that perhaps public-sector negotiations might become more successful if the incumbent Liberal government of Bourassa was replaced by the Parti Québécois. While the CSN refused to endorse officially the PQ, the FTQ decided to support the party, despite the fact that the PQ was not a working-class but rather a petty-bourgeois party. Laberge proposed to radicalize the PQ from within. In reality, the force of neo-nationalism and a common class interest were slowly eroding organized labour's distrust of the bourgeois state. An internal class conflict, reflected in divergent ideological perspectives, was being overshadowed by an ethnic conflict as reflected in the struggle over language and the role of the Québécois nation within the Canadian federal system.

CONCLUSION

The relationship between social transformation and ideological renewal was, in the case of Quebec, quite direct. *Cité libre's* liberalism, *Le Devoir's* and *l'Action nationale's* neo-nationalism, and *Parti pris'* socialist neo-nationalism articulated the aspirations of various wings of the new Francophone middle class. In time, Quebec's political parties came to represent some of these divergent ideologies. But the re-emergence of an ethnic conflict between this new middle class and the Anglophone economic elite that controlled Quebec's economy fuelled the fires of neo-nationalism and camouflaged the internal struggle over which sector of this middle class was going to control the power levers of the newly expanded state. The Lesage Liberal Party made a valiant attempt to bring liberals and neo-nationalists together but the latter gained the upper hand, forcing such *Citélibristes* as Pierre Trudeau and Gérard Pelletier to turn to the national Liberal Party to fight separatism and restore democracy to Quebec. After the Liberal defeat in 1966, those neo-nationalists favouring political independence for Quebec followed René Lévesque out of the party and helped found the Parti Québécois, a party committed to political independence and the creation of a social-democratic society in Quebec under the aegis of a Francophone bureaucratic and technocratic middle class that controlled the state. Even CSN and FTQ labour leaders and militants, committed ostensibly to socialism, eventually supported the "petty-bourgeois" Parti Québécois and helped it defeat the Liberal Party of Bourassa.

The question that some authors have been asking is: "Were the real needs of the people being served by this process of political modernization symbolized by the Quiet Revolution which has been underway in Quebec since the defeat of the Union Nationale in 1960?"[89] The answer to the question is at best a qualified yes for some and a categorical no for others. Most commentators remain cautiously optimistic. A dynamic, creative, and increasingly autonomous Quebec will survive and prosper, argues one social critic, if the various elements of the new middle class recognize and set aside their self-serving ways and a new pragmatic collective ethic comes to prevail.[90] Others feel that neo-nationalism, as demonstrated by the defeat of the sovereignty-association option in the 1980 referendum, is on the wane while liberalism and individualism are once again back in vogue throughout much of Quebec society, including the new middle class.[91] While no one can predict the final outcome of what has been a very complex process of social change, ideological renewal, and incessant struggle for political hegemony, it is always helpful to try to understand a little better the historical process of change and continuity.

NOTES

1. Gérard Filion, "Un avertissement sévère," *Le Devoir*, 9 janvier 1954.
2. *Annuaire du Québec, 1974*, 226, Tableau 3.
3. Kenneth McRoberts and Dale Posgate, *Quebec: Social Change and Political Crisis* (Toronto, 1980), 52, Table Seven.
4. Jean Hamelin et Jean-Paul Montminy, "La mutation de la société Québécoise, 1939-1976. Temps, ruptures, continuités," in Fernand Dumont *et al., Idéologies au Canada français 1940-1976* (Québec, 1981), I, 34-5.
5. McRoberts and Posgate, *Quebec*, 40-3.
6. *Report of the Royal Commission on Bilingualism and Biculturalism*, (Ottawa, 1969), IIIB, 23.
7. F. Vaillancourt, "La situation démographique et socio-économique des francophones du Québec: une revue," *Canadian Public Policy*, 5 (Autumn, 1979), 542-52.
8. Hubert Guindon "Social Unrest, Social Class and Quebec's Bureaucratic Revolution," *Queen's Quarterly*, 71 (1964), 153.
9. Pierre Dandurand et Marcel Fournier, "Développement de l'enseignement supérieur, classes sociales et luttes nationale au Québec," *Sociologie et sociétés*, 12 (avril 1980), 103-7.
10. Michael Behiels, "Le père Georges-Henri Lévesque et l'établissement des sciences sociales à Laval, 1938-1955," *Revue de l'Univer-*

sité d'Ottawa/University of Ottawa Quarterly, 52 (juillet-septembre 1982), 355-76.

11. Arthur Tremblay, Les Collèges et les écoles publiques. Conflict où coordination? (Québec, 1954), 11-12, 15-18.

12. Jacques Brazeau, "Quebec's Emerging Middle Class," in Marcel Rioux and Yves Martin, eds., French-Canadian Society (Toronto, 1964), 322.

13. Guindon, "The Social Evolution of Quebec Reconsidered," in Rioux and Martin, eds., French-Canadian Society, 157-8.

14. Brazeau, "Les nouvelles classes moyennes," Recherches sociographiques, 7 (janvier-août 1966), 157.

15. Yves Roby, Les Québécois et les investissements américains (1918-1929), (Quebec, 1976), 207-20.

16. Gérard Pelletier, "Trois paroles d'Emmanuel Mounier," Cité libre, 3 (mai 1951), 45-6.

17. Jean LeMoyne, "L'atmosphère religieuse au Canada français," Cité libre, 12 (mai 1955), 1-12; Maurice Blain, "Sur la liberté de l'esprit," Esprit, 20 (août-septembre 1952), 243-4.

18. Gérard Pelletier, "Crise d'autorité ou crise de liberté," Cité libre, 5 (juin-juillet 1952), 6-7.

19. LeMoyne, "Jeunesse de l'homme," Cité libre, 2 (février 1951), 10-12; Pierre Vadeboncoeur, "Réflexions sur la foi," ibid., 12 (mai 1955), 21.

20. Vadeboncoeur, "Réflexions sur la foi," 3-4; Pierre Elliott Trudeau, "Matériaux pour servir à une enquete sur le cléricalisme I," Cité libre, 7 (mai 1953), 31-2.

21. Trudeau, "La province de Québec au moment de la grève," in La grève de l'amiante (Montréal, 1970), 19-37.

22. Vadeboncoeur, "L'irréalisme de notre culture," Cité libre, 4 (décembre 1951); 20-1; M. Rioux, "Idéologie et crise de conscience du Canada français," ibid., 14 (décembre 1955), 3-14.

23. Trudeau, "La province de Québec," 14-37, 88.

24. This theme was developed primarily by Trudeau with the full support of his colleagues. Trudeau, "Réflexions sur la politique au Canada français," Cité libre, 6 (décembre 1952), 53-7; "Some Obstacles to Democracy in Quebec," Canadian Journal of Economics and Political Science, 24 (August, 1958), reprinted in his Federalism and the French Canadians, 103-23.

25. Trudeau, "Un manifest démocratique," Cité libre, 22 (octobre 1958), 2-29.

26. Léon Lortie et al., in L'éducation (Rapport de la troisième conférence annuelle de l'Institut canadien des affairs publique, 1956).

27. Ibid.; G. Pelletier, "Visite aux supérieurs I-III," Le Devoir, 11-12 janvier 1949; Roger Rolland, "La lettre contre l'esprit. Un témoignage sur l'enseignement secondaire, I-III," ibid., 13, 20, 27 septembre 1952; M. Rioux, "Remarques sur l'éducation et la culture canadienne-française," Cité libre, 8 (novembre 1953), 40-2.

28. P. Charbonneau, "Défense et illustration de la gauche," Cité libre, 18 (1958), 37-9.

29. Trudeau, "Le Devoir doit il préparer ses lectures au socialisme?"

Le Devoir, 2 février 1955; "Les Canadiens français rateront (encore une fois) le tournant . . ." *ibid.*, 29 janvier 1960.

30. Maurice Lamontagne, *Le fédéralisme canadien: évolution et problèmes* (Québec, 1954).

31. Trudeau, "De libro, tributo et quibusdam aliis," *Cité libre* (octobre 1954), in *Federalism and the French Canadians*, 63-78.

32. Trudeau, "Federal grants to Universities," *Cité libre* (février 1957), in *Federalism and the French Canadians*, 79-102.

33. Trudeau, "La nouvelle trahison des clers," *Cité libre*, 46 (avril 1962), 3-16; "Les séparatists: des contre-révolutionnaires," *ibid.*, 67 (mai 1964), 2-6.

34. Laurendeau, "Y a-t-il une cris du nationalisme? I," *Action Nationale*, 40 (décembre 1952), 208. Cited hereafter as *AN*.

35. Richard Jones, *Duplessis and the Union Nationale Administration* (Ottawa, 1983), 12-17.

36. Laurendeau, "Le quatrième état dans la nation," *AN*, 30 (octobre 1947), 83-8.

37. Laurendeau, "Conclusions très provisoires," *AN*, 31 (juin 1948), 414-16; "Y a-t-il une crise du nationalisme? I," 215-17.

38. Jean-Marc Léger, d'Iberville Fortier, Pierre Lefebvre et Camille Laurin, "L'ennemi dans nos murs," *AN*, 31 (février 1948), 107.

39. G. Dion et J. Pelchat, "Repenser le nationalisme," *AN*, 31 (juin 1948), 408-11; C. Ryan, "Le sens du national dans les milieux populaires," *AN*, 31 (mars 1948), 171-3; J.-P. Robillard, "Pour un nationalisme social," *AN*, 31 (avril 1948), 286-8; Laurendeau, "Conclusions trés provisoires," 413-24.

40. Léger, "Le Canada français à la recherche de son avenir," *Esprit*, 20 (septembre 1952), 261.

41. Léger, "Urgence d'une doctrine nationale," *AN*, 46 (octobre 1956), 137-8.

42. Filion, "Une double tentation," *Le Devoir*, 12 mai 1954.

43. Léger, *Notre situation économique: progrès ou stagnation* (Montréal, 1957), 1-21. Studies for the Royal Commission on Bilingualism and Biculturalism based on the 1961 census data confirmed the economic inferiority of French Canadians as individuals as well as the desperate plight of the Francophone private sector. (*Report*, IIIB, 11-60)

44. Roland Parenteau, "Quelques raisons de la faiblesse économique de la nation canadienne-française," *AN*, 45 (décembre 1955), 320-5; Laporte, "L'enjeu: notre survivance ou notre disparition," *Le Devoir*, 23 août 1957.

45. Cf. Dale Miquelon, ed. *Society and Conquest: The Debate on the Bourgeoisie and Social Change in French Canada, 1700-1850* (Toronto, 1977).

46. Filion, "La reprise de nos richesses naturelles." *Le Devoir*, 25 novembre 1953; Paul Sauriol, "Entre la servitude économique et la nationalisation," *ibid.*, 20 octobre 1958.

47. Laporte, "Une province qui se contente des miettes I-VIII," *Le Devoir*, 24-25, 27-30 janvier, 1, 3 février 1958.

48. Sauriol, "*Le Devoir* et la libération de notre groupe," *Le Devoir*,

29 janvier 1960; Laurendeau, "A l'heure des réformes," *ibid.*, 15 mars 1958.

49. Cf. Jean-Louis Roy, *La marche des Québécois: le temps des ruptures (1945-1960)* (Montréal, 1976), 245-308.

50. Arthur Tremblay, "La conjoncture actuelle de l'éducation," in *L'éducation au Québec face au problèmes contemporains* (Saint-Hyacinthe, 1958), 39-40.

51. Filion, "Crise scolaire," *Le Devoir*, 26 novembre 1955; "Il ne faut pas faire des éveques des boucs émissaires," *ibid.*, 9 novembre 1960.

52. Filion, "Il faut des techniciens, on nous donne des plaideurs," *Le Devoir*, 1 juin 1955; Laurendeau, "Le cours classique a l'école publique," *ibid.*, 25 avril 1955.

53. Laurendeau, "Premier but: l'université," *Le Devoir*, 10 juin 1955; "Où va le canada français? XIII," *ibid.*, 21 mai 1959.

54. Laurendeau, "Pour une enquete royale sur l'éducation," *Le Devoir*, 15 novembre 1960.

55. Filion, "Le fédéralisme canadien I-IV," *Le Devoir*, 21-24 juillet 1954; "Un accord, non une capitulation," *ibid.*, 29 février 1956.

56. Ligue d'Action Nationale, "Conditions d'un Etat Français dans la Confédération canadienne. Mémoire à la Commission royale d'enquete sur les relations fédérales-provinciales," *AN*, 43 (mars-avril 1954), 312-16.

57. Filion, "L'aide fédérale à l'enseignement III," *Le Devoir*, 1 avril 1952; "Le devoir du Québec envers ses universités," *ibid.*, 27 octobre 1956; "L'aide fédérale aux universités." *ibid.*, 13 octobre 1956.

58. Ligue d'Action Nationale, "Conditions d'un Etat Français," 328-44.

59. Société Saint-Jean Baptiste de Montréal, *Canada français et union canadienne* (Montréal, 1954), 54-125.

60. *Tremblay Report*, III, Book 2, 227-8, 233-7, 255-72, 294-5.

61. Pierrette Bouchard-Saint-Amant, "L'idéologie de la revue *Parti pris*: le nationalisme socialiste," in Dumont *et al.*, *Idéologies au Canada français 1940-1976*, I, 315-17; Roch Denis, *Lutte des classes et question nationale au Québec 1948-1968* (Montréal, 1979), 359-62.

62. "Présentation," *Parti pris*, 1 (octobre 1963), 2-3.

63. Bouchard-Saint-Amant, "L'idéologie de la revue *Parti pris*," 317-19. The author argues that the *Parti pris* demise can be explained by the review's inability to develop a rigorous theory of the relationship between social classes and the nation. Nationalism and socialism, in her view, can only be reconciled if they are both authentic products of the working class.

64. Paul Chamberland, "De la domination à la liberté," *Parti pris*, 1 (juin-août 1964), 64-81; Pierre Maheu, "L'oedipe colonial," *ibid.*, 20.

65. Chamberland, "Aliénation culturelle et révolution nationale," *Parti pris*, 1 (novembre 1963), 15-16.

66. "Manifeste 65-66," *Parti pris*, 3 (septembre 1965), 7-41; "Jean Lesage et l'Etat béquille," *ibid.*, 2 (février 1965), 4; Chamberland, "Aliénation culturelle," 16.

67. Jacques Dofny et Marcel Rioux, "Les classes sociales au Canada français," *Revue française de sociologie*, 3 (juillet-septembre 1962), 290-300; Guy Rocher, "Les recherches sur les occupations et la stratification," *Recherches sociographiques,* 3 (1962), 183-4.

68. Jean-Marc Piotte, "Sens et limites du néo-nationalisme," *Parti pris*, 4 (septembre-octobre 1966), 29; Maheu, "Québec politique," *ibid.*, 5 (avril 1968), 11.

69. "Manifeste 65-66," 17.

70. Maheu, "Le dieu canadien-français," *Parti pris*, 4 (novembre-décembre 1966), 45-8; "Le rapport Parent," *ibid.*, 2 (mars 1965), 7.

71. Maheu, "Que faire?" *Parti pris*, 2 (mars 1965), 54; Piotte "Sens et limites," 28.

72. "Manifeste 65-66," 20.

73. "Manifeste 65-66," 16; Piotte, "Ou allons-nous?" *Parti pris,* 3 (août-septembre 1965), 68-9.

74. Chamberland, "Les contradictions de la révolution tranquille," *Parti pris*, 1 (février 1964), 4.

75. "Manifeste 64-65," *Parti pris*, 2 (1964), 14.

76. Denis, *Lutte des classes*, 467-503.

77. Piotte, "Sens et limites," 36-7.

78. Gabriel Gagnon, "Vraie ou fausse indépendance," *Parti pris*, 4 (novembre-décembre 1966), 9-10; Gilles Bourque *et al.*, "Organisations syndicale, néo-capitalisme et planification," *ibid.*, 4 (mars-avril 1967), 5-27.

79. Gaetan Tremblay and Pierre Maheu, "L'indépendance au plus vite!" *Parti pris*, 4 (janvier-février 1967), 2-5.

80. Bourque *et al.*, "Pour un mouvement," *Parti pris*, 5 (été 1968), 30-4.

81. Jacques Rouillard, *Histoire de la CSN, 1921-1981* (Montréal, 1981), 198.

82. CTCC et FTQ, "Les centrales ouvrières du Québec et l'assurance santé," *Relations industrielles*, 13 (1958), 175-208.

83. Rouillard, *Historie de la CSN*, 198; Denis, *Lutte des classes*, ch. XII, 287-308.

84. J.-J. Simard, "La longue marche des technocrates," *Recherches sociographiques*, 18 (1977), 112-17, 129-32.

85. Réjean Pelletier, "Les parties politiques et l'Etat," in *L'Etat du Québec en devenir*, 241-61.

86. Carla Lipsig-Mummé, "Quebec Unions and the State: Conflict and Dependence," *Studies in Political Economy*, 3 (Spring, 1980), 136-7; Carol Levasseur, "De l'Etat-Providence a l'Etat-disciplinaire," in *L'Etat du Québec en devenir*, 315-25.

87. Bernard Solasse, "Les idéologies de la Fédération des travailleurs du Québec et de la Confédération des Syndicats Nationaux 1960-1978," in Dumont *et al.*, *Idéologies au Canada français 1940-1976*,

II, 233-44, 255-67.

88. Levasseur, "De l'Etat-Providence," 317-22; Rouillard, *Histoire de la CSN*, 236-42.

89. Cf. Edmond Orban, *La modernisation politique du Québec* (Montréal, 1976), 15.

90. Jacques Grand'Maison, *La nouvelle classe et l'avenir du Québec* (Montréal, 1979), 263-72.

91. Cf. Dominique Clift, *Quebec Nationalism in Crisis* (Montreal, 1980).

V
Social Control

Behaviour is controlled by a variety of mechanisms. One, the theme of Paul Axelrod's essay, is the educational system. Education helps to introduce children to the values of society, such as the virtue of hard work and self-discipline, respect for the political, economic, and social structures, and obedience to the law. As well as the emphasis on higher education discussed by Axelrod, primary and secondary education had a new prominence in Canada, especially after 1945. Education was a subject of public debate and anxious concern. This was reflected in such ground-breaking government investigations as the Hope Commission in Ontario (1950) and the Parent Commission in Quebec (1963-66.).

Control of behaviour also is exercised by more direct means. Law and order was an issue, in part because of the real problems of an urban society, in part because of a spillover of concerns in the United States over its much more serious problem of crime and disorder. Emotional debates over capital punishment led to legislation in 1967 to abolish the death penalty except for murderers of police and prison guards and to complete abolition in 1976. The abolition of capital punishment did not herald a more lenient approach in other areas of criminal justice, however. Throughout the period Canada had one of the world's higher rates of imprisonment on a per capita basis. Despite the revelation in the late 1970's of "dirty tricks" by the RCMP against suspected Quebec separatists and others, the national police force remained Canada's symbol. This is a suggestive comment on Canada's continuing concern with control.

FURTHER READING:
The standard history of education is Donald Wilson, Robert M. Stamp, and Louis-Phillippe Audet, eds., *Canadian Education: A History* (Toronto, 1970). The best work on higher education is Paul Axelrod's *Scholars and Dollars: Politics, Economics, and the Universities of Ontario, 1945-1980* (Toronto, 1982). A useful recent synthesis is Robert M. Stamp's *The Schools of Ontario, 1876-1976* (Toronto, 1982). A collection of readings on disorder, violence, and control is a good introduction to the general problem: R.P. Bowles *et al.*, eds., *Protest, Violence, and Social Change* (Scarborough, Ont., 1972). Another excellent collection of readings is William K. Greenaway and Stephen L. Brickey, eds., *Law and Social Control in Canada* (Scarborough, Ont., 1978). A very useful brief study of "deviance" and its control is John Hagan, *The Disreputable Pleasures* (Toronto, 1977).

Paul Axelrod is a member of the History Department at York University.

Higher Education, Utilitarianism, and the Acquisitive Society: Canada, 1930-1980

by Paul Axelrod

The enormous progress made in the development of Canadian education over the past century has been a source of immense pride for educators, politicians, and other school promoters across the country. One author attributes this admittedly impressive advancement to society's "never ending effort to develop an organizational structure which encourages every individual . . . to realize his fullest potentiality."[1] The massive, unprecedented expansion of post-secondary educational facilities in the 1960's seemed to confirm this faith in Canada's deep, democratic devotion to academic excellence, cultural enlightenment, and equality of opportunity.

At best this is only a partially accurate account of the recent history of higher education. At worst it is a myth that distorts the historical reality. It fails to explain the limited enthusiasm for university development both before and after the boom period of the 1960's. It removes higher education from the social and economic context within which universities have alternately struggled and prospered. And it is infused with an unjustifiably rhapsodic spirit about the purposes, accomplishments, and prospects of post-secondary education in Canada.

The experience of Canadian universities since the 1930's reveals that if cultural enrichment and democratic achievements were the periodic products of university life, they were never the major social forces that shaped the development of higher education as a whole. Instead, politicians, businessmen, and the public at large demanded more tangible "returns" on the dollars "invested" in post-secondary education. When these appeared lacking then the universities languished.

On the eve of the Great Depression few Canadians thought

twice about the state of the country's two dozen universities and small colleges, although in the Maritimes at least the Rockefeller and Carnegie foundations were showing considerable interest. The important work of Banting and Best had placed scientific research in the spotlight for a time in the early 1920's, but public attention in that decade belonged mainly to ostentatious investors, militant farmers, and fad-crazed teenagers. In an apparently prosperous and potentially frivolous world, Canadian educators were preoccupied with both the behaviour and productivity of post-war youth. When parents were not fretting about the corrupting influence of alcohol and the automobile, they were reminding their young that "each day in high school adds $25.00 to [a student's] life earnings."[2] As both public custodians and agencies of economic development, high schools dramatically increased their enrolments and soon became, in Robert Stamp's phrase, "the universities of the people."[3]

The universities themselves, however, were still the cloistered halls of possibly respected but mostly ignored intellectual and ecclesiastical elites. To the vast majority of Canadians the universities were inaccessible and distant dinosaurs, preoccupied with classical education, steeped in conservative values, and, with the exception of the handful of professional schools they housed, insulated from the more pragmatic and materialistic concerns of the day.[4]

When the depression hit, Canadian universities were shaken by the impact. This, of course, was not their experience alone. Few institutions escaped the ravages of the depression economy. But by virtue of its inferior position on the scale of social priorities, higher education did well simply to survive. That it did survive was despite, not because of, the support of provincial governments. Across the country grants to universities were slashed severely. On many campuses faculty salaries were reduced or payments deferred. The University of Saskatchewan forced some professors to take extended leave without pay or face outright dismissal. Everywhere, plans for program expansion were delayed or cancelled; at McGill, courses in social work, pharmacy, and Chinese studies were withdrawn.[5]

Were it not for some $6 million in grants from the American-based Carnegie Foundation, a number of smaller colleges might well have closed. Dalhousie, for example, which had received no direct operating grants from the Nova Scotia government between 1920 and 1940, was especially dependent on a combination of private donations and Carnegie aid. The public image of the University of Manitoba was not enhanced by the discovery in 1932 that its board chairman, John Machray, a distinguished lawyer and university investment counsellor, had cost the university over $970,000 through fraud and embezzlement going back to 1903. He was tried, convicted, and jailed, leaving in his wake a decimated endowment fund and the need to lay off faculty and raise tuition fees.[6] Few politicians were as openly hostile to the academic world as Ontario Premier Mitchell Hepburn, but when he defended grant reductions in 1939 with the claim that provincial governments had been too generous to the universities, and that the problems of primary schools were far more important, he captured the general mood of voters and taxpayers.[7]

It is not that the universities went out of their way to trouble the politicians. In fact, the reverse was generally true. Even during the depression, when the country's economic system floundered and failed, few social critics, let alone revolutionaries, could be found among Canadian academics. Amid fears of social and political unrest, universities attempted to perpetuate their role as "sanctuaries of truth" and guardians of tradition. Historian George Wrong assured business magnate and University of Toronto governor Joseph Flavelle that "in the main the universities of the western world are strongholds of conservative thought and a steadying influence on our society. This is not less true of McGill and Toronto than of Oxford and Cambridge."[8] Thus, when reform-minded Fabian socialists like Frank Underhill, King Gordon, and George Grube associated themselves with the fledgling League for Social Reconstruction and spoke publicly on "controversial" issues, they were denounced, censured, and even threatened with dismissal.[9] The weight of tradition, their accountability to established interests, and the absence of a well-defined and tested history of academic freedom ensured that Canadian universities would uphold, not challenge, the dominant ideological values of the day, even if their activities touched relatively few in the community.

World War II, which transformed so many facets of Canadian life, was instrumental in altering public perceptions about the respectability and value of higher education. Politicians, editors, businessmen, and academics enthusiastically joined the crusade to serve the country's wartime needs. Teachers and university professors were especially well placed to play an influential role. Above all, argued Duncan McArthur, the Minister of Education in Ontario, students must be lectured on the reasons for the war itself. Democratic parliamentary government was in peril, he claimed, unless prospective voters and leaders appreciated its value and were prepared to defend it against dictatorial challenges. For the moment, exhorted the minister in 1940, the student's pursuit of individual fulfilment in school must be supplanted by the teaching of "community responsibility." [10] In the same year ministerial representatives of education departments from across the country met at a conference on "Education for Citizenship" and resolved "to stimulate in the minds of all Canadians a greater appreciation of democracy as a way of life to the end that they may better understand the present struggle and thereby make the maximum contribution to the war effort of the nation." [11]

Enlisting the classroom as an agent of pro-war socialization was thus one important function of schools during the hostilities overseas. Given their centralized organization, primary and secondary schools could carry out this task more easily than the universities, where the tradition of institutional autonomy had generally kept government out of the lecture halls and laboratories of the nation. It is all the more significant that, because its spokesmen readily committed themselves to the patriotic cause, the university was perceived to have a role in the prosecution of the war effort as vital as that of any institution in society. In his annual report of 1941, H.J. Cody, the president of the University of Toronto, noted that "In all the relevant departments, special efforts have been made to teach the fundamental issues at stake in the present struggle and to emphasize the spiritual values which make democracy possible and desirable, and make human life livable." [12] And "with other universities," Queen's claimed "to share the responsibility of demonstrating to the world that universities are an essential factor in upholding, maintaining, and strengthening our democratic way of life." [13]

To realize these ends, every Canadian university imposed compulsory military training on all males over eighteen in the Officers' Training Corps or in Training Centre Battalions. All young men received at least six hours a week in military drills and lectures. Female students, as well, were required to play their part by engaging in such war-related work as the Red Cross or auxiliary service training. In 1942, in an admirable fit of patriotic fervour, hundreds of male students from eastern universities responded to the federal government's plea for aid to Saskatchewan wheat harvesters. For those returning to university late as a result of this project, the beginning of the academic year was delayed. [14]

World War II produced not only expressions of patriotism but also sophisticated forms of organizing for the war itself. With remarkable facility and speed, the federal government mobilized citizens through institutions created for specific wartime functions and through those that were already in place. It was in this latter context that universities were enlisted to serve the nation in very concrete terms. Indeed, admitted Sherwood Fox, the president of the University of Western Ontario, "with regret we must face the stern fact that exigencies of war have compelled all universities of the allied nations temporarily to relegate many basic principles of education to second place." [15]

The National Conference of Canadian Universities (NCCU), the administrative umbrella organization of the country's universities, co-ordinated much of this effort by responding to government initiative for the production of trained technicians and professionals capable of turning their skills to the pressing national need. So impressive was the universities' role that an annual report of the Wartime Bureau of Technical Personnel exclaimed: "It was evident in all their dealings with the Department of Labour that [the universities'] attitude was one of simple readiness to carry out any task which they might be called upon by the government to undertake." [16]

Among a number of projects, the federal government set aside $300,000 for the purpose of attracting high school students into engineering and science, the graduates then being assigned to various jobs by the National Selective Service with the army having first choice. At the 1942 NCCU conference, while some academics expressed fears that the universities might become mere trade schools as a result of the special tasks they were called upon to perform in the war, the delegates nonetheless passed the following resolution: "The universities' conference should see to it that our war potential does not fall short of maximum realization for lack of full use of our technical facilities." [17]

To achieve this end, universities revised their entrance requirements so that the Defence Training Course taught in high schools could be substituted for other less "practical" credits, including Latin, geography, history, or a foreign language. [18] In courses not considered essential to the immediate national interest (mainly those in the arts and humanities), by federal order only the members of the upper half of such classes were allowed to remain at university until after graduation. No student was permitted to proceed to graduate work or to transfer from one faculty to another without the approval of the National Selective Service. [19] A former president of the University of Saskatchewan recalls a member of the Wartime Bureau of Technical Personnel participating in deliberations about which students would be forced to drop their studies and enter war-related vocations. [20]

Some academics, led by F.C. James, the principal of McGill, and R.C. Wallace, the principal of Queen's, were so enthusiastic about the practical role the universities were capable of playing that in late 1942 they recommended to the federal government that all teaching in commerce, arts, law, and education be suspended for the duration of the war. Only after an emergency meeting called by another group of professors, headed by Harold Innis and J. Watson Kirkconnell, in which a brief was drawn up and presented to Ottawa defending the teaching of humanities even in wartime, was the implementation of this astounding recommendation prevented.[21]

Aside from the training of manpower and the socialization of students, the universities performed another highly acclaimed wartime function: scientific and military research. One observer went so far as to claim that, during the war, the "laboratory became the first line of defence and the scientist, the indispensable warrior."[22] Scientists conducting research at the National Research Council and in university labs made impressive advancements in such areas as the adaption of radar for land, sea, and air use; the optical glass industry; the refrigeration of foodstuffs for transport overseas; and the technology of war gases and ballistics.[23] Universities that could boast of scientists engaged in top-secret research enhanced their prestige during the war and sought to raise private funds on the strength of such patriotic activities.[24]

In the immediate post-war period, higher education proved itself to be of considerable practical value in one additional area. Canadian universities attracted much public attention by agreeing to educate, in a type of emergency program, thousands of post-war veterans, many of whom had interrupted their schooling to serve overseas. As part of its program to resettle and retrain ex-soldiers, and to avoid the economic and social displacement that had occurred at the end of World War I, the federal government subsidized both the tuitions and living expenses of veterans pursuing post-secondary education. As a result the student population of Canadian universities jumped from 38,000 in 1944-45 to just over 80,000 by 1947-48.[25]

After years of unrelieved poverty, then, it appeared that the universities had finally achieved the public prominence and financial security to which they felt entitled. But this was an illusion. Universities received very little funding for building projects, and operating support was intended primarily to address the immediate needs first of the war and then of the veterans. Once the war ended, and after the last of the veterans had passed through the system, the universities faced the dismal prospect of returning to the earlier state of genteel poverty. One authoritative source lamented in 1951 that "our universities are facing a financial crisis so great as to threaten their future usefulness."[26]

The universities received short-term reprieve in 1951 following the publication of the Report of the Royal Commission on National Development in the Arts, Letters and Sciences. Reflecting the growing concern in post-war Canada over the need to preserve and nourish indigenous culture, the Massey Report recommended, among other things, that the federal government provide direct financial support to Canadian universities. The vital services they had performed in the war, the role they played in training professionals and civil servants, and their importance as cultural outlets, especially in small communities, had earned the country's universities the right to economic security.[27] Although the federal government rejected the Commission's proposal for a series of national scholarships for Canadian students and delayed for six years the creation of the Canada Council (also recommended by the Commission), Ottawa did allot over $7 million in direct aid to higher education, to which the struggling universities gave a collective and gratified sigh of relief.[28] They had been rescued from imminent financial disaster, but the piecemeal nature of even this support would become shockingly evident in a few short years.

Only the romantic and naive would attribute the massive expansion of educational facilities in post-war Canada to a sudden burst of renaissance-type enlightenment among the Canadian public and its leaders. Even the most cursory appraisal reveals that the basic motives were undeniably utilitarian. As they had on rare occasions in the past, Canadians invested heavily in higher education in the hope of realizing concrete, profitable returns.

The war's conclusion left Canadian society in a peculiar and perhaps paradoxical state of smugness and uncertainty. Canadians were justifiably proud of their contributions and sacrifices in checking the cancerous spread of European fascism, in preserving traditional institutions, and in upholding the "democratic way of life." Yet as their compulsive interest in overseas politics receded, they seemed unprepared to restore domestic life to its pre-war condition. The miseries of the depression were deeply embedded in the country's collective memory and Canadians were grimly determined to extend the material security that the war had provided well beyond V-E Day.

The tranquility, apathy, and political quiescence that has characterized images of the 1950's should not overshadow the reality of a people hard at work, seizing upon opportunities that had been vanquished by the depression and delayed by the war. The enormous success of the post-war veterans' educational program was one indication of this determined spirit. The educational system as a whole was swept up in this surge of optimism as Canadian parents sought to achieve vicariously through their children what had slipped away from their own generation in nearly two decades of economic and military turmoil. The post-war baby boom, from which were derived the hordes of students who would fill the schools and universities in the fifties and six-ties, can itself be viewed as the product of delayed marriages and confidence for the coming years. While this event deserves greater examination, most scholars attribute such population surges to a popular belief that the future will be better than the past. [29]

As early as 1947 a national Gallup poll pointed to the ten-dency among Canadians to tie educational training to pragmatic ends. Sixty per cent of those sampled felt that schools should teach "more practical subjects." That education itself was treated with great deference – a result, at least in part, of the positive role the schools had played in the war – was suggested in a poll in which 60 per cent of Canadians claimed to be satisfied with school facilities and an equivalent number believed teachers to be as capable as they should be. A few years later, once the desperate shortage of educational facilities had become ap-parent, 51 per cent of Canadians said teachers should be paid more and 58 per cent agreed that taxes should be raised in order to alleviate the problem. In Ontario, the nation's most heavily populated and industrialized province, 62 per cent favoured rais-ing taxes. That educational training in the public mind was linked to the goals of personal security and industrial progress was indicated in a 1957 poll in which the largest minority of Canadian men questioned said that they would choose a career in engineering over any other. [30]

If any date can be isolated as pivotal in raising to unprece-dented levels public consciousness over the value of education, especially over the increasing importance of higher education, 1956 would surely qualify. In the previous year, Edward Shef-field, a federal government consultant, released a study to the National Conference of Canadian Universities projecting that, through demographic pressure alone, university enrolment would double to over 120,000 by 1965. [31] The report sparked a period of frenetic activity among educators and businessmen. The NCCU sponsored a special conference on "Canada's Crisis in Higher Education" in the fall of 1956, in which the very survival of the country was pinned to the expansion of educational facili-ties. Papers, speeches, and conference resolutions from some of Canada's most prominent academic figures underlined the crisis. To reach the nation's information nerve centre, the NCCU struck a committee under Claude Bissell, the president of Carleton University, which employed an "effective and simple device" of sending a one-page letter to the editors of all the newspapers in Canada presenting the statistical case of the Sheffield report and "underlining that in ten years we would have a doubling of our university population."[32] In the same year a conference of renowned educators, businessmen, and scientists was convened at St. Andrew's, New Brunswick, where similar statements thickened the air and received wide publicity.[33] The conference established a private business-run organization called the Industrial Foundation on Education whose expressed purposes were to promote the cause of and raise money for higher education in Canada.[34] In 1957, the Report of the Royal Commission on Canada's Economic Prospects drew these threads together, reinforcing the link between Canada's educational development and the country's economic fate. Universities, asserted the Commission, "are the source of the most highly skilled workers whose knowledge is essential in all branches of industry . . . . It is incredible that we would allow their services to society. . . to lapse or lag."[35]

Virtually every aspect of education was explored in scores of publications during this period, but for public consumption certain prominent themes stood out. The quietude of the 1950's had been regularly disturbed by lurid accounts of Soviet political ambitions, coldly and at times hysterically documented in the nation's media. Indeed, aside from the public preoccupation with economic growth and material security, the simmering Cold War constituted the other major issue that absorbed the attention of North Americans in the post-war period. In 1951 one opinion poll identified the fear of war as the major concern of Canadians (53 per cent). Following the sensational American espionage trial and executions of Julius and Ethel Rosenberg in 1953, 62 per cent of Canadians were prepared to deny Communists freedom of speech; only 26 per cent of the public favoured upholding such a fundamental democratic right. And in 1961, while 42 per cent of Canadians felt that the "free world" could live peacefully with the Russians, fully 48 per cent predicted a new world war.[36]

How did this issue relate to the incessant demands for improved educational facilities? Soviet progress had been generated by a remarkably sophisticated technology, if not equalling, then at least approaching that of the United States. For North Americans, the successful launching of the Sputnik satellite in 1957 underscored these extraordinary developments in a frightening way. Such advances were based on the speedy training of technologists, engineers, and scientists, financed by the government and trained in universities. One researcher, citing Allen Dulles, the director of the Central Intelligence Agency, reported that the Soviet Union would graduate 1,200,000 students in pure science during the 1950's, while the United States would graduate only 990,000.[37] A statement to the St. Andrew's Conference by James Duncan, a former president of Massey-Ferguson, chairman of Ontario Hydro, and a member of the Industrial Foundation on Education, suggested that the connection between the economy, the Cold War, and higher education was apparent to many:

> In my opinion we are in danger of losing the cold war unless we do something very drastic about it and education is very close to the core of our problem. Science and engineering have made such remarkable progress in recent decades that the nation which holds the lead in these fields holds the initiative in world affairs.

The conference concurred and passed the following resolution:

> The representatives of the universities express their considered opinion that it is their urgent duty to warn the people of Canada that the problem of the universities has become an emergency of grave national concern to the certain disadvantage of our progress as a nation, and can only be solved by energetic and immediate assistance and cooperation of all governments in Canada, of business and industry and of private benefactors.[38]

Without this type of commitment, echoed the Royal Commission on Canada's Economic Prospects, Canada, along with other non-Communist nations, risked falling victim to Soviet "ecumenical ambitions."[39] On the heels of the Sputnik launching, the Minister of Education in Ontario called a meeting of the province's university presidents and told them: "it is essential that we do everything we can to reassure those of the public who are anxious about present conditions that everything is being done and will be done to strengthen and to support the services rendered by the Ontario universities."[40]

In demonstrating from an academic perspective that the Cold War raised questions about the state of the national culture as much as it did about the condition of technology, Claude Bissell, the new president of the University of Toronto, published an article in *Maclean's* in April 1958, "Universities Must Answer

Sputnik with Higher Standards." The NCCU brief to the Royal Commission on Canada's Economic Prospects claimed that the humanities and arts, "from which the soul of man is fed, and through which the heritage of civilized communities is passed to mortal generations," also deserved greater financial support.[41] Senator Donald Cameron, the director of the Banff School of Fine Arts, cited Robert Hutchins of the University of Chicago on the same theme. "It seems useless to hope that democracy can survive unless all people are educated for freedom. Mass stupidity can now mean mass suicide."[42]

But the appeals of the academics were, for the most part, as intensely practical as those of the business community and underscored the utilitarian impulses of the Canadian people. According to the NCCU, "The demand for expert persons, for intelligent persons, with background and perspective, increases with every increase in the population, with every increase in the gross national product, with every requirement for increased investment."[43] No one, in fact, disputed the Ontario government's claim that educational investment was necessary for Canada to become a "modern industrial power."[44]

The task ahead entailed not merely waging ideological war against the nation's potential enemies but securing as well Canada's competitive advantage over the country's economic rivals. The Industrial Foundation on Education both marvelled and panicked at the incredible progress Germany and Japan had made since the war. "In 1945 Western Germany lay in ruins and a starving people wandered through the rubble of her devastated cities. Today Germany competes successfully in foreign markets with finished products incorporating the latest technology." The weakness of Canada's educational training facilities was demonstrated by her heavy reliance on skilled immigrants and refugees from other countries. In the first nine months of 1957, disclosed the IFE, Canada brought in nearly 2,150 engineers. For the whole year this would prove to be some 3,600, "over twice as many as graduated from all Canadian universities in 1957."[45] According to the president of Polymer Corporation, "over the next 25 years we will need a minimum of three to four times as many engineers and scientists as are now employed and ten times as many technicians."[46] Indeed, Canada was so far behind her rivals that she spent proportionately one-third of funds allotted in the United States to industrial and scientific research and only three-fifths of those in the United Kingdom.[47] In a survey that revealed in direct terms the perceived relationship of educational training to corporate performance, the Department of Labour found:

The shortage of professional personnel is evident and is not a matter of conjecture. 50 percent of Canadian employers of professional personnel are experiencing difficulty finding staff. Of the companies surveyed, 47 percent reported curtailment of production and expansion plans, 33 percent curtailment of planning and research, 21 percent overloading of present personnel, 14 percent inability to offer adequate training, and 11 percent a shortage of future executives.[48]

On a personal basis, the message cut deeply and effectively, as economists were able to prove in simple and compelling terms that Canadians who were well-educated would earn more money than those who were not. "Estimates have shown," noted the Economic Council of Canada, "that better education appears to have raised labour earnings per man by about 30 per cent from 1911-1961."[49] In a 1963 poll, the public revealed how completely it had absorbed such information over the years: 60 per cent of Canadians agreed that a boy should not leave school at age sixteen even if he wanted to, while only 30 per cent said he should be permitted to do so. As if to convince by example, 39 per cent of Canadians in a 1956 poll confessed that leaving school early had been their biggest mistake in life.[50]

Who should pay for the massive expansion of higher education? According to Canadian businessmen, only government could do the job. Contending that students should continue to finance at least part of the education, the editors of the Bank of Montreal *Business Review* admitted that "students can't provide more than a fraction of the increased income that will be required."[51] Similarly, as the president of Falconbridge Nickel of Canada argued, corporations were equally handicapped in their ability to pay.

The financial problem is entirely beyond the means of philanthropic corporations. It must be remembered that corporations handle the funds of individual investors and have the duty and responsibility of using these funds only for the proper purposes of the businesses and in the best interests of the shareholders . . . . Our educational problem is a national problem.[52]

Lest their corporate brethren were unconvinced by the Gallup polls, the politicians' speeches, or the academic lobbyists, prominent company spokesmen argued the case of higher education in starkly practical terms, which all businessmen could readily understand and would ignore only at their peril. An editorial in

Trade and Commerce claimed that "in supporting higher education business is to a certain extent just buttering its own bread . . . . Graduates of engineering and science faculties are being channelled directly into the service of business so that universities are actually saving the businessmen considerable expense that might be encountered in on the job training." [53] "It is out of the universities," emphasized A.A. Cumming, the president of Union Carbide Canada, "that we shall get the professional engineers, geologists, research scientists and others who can lead us forward in the search for technological excellence. They are also the place from which will come the economists, the accountants, the investment people and others for whom a professional economic training is essential." [54]

Equal enthusiasm greeted the passing of the Technical and Vocational Assistance Act in December 1960, which produced a massive infusion of federal funds into programs designed to upgrade and retrain the Canadian labour force. As a result thousands of Canadian students enrolled in technical education courses; and the provinces, eagerly consuming federal grants, established community colleges for job-hungry high school graduates unable or unwilling to pursue careers dependent on university training. Through this process a new (and less prestigious) level of post-secondary education evolved to meet industry's demands for technicians and office and service workers.

Apart from the "products" it turned out in the form of skilled employees, educational investment was itself seen by Canadian business as a fabulous boon to the construction industry. "If the education industry had not increased its investment in construction from 1961-63 by some $211 million, or a gain of nearly 70 per cent above 1961 levels, our $6 billion construction industry would have shown only about half the gain it made during the past two years." [55] Thus universities were considered essential to the fuelling and sustaining of a free enterprise economy. Academics were certainly not unaware of the rampant pragmatism that shaped government policy in the area of higher education. But they were comforted and in some ways deceived by the expansion of the "non-utilitarian" areas of university life that accompanied the growth of the professions. After all, did the 1960's not witness the explosion of university general arts programs whose function was cultural, not economic? And did Canadian universities thereby not fulfil the dream of the Massey Commission of 1951 of preserving and promoting indigenous culture? In short, was the support extended to general arts not a perfect and powerful indication of society's commitment to the classical educational cause of pursuing truth for its own sake?

The evidence suggests something quite different. Those who viewed the importance of higher education in primarily economic terms *included* arts programs in their prescriptions. In virtually every major industrial and commercial enterprise, businessmen were firm in their conviction that intensive student exposure to the liberal arts was as vital to the well-being of the economy as was specific professional training. This perception was born of the very complexity of the economy itself, which rendered inadequate narrow, specialized learning, even in the major professions. What employers sought from the universities was the imaginative student who would become the adaptable employee. According to the *Canadian Chartered Accountant*, business training must include not only the tools of the trade, but also such knowledge as "the nature of life in foreign countries, more than one language, and academic work that broadens students' bases of information and makes them generally analytical in their approach to the world in which the businesses they serve operate" – all talents that would best be provided by a good general arts background.[56] And in the words of the president of Imperial Oil, "industry has found that it can train an educated man, but it cannot necessarily educate the trained man."[57]

Although they had different concerns, then, the views of businessmen reinforced those of academics on the issue of the liberal arts. The latter could not but be enthralled at the expansion of their own professional opportunities in the humanities and social fields during the 1960's. While arts professors may not intentionally have been preparing their students for careers in business and science, it is clear that the subjects they taught were viewed as essential by the business community itself. This symbiotic relationship explains a great deal about the depth and nature of support for the expansion of higher education in Canada.

Because the demand for graduates was strong, whatever their academic degrees, all forms of post-secondary education – from engineering to fine arts – were seen as profitable forms of public investment (in a booming economy). If proponents of general education were committed to creating modern-day renaissance men, business did not object so long as these new renaissance men had among their array of talents the capability of working within and contributing to the management of a complex corporation. As business analysts Peter Drucker and John Galbraith observed, knowledge itself was power, and higher education was useful mainly because it had something to sell.[58] None of this is to deny the cultural achievements of the 1960's spurred on in part by university arts courses. But the arts thrived on the coattails of a university system designed primarily to serve economic ends.

The marriage of economic and cultural forces was especially evident in Quebec, where post-secondary education went through a fundamental reorganization during the Quiet Revolution of the 1960's. The Parent Commission Report, a massive investigation of the province's educational system (initiated in 1961), laid the basis for the attempted integration of schooling with the processes of secularization and economic development. The Commission condemned the failure of the old church-run classical colleges to provide students with adequate technical and practical training. By 1970 over thirty CEGEPs (colleges d'enseignement général et professionnel) had been established under the authority of the Ministry of Education. Intended to qualify students for skilled and semi-skilled employment, the colleges quickly discovered that Quebec's economic growth had not kept pace with educational change, leaving large numbers of college graduates with limited opportunity to practise their trades. Seeking better career prospects, thousands went on to the province's first public (French-speaking) university, the Université du Québec, opened in 1969 with branches in several cities. In Quebec, cultural life thrived in and was nurtured through higher education, but as in English Canada, economic priorities provided the rationale, the funding, and the institutional settings for the diverse activities in which teachers and students engaged.[59]

While support for the expansion of higher education was shaped by broadly based economic demands, the system felt as well the impact of pressures to "democratize" access to Canadian universities. Indeed, the "equality of opportunity" argument, heard increasingly in the late 1950's, became almost an article of faith among liberal-minded citizens and politicians in the 1960's. And in 1972 both the reports of the Commission on Educational Planning in Alberta and the Commission on Post-Secondary Education in Ontario reiterated this commitment. According to the former, in order for native people and the poor "to be set free, and to be able to function normally in our society, educational opportunities should be made available to them – and to every individual within our province."[60]

Certainly the democratization theme accounts, in part, for the ability of university promoters to elicit the support of those with different interests and competing political persuasions for the central goal of expanding the university system, and it would be foolish to deny its import. But in a period when all investment in higher education was viewed as inevitably profitable, it was unnecessary for official spokesmen to distinguish between the democratic and economic benefits of post-secondary education. For the middle and upper classes, universities were the vehicles to professional status. For the less privileged, they held out the promise of upward social mobility. Both of these goals could be rationalized as worthwhile investments in the future of a country starved for highly trained and locally educated professionals. In the context of the overall economic value of higher education to society at large, student-aid schemes were themselves considered investments worthy of public support. There was considerable debate, however, over the form these programs should take. Despite their increasing interest in the question of equal opportunity, the governments of Canada imposed severe limitations on the types of student-aid plans introduced. Conceived and implemented within the context of a capitalist culture, the programs themselves reflected and reinforced the utilitarian objects and ideological corollaries of a free-enterprise society.

During the 1950's, educators and parents expressed considerable concern about the academic performance of students at all levels of the school system. In a society so conscious of the importance of education to the country's economic fate, it was considered vital for schools to encourage students both to continue their education for as long as possible and to perform at the highest possible level of achievement. Student retention rates increased steadily throughout the 1950's and, when the dropout rate showed signs of rising, educators were quick to draw attention to the problem.[61]

Indeed, one businessman was so concerned about the "lack of student motivation" among Canadian young people that he asked the disturbing question: "Are we raising a generation of failures?" He explained the phenomenon in (unproven) sociological terms by suggesting that Canadian society was becoming so prosperous that students, on the example of their parents, were unwilling to work hard for minimal immediate rewards; just as parents demanded higher wages, so many students were unprepared to bear the drudgery of homework and self-discipline.[62] Similarly, the Industrial Foundation on Education noted that while Canadians spent several billion dollars a year on consumer items, they apportioned only $115 million to industrial and scientific research. This compared unfavourably and dangerously with the situation in the Soviet Union, where a very different spirit prevailed. "We are competing with an ideology whose principals believe in it with a religious fervour. The question we must answer deals with whether or not we can combat

this system with lukewarm attitudes toward our own beliefs."
While no one recommended emulating the methods used by the
Soviet Union to achieve its ends, there was, even among certain
business spokesmen, a curious respect for the enormous education accomplishments of that nation. Unlike Canada, Russia
seemed free of "laggards" and "intellectual duffers" in the educational system.[63]

In light of these perceptions, the main problem became one of
encouraging the best students to pursue their education. In a
confidential report submitted to the Ontario Minister of Education, the IFE documented the extremely high "casualty rates"
among students in several Ontario communities. In one city, 35
per cent of those students with an IQ level above 110 had no intention of going to university. Only 23.9 per cent of all Ontario
students planned to obtain a higher education. In fact, only 7
per cent of grade 13 students actually did. Once in university,
over 40 per cent of students were found to drop out before com-
pleting their degrees. According to the IFE, through a combination of financial problems and lack of motivation, Canadian
students were simply not performing to the best of their
abilities.[64] This attitude and these conditions could hardly be tolerated by the achieving society.

In order to search out the competent from all social classes,
commentators talked increasingly of the need to improve the ability of lower-income families to send their children to university. If universities maintained high standards, and if the poor
were given financial assistance, then society would be well served
by those qualified but traditionally unable to afford post-
secondary education. When financial pressures forced universities across the country to raise tuition fees in 1951, many presidents lamented the deleterious effect this would have on students
from low-income families. The fact that the student's share of
educational costs had increased intolerably and compared
unfavourably with those of Britain and the U.S. provided a po-
tent argument for increasing public aid to higher education.[65]

In a well-written brief, the National Federation of Canadian
University Students argued in 1960 that, since the role of the
state had increased in other areas of health and welfare, it was
logical for similar aid to be extended to such a valuable social
service as higher education. In fact, the student organizations argued, as they would with increasing vigour throughout the
1960's, that higher education should be tuition-free, both on
principle and as a practical vehicle for raising the participation
rates of lower-income students in institutions of higher learning.
This view was endorsed, in slightly more qualified terms, by

spokesmen for the Canadian labour movement. At successive biennial conferences, the Canadian Labour Congress recommended "free university education for all students who are qualified and who maintain standards of achievement."[66]

With one brief exception, however, no provincial government or university ever adopted a policy of free tuition,[67] although every politician paid deference to the need for democratizing access to higher education. The argument against such a radical step in the late 1960's was based largely on the problem of prohibitive cost.[68] By that time it was simply too expensive a proposition. But in the late fifties and early sixties, when the elimination of fees would not have been so financially burdensome, the argument was rationalized in very different terms. Despite the enormous growth of the public sector, Canada remained fundamentally a free-enterprise society. "Rugged individualism" was still a cultural staple of the system and thus the need for students to learn the value of individual responsibility by paying their way through university was proclaimed consistently.

The comments of businessmen and politicians were a revealing insight into this state of mind. That higher education was recognized by corporate leaders as a valuable investment was incontestable. Furthermore, as if to prove their commitment, many companies in the late 1950's donated money to universities through direct grants and scholarship programs. Though the motives of individual business leaders might have varied widely, they appeared less impressed with the moral import of the democratization and accessibility arguments than with the very pragmatic contention that increasing the participation rates of the brightest Canadian students was an absolute necessity in light of the prevailing "national emergency." While some students, social democratic politicians, and labour leaders talked about the need to eliminate income disparities through increased educational opportunities, businessmen believed that financial barriers to post-secondary education should be reduced for the essential purpose of training as many Canadians as possible. But higher education must never be free. As Stanley Deeks of the IFE exhorted, "In a free country such as ours, motivation must be provided through incentive only."[69] By eliminating fees, the universities would only be increasing "our trend toward becoming a soft society, and our propensity to expect to obtain something without making the effort to earn it."[70] Leaving the private family unit with prime responsibility for financing university education, yet buttressing this support with material incentives for the best students, was perfectly consistent with the free-enterprise view that the most competent, competitive, and ambitious students would succeed in the outside world. Ontario Premier John Robarts articulated a similar justification in 1963 for refusing to abolish tuition fees.[71] Unlike the student groups and labour spokesmen, businessmen and most politicians were not interested in eliminating the class system; for them the market would judiciously weed out the strong from the weak. They favoured a meritocracy, not equality.

Student-aid programs of the late fifties and early sixties reflected this mix of cultural and political values. After persistent opposition, the Ontario government introduced a program in 1958 providing $500 loans, interest-free until graduation, for all needy students with at least a third-class standing. Premier Leslie Frost defended the program in this way: "I think that no person in this country who has the potential to make good in the university world and the things that lead from the university should be denied that education."[72] The democratic thrust of this statement, however, was somewhat undermined in a different speech by Frost in the same year. In it he exposed the overriding importance of economic considerations behind government funding policies.

> The policy of the Ontario government towards higher education has always been the same . . . to expand and improve the facilities for higher education in this province. I must admit, that although this policy was motivated to a great extent by our desire to assist young people to develop their intellectual potential and to develop into well informed citizens, it was motivated by our early realization that if this Province was to advance, it would need more than will, it would need brain power – and this perhaps is the world's most scarce resource.[73]

Further provision for student aid was made by the federal government in 1964, when loans of up to $1,000 were extended to needy students meeting minimum university entrance requirements. In defending the program, Finance Minister Walter Gordon once again demonstrated the vital relationship between the democratic and utilitarian themes.

> A university education or its vocation equivalent is the highest achievement of our educational system and it should be within the financial grasp of every young Canadian who is capable of making good use of it. If we do not provide the means whereby all children with necesssary abilities can share the privilege of higher education, then we are doing them a great injustice and denying our country a source of economic and intellectual benefit which we can ill afford to sacrifice.[74]

Critics protested that aid programs based solely on loans were usurious and self-defeating and would do little to facilitate the entry of lower-income students into the post-secondary system.[75] In order to address these concerns, most provinces supplemented the federal loan scheme with aid packages that provided non-repayable grants to the poorest students. Despite such obvious improvements, tuition fees were still not abolished. The programs also retained the immovable principle that the family was primarily responsible for financing the student's education, and the qualifications a student had to fill to be considered independent from his or her parents were damned by critics as excessively stringent. Finally, the debt factor still loomed large for the poor since in most provinces they had first to commit themselves to sizable loans to qualify for grants.[76] All of this produced a complex student-aid approach mirroring the values of a mixed economy in a prosperous age, in which governments driven partially by moral pressures but mainly by practical imperative would provide limited financial assistance to students, leaving them exposed to the debts, rigours, and uncertainties of the marketplace.

Propelled by buoyant economic conditions, favoured by free-spending politicians, and buttressed by widespread public support, higher education during the 1960's became one of Canada's major growth industries. Between 1960 and 1970 full-time enrolment across the country almost tripled to 316,000. In the same period expenditures by Canadian universities increased 600 per cent to $1.6 billion. And between 1945 and 1970 the number of institutions offering university-level training doubled to sixty. All of this was to say nothing of the massive expansion of community college education for the training of students in technical and vocational areas. The spinoff effects of educational investment into other areas of regional economic life, if uncalculated, were unmistakably evident. Popular faith in the economic value of post-secondary education reached unprecedented heights.[77]

And then the balloon burst. Throughout most of the 1970's and into the early 1980's, the country's universities endured a state of permanent underfunding. Despite the fact that enrolments climbed consistently (contrary to public belief), full-time (tenure-stream) teaching appointments all but vanished, support staff were laid off, library budgets were ravaged, and new program plans were postponed or cancelled.[78] In 1977 the government of British Columbia closed down Notre Dame University, and five years later the government of Nova Scotia withdrew all funding to the Atlantic Institute of Education. Throughout the country the fate of other small, "marginal" universities hung in the balance in the face of inadequate funding.

Like other publicly funded institutions, universities felt the impact of the deepening recession that Canada had been experiencing for more than a decade. Fearful that public spending and higher deficits would only fuel inflation without reducing unemployment significantly, the federal and provincial governments chose instead to restrain wages, particularly in the public sector, and to encourage the expansion of private corporations through direct grants and tax relief. This strategy had not worked by the early 1980's, but the damage to schools, universities, hospitals, social services, and the arts was obvious and profound.[79]

For universities, however, the problems were exacerbated by growing public suspicion about their value as economic instruments. Reports of "surplus" university graduates, especially in the arts, received wide play throughout the 1970's. In 1972 the Manpower and Immigration Department discovered that the 735 companies it surveyed had hired 38 per cent fewer arts graduates than in the previous year, which itself had been 37 per cent below the 1970 figure. A Statistics Canada survey of 1976 university graduates found that two years after graduation, 8.2 per cent were unemployed and only 42 per cent of those with jobs believed that their university training was directly relevant to the positions they held. For those with doctorates in the arts, the problem of underemployment (that is, the occupation of positions for which they were overqualified) was especially severe.[80]

These conditions, combined with the wide belief that universities had been bathed in luxury for far too long, led a number of economists, including those working for the Economic Council of Canada, to reverse their positions on the value of investing heavily in higher education. Claiming to have "refined" their earlier models measuring the "rate-of-return" on educational spending, economists produced conclusions consistent with the growing demand for restraint in the public funding of higher education.[81] Politicians used these studies to rationalize their imposition of higher tuition fees. Students, they now argued, benefited more from higher education than society did as a whole. Therefore, they should pay a larger share of the cost. No one put the argument more crudely than the Ontario Minister of University Affairs, who introduced his restraint program in 1971 with the demand that universities should produce "more scholar per dollar."[82]

Revolted by student unrest, worried about the "productivity" of the universities, and convinced that professors "spend too little time teaching . . . . and too much time researching books and articles for a fee," Canadian businessmen added their own voices to this obsessive concern with efficiency and profitability in the workings of the country's universities. Annual surveys of approximately 300 major companies between 1971 and 1978 revealed that the proportion of the corporate donation dollar going to higher education fell from 37 to 25 per cent.[83] Once extolled as the most vital of public investments in a growing economy, post-secondary education had become, in the eyes of many, a major part of the economic problem. This was not to suggest that the universities of Canada were in imminent danger of being closed down – *en masse*. Despite the uneven demand for graduates, certain areas of higher educational training still served the private sector well. The demand for engineers, business graduates, and computer scientists remained relatively strong throughout the 1970's and early 1980's, though in the face of enduring recession the future of even these fields was uncertain. Students responded to their perceptions of the market by enrolling increasingly in the "pragmatic" disciplines at the expense of arts and general education.[84]

The stated priorities of the federal and provincial governments reflected this selective interest in the activities of Canadian universities. In the fall of 1981, Ottawa promised to reduce dramatically its support of higher education through the Established Programs Financing arrangement and to redirect its funds toward university programs and research designed to serve the country's economic needs.[85] And in every region, provincial governments took initial steps to control the growth of academic programs, to avoid "duplication" of facilities, and to encourage universities to "rationalize" their development in accordance with economic demand. Perhaps the most extreme example of this approach was in British Columbia, where an Academic Council created in 1978 was assigned unprecedented authority over colleges and universities.

It provides for articulation committees to recommend on the equivalency of courses given at one institution or university as compared to courses given at another institution or university. In cases of dispute the Academic Council is to have power to make a ruling on the matter, apparently in this respect being able to override university decisions on admissions. This power, if exercised, might well conflict with provisions of the Universities Act, and it certainly flies in the face of widely accepted and indeed minimal notions of the academic responsibilities of the university.[86]

Recession, rationalization, and restraint – these were the watchwords that shaped higher education in the 1970's and early 1980's. Against such odious and debilitating pressures, the goals of widening accessibility, fostering social criticism, enhancing cultural development, and preserving institutional autonomy struggled to assert their priority in the framing of post-secondary educational policy. But as history proved, higher education had always been vulnerable to the materialistic demands and economic exigencies of the Canadian political economy and political culture. During the 1960's unprecedented prosperity deceived many into believing that universities were valued highly for their democratic promise and cultural benefits. This was a myth. Amid the recession that followed, the mask was lifted and the myth dissolved.

NOTES

1. R.S. Harris, *Quiet Evolution: A Study of the Educational System of Ontario* (Toronto, 1967), 148.
2. *Maclean's*, 8 September 1925, cited in R. Stamp, "Canadian High Schools in the 1920's and 1930's: the Social Challenge to the Academic Tradition," *Historical Papers* (1978), 79.
3. D. Wilson, R. Stamp, and L.P. Audet, *Canadian Education: A History* (Scarborough, Ont., 1970), 325.
4. Robin Harris, *A History of Higher Education in Canada: 1663-1960* (Toronto, 1976), part IV; Michiel Horn, *The League for Social Reconstruction: Intellectual Origins of the Democratic Left in Canada, 1930-1942* (Toronto, 1980), ch. 1.
5. W.P. Thompson, *The University of Saskatchewan: A Personal History* (Saskatoon, 1970), 124; Harris, *History of Higher Education*, 357; J.J. Talman and R.D. Talman, *Western: 1878-1953* (London, Ont., 1953), 111.
6. Harris, *History of Higher Education*, 355; W.L. Morton, *One University: A History of the University of Manitoba 1877-1952* (Toronto, 1957), 147-52.
7. Talman and Talman, *Western*, 112; E.E. Stewart. "The Role of the Provincial Government in the Development of the Universities of Ontario: 1791-1964" (D.Ed thesis, University of Toronto, 1970), 355-69.
8. Horn, *The League for Social Reconstruction*, 178, 182.
9. *Ibid.*, 61-2, 184; see also D. Francis, "The Threatened Dismissal of Frank H. Underhill from the University of Toronto: 1939-1941," *CAUT Bulletin* (December, 1975); M. Horn, "Academic Freedom and the Canadian Professor," *CAUT Bulletin* (December, 1982).
10. "Education for Democracy," *Saturday Night*, 7 December 1940.

11. "Do You Deserve Democracy? A Letter to a Young Canadian Citizen," *Food for Thought* (October, 1940).

12. University of Toronto, *President's Report* (1941), 1.

13. Queen's University, *Principal's Report* (1941), 2-3.

14. University of Western Ontario, *Report of the President* (1943), 6.

15. *Ibid.*, 4.

16. Wartime Bureau of Technical Personnel, *Annual Report*, (Ottawa, Department of Labour, 31 March 1944), cited in G. Pilkington, "A History of the National Conference of Canadian Universities: 1911-1961" (D.Ed thesis, University of Toronto, 1974), 304.

17. Pilkington, "A History," 311.

18. "Report of Committee," a Proposed Defence Training Course, drawn up by the General Committee's Sub-Committee on Courses, Ontario Department of Education, 13 November 1941; R.C. Wallace to G.F. Rogers, 19 December 1941, W. Sherwood Fox to G.F. Rogers, 20 December 1941, RG-2-P3, Archives of Ontario.

19. Queen's University, *Principal's Report* (1943), 14.

20. Thompson, *University of Saskatchewan*, 129.

21. Pilkington, "A History," 329-33; A.G. Bedford, *The University of Winnipeg: A History of the Founding Colleges* (Toronto, 1976), 230.

22. Charles E. Burke, "Science, Technology and Research in the Canadian Democracy," pamphlet in McMaster University Archives, 1948.

23. M. Thistle, ed., *The MacKenzie-McNaughton Wartime Letters* (Toronto, 1975), MacKenzie to McNaughton, 27 October 1941, and xix-xx; Vernon Hill, "Canadian Universities Train Youth for War and Leadership in Critical Post-War Period," *Saturday Night*, 20 January 1945; Queen's University, *Principal's Report* (1941), 11.

24. McMaster University, "A Frank Statement of its Origins and Developments Present Status and Future Needs," McMaster University Archives, 1944.

25. Harris, *Quiet Evolution*, 456; E.F. Sheffield, "The Post-War Surge in Post-Secondary Education, 1945-1969," in Wilson *et al.*, *Canadian Education: A History*; D. Stager, "Federal Government Grants to Canadian Universities, 1951-1967," *Canadian Historical Review*, LIV (1973), 287-90.

26. Report of the Royal Commission on National Development in the Arts, Letters and Sciences (Ottawa, 1951), 141.

27. *Ibid.*, 132-7.

28. See *President's Report*, University of Toronto (1951); *President's Report,* University of Western Ontario (1951).

29. See R.A. Easterlin, "An Explanation of the American Baby Boom following World War II," in D.M. Heer, ed., *Readings in Population* (Englewood Cliffs, N.J., 1968); Alan Sweezy, "The Economic Explanation of Fertility Changes in the United States," *Population Studies*, 25, 2 (1971); W.E. Kalbach and E.M. McVey,

The Demographic Bases of Canadian Society (Toronto, 1971); B. Macleod *et al., Patterns and Trends in Ontario Population* (Toronto, 1972); R. Bothwell *et al., Canada Since 1945: Power, Politics, and Provincialism* (Toronto, 1981), ch. 3.

30. *Public Opinion News Service*, 30 August 1947, 29 August 1950, 7 August 1954, 4 January 1956, 2 January 1957.

31. "Canadian University and College Enrollment Projected to 1965," NCCU, *Proceedings* (1955), 34-6.

32. C.T. Bissell, ed., *Canada's Crisis in Higher Education* (Toronto, 1957); Bissell, *Halfway Up Parnassus: A Personal Account of the University of Toronto, 1932-1971* (Toronto, 1974), 44.

33. Stanley Deeks (an organizer of the conference and an employee of the IFE), private scrapbook of newspaper clippings and interview, 12 May 1976.

34. IFE, *The Case for Corporate Giving to Higher Education* (1957). See also P. Axelrod, *Scholars and Dollars: Politics, Economics, and the Universities of Ontario, 1945-1980* (Toronto, 1982), ch. 2.

35. *Final Report of the Royal Commission on Canada's Economic Prospects* (Ottawa, 1957), 452.

36. *Public Opinion News Service*, 6 January 1951, 16 May 1953.

37. Wilson Woodside, *The University Question* (Toronto, 1958), 30.

38. Cited in IFE, *The Case for Corporate Giving*, 4, 5.

39. *Final Report on Canada's Economic Prospects*, 19.

40. "Colloquium held in the Senate Chamber of the University of Toronto, 17 January 1958 with the Principals and Presidents of Ontario Universities and the heads of mathematics departments," RG-2 P3, Archives of Ontario.

41. Submission of Canadian Universities to the Royal Commission on Canada's Economic Prospects, presented by representatives of NCCU, 6 March 1956, 5.

42. "Education: the Key to Survival," *Cost and Management* (July, 1961).

43. Submission of Canadian Universities, 5.

44. Submission of Ontario to the Royal Commission on Canada's Economic Prospects (1956), 57.

45. IFE, *The Case for Corporate Giving*, 3, 10.

46. J.D. Barrington, cited in *Financial Post*, 15 September 1956.

47. IFE, *The Case for Corporate Giving*, 18.

48. Cited in H.J. Somers, "Private and Corporate Support of Canadian Universities," in Bissell, ed., *Canada's Crisis in Higher Education*, 20.

49. G. Bertram, *The Contribution of Education to Economic Growth*, a study prepared for the Economic Council of Canada (Ottawa, 1965), 61-2; see also Economic Council of Canada, *Second Annual Review* (Ottawa, 1965), 87.

50. *Public Opinion News Service*, 7 April 1965, 29 June 1963.

51. "Canada's Expanding Universities," *Business Review*, 27 November 1961.

52. H.J. Fraser, "The University and Business," in *Canadian Univer-*

sities Today (Toronto, 1961).

53. "What Does Business Owe to Education?" *Trade and Commerce* (August, 1960).
54. A.A. Cumming, "The Business Community's Responsibility to Higher Education," *Monetary Times* (September, 1964).
55. Richard Edsall, "Education: the Boom that Never Goes Bust," *Canadian Business* (October, 1963). See also "The Employer's View," *Report of the Royal Commission on Education*, Province of Alberta, 1959.
56. "Education and Training Power," *Canadian Chartered Accountant* (October, 1963).
57. *Imperial Oil Review* (September, 1959).
58. See John Galbraith, *The New Industrial State* (Boston, 1967), 377-80.
59. K. McRoberts and D. Posgate, *Quebec: Social Change and Political Crisis* (Toronto, 1980), 54-7; Roger Magnuson. *A Brief History of Quebec Education* (Montreal, 1980), ch. v.
60. Report of the Commission on Education Planning, *A Future of Choices – A Choice of Futures* (Edmonton, 1972), 60; Report of the Commission on Post-Secondary Education in Ontario, *The Learning Society* (Toronto, 1972), 147.
61. *Canadian School Journal* (1954), 28.
62. Robert Warner in *Imperial Oil Review* (February, 1961).
63. Stanley Deeks in the *Port Arthur News Chronicle*, 14 August 1958; *Prince Rupert Daily News*, 26 June 1958; *Financial Post*, 28 May 1960 (editorial).
64. IFE, *The Case for Corporate Giving*, 6; IFE, "Academic Casualty Rates and Student Aid," RG-2 P3, Archives of Ontario.
65. Queen's University, *Principal's Report* (1951), 13; University of Toronto, *President's Report* (1951), 4.
66. National Federation of Canadian University Students, "Brief on Education," 1960, RG-2 P3, Archives of Ontario; CLC, *Proceedings* (1962), 23.
67. Tuition fees were eliminated at Memorial University of Newfoundland in 1966. In 1968 tuition was subject to means tests and later introduced for all students. See F. Rowe, *Education and Culture in Newfoundland* (Scarborough, Ont., 1976), 68.
68. See, for example, the remarks of E.E. Stewart, the Deputy Minister of University Affairs, *Globe and Mail*, 14 March 1969.
69. *Toronto Star*, 10 October 1958.
70. IFE, *The Case for Increasing Student Aid* (1958), 14; see also W.J. McCordiac in *Canadian Banker*, 69 (1962), 93.
71. Ontario Legislative Assembly, *Debates*, 25 March 1963, 2134. See also *ibid.*, 19 February 1965, 641, where both Davis and Robarts are quoted as opposing free tuition on the grounds that such a policy would violate free enterprise. A similar position can be found in IFE, *The Case for Increasing Student Aid* (1958), 7.
72. *Debates*, 10 February 1958, 70.
73. Speech at Waterloo College, 3 December 1958, RG-2 P3, Archives of Ontario.

74. House of Commons, *Debates*, 14 July 1964, 4442.
75. T.C. Douglas, House of Commons, *Debates*, 14 July 1964, 4467.
76. For an overview of these programs, see Robert Pike, *Who Doesn't Get to University . . . and Why* (Ottawa, 1970). See also G. Cook and D. Stager, *Student Financial Assistance Programs* (Toronto, 1969).
77. See, for example, J.R. Nininger with F.W.P. Jones, *A Survey of Changing Employment Patterns at Lakehead Cities of Port Arthur and Fort William* (Toronto, 1964), which relates economic growth to educational development. See also J.A. Cleworth *et al.*, *The Economic Impact of McMaster University on the City of Hamilton and Surrounding Localities* (Hamilton, Ont., 1973).
78. See, for example, Ontario Council on University Affairs, *System on the Brink: A Financial Analysis of the Ontario University System* (1979); The Maritime Provinces Higher Education Commission, *Second Annual Report, 1975-76* (Fredericton, 1976); "Cuts, Cuts, Cuts, Restraint, Restraint . . .," *University Affairs* (November, 1982); Peter Leslie, *Canadian Universities: 1980 and Beyond* (Ottawa, 1980), 65-129.
79. For a lucid discussion of the economic crisis of the 1970's, see Cy Gonick, *Inflation or Depression* (Toronto, 1975).
80. *Financial Post*, 23 September 1972; W. Clark and Z. Zsigmond, *Job Market Reality for Post-Secondary Graduates: Employment Outcome by 1978, Two Years After Graduation* (Ottawa, 1981).
81. David Dodge, *Returns to Investment in University Training: The Case of Canadian Accountants, Engineers and Scientists* (Kingston, Ont., 1972); David Sewell, "Educational Planning Models and the Relationship Between Education and Occupation," in S. Ostry, ed., *Canadian Higher Education in the Seventies* (Ottawa, 1971); Economic Council of Canada, *Design for Decision Making – Eighth Annual Review*, (Ottawa, 1971), 210, 212. See also Ivar Berg, *Education and Jobs: The Great Training Robbery* (New York, 1970).
82. *Toronto Telegram*, 8 March 1971; Minister of University Affairs, "Statement on Operating Support of Provincially Assisted Universities for 1971/72 and 1972/73," April, 1971.
83. Institute of Donations and Public Affairs Research, *Corporate Giving in Canada, 1971-1978* (Montreal, 1978).
84. Statistics Canada, *From the Sixties to the Eighties: A Statistical Portrait of Canadian Higher Education* (Ottawa, 1978), 35.
85. Canada, *Fiscal Arrangements in the Eighties: Proposals of the Government of Canada* (Ottawa, 1981); *Financial Post*, 21 November 1981.
86. Leslie, *Canadian Universities*, 76.

VI
Women

The development of women's history as an important, new component of Canadian historiography has occurred in the last decade. The rise of the women's movement in the late 1960's and early 1970's has led to a vigorous and ongoing re-examination of women's roles in Canada – both contemporary and historical. While much of this work initially focused on the institutional history of the women's movement and of women's organizations or on biographies of important individuals, increasing scrutiny is now directed at women's work, waged and unwaged, and at the ideology of male supremacy.

Since the 1930's women have entered and remained in the paid labour force in far larger numbers than was the case in the older pattern of paid work as an expression primarily of one state of the life cycle – the period bridging the gap between puberty and marriage. This older pattern has broken down almost completely. The expansion of office work, the growth of the civil service, and, generally, the development of service and public-sector employment have dramatically transformed women's labour market roles. These economic changes, when combined with the concomitant demographic revolution of the twentieth century, evident even before the Pill, have brought to the fore significant social and ideological conflicts.

These conflicts, eminently apparent in the political realm, also have affected Canadians' private lives. Relationships between men and women and the nature of family life have become conflict-laden and highly contentious areas of dispute. Ironically, while the role of the expert and the professional has been augmented by the insecurities that accompany this painful re-examination of basic premises about social life, the renewed debate has also led to deeper scrutiny of the unstated assumptions and underlying ideologies of the previously sacrosanct "helping" professions.

This questioning also extends to the role of the state and the nature of governmental programs. The following essay is a good example of one such re-examination of state employment-training programs, which, despite their rhetoric of change, display a disconcerting continuity in official ideology about women's place in Canadian society. In the process, the authors raise important questions also about the impact of World War II on women's roles, suggesting that it was not as profound as is generally assumed.

Without doubt, however, the major event for the history of women in the period since 1930 is the emergence and development of the women's movement. The resurgence of feminism in the 1960's and 1970's in Canada awaits its historian. The insights of women's history, meanwhile, are beginning to make their impact on our general view of Canadian history.

FURTHER READING:
On women in the labour market, see Pat and Hugh Armstrong, *The Double Ghetto* (Toronto, 1978); and Graham Lowe, "Class, Job, and Gender in the Canadian Office," *Labour/Le Travailleur*, 10 (1982), 11-37. On the relationship between paid and unpaid labour, especially helpful is Meg Luxton, *More Than a Labour of Love: Three Generations of Women's Work in the Home* (Toronto, 1980). Women and World War II are the subject of a number of Ruth Pierson's articles: "'Jill Canuck': CWAC of All Trades but No 'Pistol Packing Momma,'" *Historical Papers* (1976), 141-74; "'Home-Aide': A Solution to Women's Unemployment After World War II," *Atlantis*, 2 (1977), 85-96. Also useful is Gail Cuthbert Brandt, "'Pigeon-Holed and Forgotten': The Work of the Sub-Committee on the Post-War Problems of Women, 1943," *Histoire Sociale/Social History*, 29 (1982), 239-59. For good overviews of contemporary debates in the Canadian women's movement, see Margie Wolfe, ed., *Still Ain't Satisfied* (Toronto, 1983); and Geraldine Finn and Angela Miles, eds., *Feminism in Canada* (Montreal, 1983).

Ruth Roach Pierson is an historian at the Ontario Institute for Studies in Education. **Marjorie Cohen** teaches in York University's Social Science Division.

Educating Women for Work: Government Training Programs for Women before, during, and after World War II

by Ruth Roach Pierson
and Marjorie Cohen

Some contemporary opponents to women's employment in non-traditional occupations argue that women are not in such jobs because they choose not be be.[1] Underlying that argument is an assumption of freedom of choice and equality of opportunity that flies in the face of historical experience, for even the briefest look at the historical record reveals the powerful social and economic forces channelling women's labour into certain areas and erecting barriers to keep it out of others. The type and accessibility of job training constitute one such force, at the same time as it is linked to, influenced by, and indicative of others. An examination of three vocational training programs developed in Canada under federal legislation between 1937 and 1947 – the Dominion-Provincial Youth Training Program of 1937-40, the War Emergency Training Program of 1940-44, and the rehabilitation component of the Canadian Vocational Training Program, 1945-47[2] – demonstrates the relationship between economic conditions, social definitions of femininity, and women's employment.

During this ten-year period, Canada underwent three distinct labour market phases. Of particular interest are the effects on women as training programs changed to accommodate labour glut, labour scarcity, and the transition from wartime to peacetime economy. The type of training provided for women did indeed vary with changes in demands on the labour market, but what was considered "normal" work for women remained surprisingly constant, even after the experience of war. In fact, throughout the period the training possibilities for women were limited by conceptions of women's social role and fears of female competition for men's jobs. Furthermore, it will be seen that middle- to upper-class women's organizations,[3] recognized by government as the representatives of women's interests, placed their influence behind the prevailing inclination of public policy to preserve sex-typed occupations, the sexual division of labour, and the class-based occupational structure.

THE DOMINION-PROVINCIAL
YOUTH TRAINING PROGRAM

The first program, the Dominion-Provincial Youth Training Program, was introduced in 1937 as a means of alleviating unemployment among people between the ages of sixteen and thirty. Four main types of training project were developed: (1) training in the primary resource industries of forestry and mining; (2) urban occupational training, for "skilled" or "semi-skilled" jobs; (3) rural training designed to keep young people on the land; and (4) physical recreation and health training. Within the program as a whole, the courses for men and the courses for women were kept separate and distinct. Women were totally excluded from training in mining and forestry. The fourth was not really vocational training at all, but rather physical education intended to raise the morale and increase the physical fitness of Canada's young people, with only two provinces, Alberta and British Columbia, participating. Domestic training for women predominated in the remaining two categories, especially in the rural training courses for women, where it was seen as preparatory to a life as farm wife. While young men were given courses in general agriculture, farm mechanics, rural community leadership, and even egg and poultry grading and bee-keeping (occupations traditionally within the preserve of farm wives and daughters), young rural women were offered courses in handicrafts and homecraft. Domestic training for women also came first in urban occupational training. While men were offered industrial apprenticeships, and training courses in such fields as motor mechanics, carpentry, electronics, machine shop, building construction, welding, and even ski instructing, the most prevalent form of training for women in almost all provinces was that provided in Home Service Training Schools. Indeed, approximately 60 per cent of the women in urban occupational training were enrolled in these schools to be trained as domestic servants. The remaining 40 per cent were scattered through an array of other sex-typed courses including dress-making, retail selling, catering for tourists, waitressing, home nursing, interior decorating, "commercial refresher," and "in-dustrial learnerships" in power sewing machine operation.[4]

This emphasis on domestic training as primary vocational training for girls and women was no historical aberration. Faced with a chronic shortage of domestic servants since the late 1800's, organized women, both urban and rural, pressured governments to meet the need through immigration policies favouring female domestics and through the promotion of domestic science instruction in the public schools.[5] With immigration restricted after the onset of the depression, emphasis by necessity shifted onto training as the method of recruiting domestics, and many women's organizations, such as the National Council of Women and the YWCA, appealed to the government with a new urgency for the establishment of state-supported schools for domestic servants. Members of women's organizations were believed to have special knowledge of training requirements, as well as the ability to influence potential employers regarding working conditions. Thus, they were directly incorporated into the program's administration once the schools were established.

Setting up schools for domestic servants had also been the advice of the Women's Employment Committee of the National Employment Commission.[6] In studying the effects of the depression on women's employment opportunities, the Women's Employment Committee had found unemployment in almost every classic women's occupation except domestic service.[7] Indeed, domestic service was one of the few areas in which there was actual expansion in employment for women.[8] Contributing to this were the changes in income distribution during the depression: some lower-middle-class housewives could now afford a maid, given the low pay many desperate women were forced to accept.[9] Despite the employment opportunities in domestic service, the supply did not outstrip the demand, primarily because of the unattractiveness of the occupation: the low pay, irregular and long hours, isolation, poor working conditions (including employer-employee relations), and social stigma.

The Home Service Training School program had as its objective eliminating all those rebarbative features and raising the status and prestige of domestic work. A presupposition underpinning the program was that proper training was necessary, not to stimulate demand for female domestic workers but to stimulate supply. The architects of the household training schemes reasoned that once women were properly trained and certified, then employers would begin paying them higher wages and more respect, with the result that more women would seek jobs as domestics. [10]

The Home Service Training Schools drew on the model of servant courses set up by such women's voluntary organizations as the YWCA earlier in the depression. Approximately half the schools were fully residential; in the others, trainees took turns living in a "practice house." Instruction was provided in the basic skills of housework: preparation and serving of food, daily and weekly cleaning of rooms, laundry, sewing and mending, and answering the door and telephone. Certain subjects, such as table setting and use and care of electrical equipment, clearly indicate the perceived gap between the accustomed standard of living of the trainee and that of her prospective employer. Marketing and budgeting were not taught universally; and child-care training, where it appeared, was connected with home-nursing and occupied a relatively insignificant place on the curriculum. Classes on deportment, personal attitude, employer and employee relationships, and personal habits and appearance were designed to promote "the development of right attitudes to work, clearly, a high priority among employers." [11]

The term "hostess method" was applied to the approach adopted by some schools of having the trainees go out to work in selected local homes to obtain practical experience. The federal Department of Labour official report of November 1938 acknowledged that the possible benefits of the hostess method could well be outweighed by its inherent dangers, the chief of which being that the trainees could too easily be exploited and used to replace char-women or other casual household help.

Despite the project's stated objective, the Home Service Training Schools had limited success in improving the status, pay, working conditions, or employer-employee relations of domestic service. One report noted that talks to women's organizations were necessary to educate "employers to their responsibility in the treatment of girls who come into their homes for home service work" for it was "quite apparent that some employers have much need of education along this line." [12]

On the issues of working conditions and pay, there were clear differences in perspective between labour and management. [13] While the women in Vancouver who organized the Domestic Workers' Union No. 91 in 1936 were demanding a forty-eight-hour week and inclusion in the minimum wage laws, the Victoria Branch of the YWCA, the first in Canada to inaugurate a "Household Training Course" to train young women for domestic service, was recommending that the hours of work for "girls" employed in homes should not exceed sixty per week and the national YWCA was only willing to endorse a recommendation for a maximum eleven-hour day or sixty-nine-hour week.[14] Similarly, while the Saskatchewan Provincial Executive of the Trades and Labour Congress of Canada sought inclusion of domestic workers under the Minimum Wage Act, the 1940 Household Employment Study Group of Preston, Ontario, composed of housewife employers of domestic help, concluded "that the situation is not ready for legislation as to hours and wages" since "it is better for a girl to be in a home with room and board, even at low wages, than to be without work."[15] Clearly, self-interest motivated such pronouncements.

Nor did the Home Service Training School project succeed in removing the social stigma attached to domestic service in the eyes of prospective household workers. The November 1938 survey reported that:

> In many localities it has been found difficult to get girls from families in receipt of direct relief to undergo such a course of training, or to accept work on its conclusion. There is a deep-seated prejudice against this type of work, not only among the young women themselves, but among their parents.[16]

Although the Youth Training Program was implemented specifically to help young people "not gainfully employed and certified as being in necessitous circumstances, including deserving transients,"[17] the administrators of the Home Service Training Schools took a dim view of recruits who were overly "necessitous," such as "'problem' girls" sent to the schools for training by social welfare agencies. A general assumption in operation by late 1938 was "that the more necessitous the trainee, the less suitable she is for the work."[18] There thus remained an unresolved contradiction between the employer's desire for "a finer type of girl" and the stubbornly unattractive nature of the live-in servant's job, which repelled all but the most vulnerable and least advantaged women in the labour market. While official reports at the time stated that the Home Service Training School project was successful, the small number trained (3,683 by May 1940) and the fact that the schools' enrolments rarely reached capacity indicate that it was not the raging success its planners had hoped it would be.[19]

This solution to female unemployment was generally viewed, however, as both sensible and feasible. Domestic service was an occupation traditionally associated with women where there would be no competition with men and where demand perpetually outran supply. Members of women's organizations found the promotion of domestic training compatible with their conception of the proper niche for a certain class of women; with their perception of the only alternative for unfortunate women forced onto the job market; and with their charitable impulse to help needy women find work during difficult economic times, an impulse that dovetailed more often than not with their own demands for domestic help. Neither government nor women's groups questioned the assumption that housework was women's responsibility, whether performed directly or supervised by women, and neither questioned the class structure that made paid housework the obvious occupation for poor females. Moreover, that women's organizations pushed for domestic training programs was as much a function of the members' own confinement to the domestic sphere and of their own responsibility for housework as it was of the lack of alternative job opportunities for women.

THE DOMINION-PROVINCIAL WAR EMERGENCY TRAINING PROGRAM

The second program, the War Emergency Training Program, formally came into being in 1940. Under it women were trained for employment in some trades previously operated as male enclaves, but that training was still designed to prepare women differently from men, above all for a more circumscribed working life.

As early as 1938-39, when war was only a strong possibility, the government began adapting the Youth Training Program to national defence purposes. Specifically, in 1938, arrangements were made for certain provinces to train men in aircraft manufacture and, in the spring of 1939, to train ground mechanics for the air force. With the actual outbreak of war in September 1939, the Youth Training Program was further altered to meet the growing needs for war industrial training and trades training in the armed forces. A plan for a special War Emergency Training Program was drawn up during the summer of 1940, and the War Measures Act was invoked to make it possible for the federal government to assume most of the cost of war-related training projects.[20] Provinces and municipalities contributed the shops of their vocational and technical schools during summer vacation and after regular school hours. By the end of 1940, "the War Emergency Training Programme . . . formally came into being after a year and a half of progressive evolution

. . . ."[21] Projects formerly carried on under Youth Training were allowed to lapse while schedules of new projects to be undertaken were attached to new federal-provincial agreements.[22]

Labour power *per se* did not become a problem in Canada until almost two years after the start of the war. By the late 1930's the depression had eased somewhat, but in September 1939 the official unemployment rate still included some 600,000 to 900,000 unemployed, depending on the source. In the early stages of the war, Canada's production effort, principally in the primary sector providing raw materials and food, was not strained, but after the fall of France in June 1940, as Canada's production of war equipment for allied armies was stepped up, her industrial sector began increasingly to suffer shortages of skilled and semi-skilled labour. Hence, there was a need to expand and formalize a War Emergency Training Program.

At the outset practically all the trainees were male. "All other factors being equal unemployed men will be first assigned provided they have the requisite capacity to benefit from the training or to perform the work," the *Labour Gazette* reported in January 1941 as one of the principles that would govern the implementation of the War Emergency Training Program.[23] Preference was to be shown to veterans of the Great War, soldiers discharged from the armed forces in the current war, and men over forty years of age. The minimum age of admission was sixteen.[24]

Female trainees were enrolled only in Ontario classes, and they numbered a mere 271 out of a total 10,156 enrolled in classes throughout Canada during the first four months of 1941.[25] At that time women were being accepted for training only when "specifically sponsored by employers."[26] In such cases, the employer would select the trainees and specify the kind of training desired. Since training was usually quite specialized, the time the trainee spent at the school could be as little as two weeks, in contrast to the normal course of more general training, which lasted three months.[27]

At least until the end of 1941 women continued to be trained for domestic service under the Youth Training Program. More than 847 received training in Home Service Schools in Manitoba, Quebec, Alberta, and British Columbia in 1941.[28] During that year women in New Brunswick, Quebec, Manitoba, Alberta, and British Columbia were also given specialized training in dressmaking, power sewing machine operating, and handicrafts. In November, however, the Director of Training in the Department of Labour informed the Minister that instructions had been sent out to all regional directors to arrange for war industrial training for women as soon as the local supply of male applicants ran out.[29] By the end of 1941 war industrial training had been given to 3,341 women, albeit mostly in Ontario, and they constituted approximately 17 per cent of the total then enrolled.[30]

The industrial training program itself was expanding. In June 1941 training was being offered at seventy-five vocational schools across the country. By the end of the year there were 101, located in all provinces except Prince Edward Island.[31] The number of training centres in operation fluctuated with the changes in demand in different areas, but settled by mid-1943 to an average of about 120. Where there were not enough vocational shops in existing technical schools, former Youth Training centres were taken over for the War Emergency Training Program or additional special centres were opened and equipped. "When the demand for training was at its peak most of the centres operated two shifts and some of them three shifts per day."[32] For instance, Toronto's Central Technical School, which helped pioneer the Program, operated on a three-shift, twenty-four hour basis, with regular public school classes for boys and girls from 8:45 a.m. to 3 p.m., and two shifts for war trainees, the first from 3:30 to 11:20, and the midnight shift from 11:30 p.m. until 7:30 a.m. No women were allowed to attend the midnight class.[33]

In September 1941, training within industry was also brought under the jurisdiction of the Training Branch of the federal Department of Labour. And in early 1942 the War Emergency Training Program acquired authority to co-operate with industry in the organization and operation of plant schools that would provide types of training not available in the pre-employment centres. By mid-1943, 105 approved plant schools were in operation and receiving financial and technical assistance from government. In addition, part-time classes to facilitate the upgrading and promotion of persons already employed in industry were started and quickly expanded during 1942.

Besides training for war industry, the War Emergency Training Program was also designed from the start to supplement the trades training of the armed forces. Shortly after the creation of the women's services[34] – the RCAF (Women's Division), the Canadian Women's Army Corps, and the Women's Royal Canadian Naval Service – between the summers of 1941 and 1942, female personnel also became eligible for training. The trades training in the service was offered in separate classes for men and women, and, although it increased over the years, the number of trades in which women could be trained remained only a fraction of those open to men. A large proportion of servicewomen were trained as clerk stenographers for the army and air force. In the spring of 1942 a class of women cooks was receiving instruction at Toronto's Central Technical School in preparation for service with the Canadian Women's Army Corps.[35]

As the expansion in the War Emergency Training Program was occurring, Canada's sources of labour supply among men, however preferred, continued to decline steeply. When Prime Minister Mackenzie King announced on March 24, 1942, the establishment of National Selective Service to co-ordinate and direct the near total mobilization of Canada's labour power for the war effort, he designated bringing women into industry as "the most important single feature of the program," and specified a series of ten measures to be undertaken, including the provision "of training programs specifically designed for women."[36] Even before he spoke, arrangements had been made to increase the numbers of women in pre-employment industrial training, especially in Ontario but elsewhere as well. By the end of February 1942, training schools in Quebec, Saskatchewan, Alberta, and British Columbia were also enrolling women in industrial classes. From April to December of 1942 the female proportion of full-time pre-employment trainees overall rose to 48 per cent (total men: 12,453; total women: 11,579). Meanwhile the proportion of female trainees in full-time and part-time plant school classes as well as in part-time classes in technical schools was also increasing.[37]

The trades in which instruction was being given to women included: machine shop practice; ammunition filling; fine instrument mechanics; power machine operating; welding (arc and acetylene); aircraft sheet metal and aircraft woodworking; aircraft fabric and doping; bench fitting and assembling; electric wiring and radio and electric assembly; industrial chemistry; drafting and mechanical drawing; inspecting; and laboratory technician work.[38] Clearly, women were being trained in skills previously confined to males. Nonetheless, the policy was to protect men's privileged position as "skilled" workers in industry and thus keep women's admission to "skilled" jobs to a minimum.[39] This policy was implemented in a variety of ways.

First, there was the general policy of giving priority to eligible men over eligible women. The first Director of National Selective Service made assurances to that effect in April 1942, when he explained that "we don't intend to bring women in one door and have skilled men forced out the other." Acknowledging that skilled male workers were still unemployed in some sections of Canada, he agreed that "it would be folly to recruit women in these places, until the men have been absorbed." Furthermore, he declared that it would be "contrary to the principles of the selective service regulations that an employer utilize those regulations to replace men with women merely for the sake of having the same work done at lower cost." He ended with an emphatic endorsement of the principle of the primacy of the male breadwinner.[40]

Another way in which women's access to skilled work was circumscribed resulted from a reorganization of production. This was most easily effected in plants that had to undergo considerable reorganization in any case to convert from peacetime to wartime production. Impressed by "scientific management schemes" developed in Britain and the United States, the Inter-Departmental Committee on Labour Co-ordination recommended in December 1941 that, to reduce the demand for skilled labour,

> Jobs will be broken down, and the trained mechanics will devote their time to the most skilled part of the work. The rest of the work will be divided among others next [to] the mechanics in line, each of whom ought to be broken in on his part of the job with a few weeks training. New employees will be taken on at the bottom on the least skilled jobs and moved up as rapidly as circumstances and their abilities permit.[41]

This increased subdivision and stratification of the production line made it possible to reserve the most "skilled" jobs at the top for long-term male employees while bringing in at the bottom new employees to perform minute and monotonous operations requiring a minimum of training.[42] Despite the promise of advancement contained in the Report of the Inter-Departmental Committee on Labour Co-ordination, the actual possibility of many of the minimally trained new workers moving very far up the ladder of skill was strictly limited by the imperatives of the war emergency with its short-term goals.

The introduction of improved machinery facilitated reorganization. Praising the revolution in technology necessitated by the war effort, a *Maclean's* article spoke reverently of the new machines developed to remove the responsibility for accuracy from human beings and rigged with so many stops and checks that the possibility of error was reduced almost to the vanishing point. The novice operator, "schooled in a few simple tasks and motions," could hardly go wrong unless he or she fell asleep on the job.[43] These changes in the organization and technology of production meant that industry could rely increasingly on inexperienced and minimally trained workers. By 1942-43, as production was stepped up in munitions, ammunition, aircraft, and fine instrument manufacture, their ranks were increasingly female.

The media played up the connection between the greater use of women in war industry and the introduction of machines compatible with women's learning capacities. Thus a female trainee was quoted in *Maclean's* as saying of her lathe, "with a look of amazed delight on her face, 'Why, it's easier to run than a sewing machine.'"[44] And according to *Canadian Aviation*, Vultee Aircraft Incorporated had made a careful study of the problems involved in employing women and found that if machines could be developed to compensate for women's alleged inferior co-ordination and inferior weight, height, and strength, then "women make loyal and productive workers, and can handle a surprising number of type of jobs."[45] Another *Canadian Aviation* article gave detailed examples of "methods improvements" introduced into the production of the Harvard advanced trainer at Noorduyn Aviation Limited, which allowed female operators to work more efficiently than male operators using the old methods.[46]

Training provided for women under the War Emergency Training Program was designed to fit them for specific jobs for the duration of the war, not for lifetime careers as skilled workers, much less skilled mechanics who might compete with men in the post-war job market. This was obvious in the generally shorter training period for women. At the beginning of the program the length of the normal course was set at three months, but increased specialization in industry and the attendant need for workers trained in a very narrow range of skills led to the introduction of a wide variety of shorter courses. Two weeks was set as the minimum training period. This reduction in the training period, as the *Labour Gazette* reported, was "particularly evident in regard to women, where the majority of the training courses last from two to six weeks." "Inevitably," the *Labour Gazette* continued, "this type of training produces people who can only perform one job and are lacking in a wider range of skill."[47]

At Toronto's Central Technical School, the average length of industrial training courses was from ten to twelve weeks, but some highly technical subjects, such as industrial chemistry and machine drafting, went on for twenty weeks. "On the other hand," a *Maclean's* article noted, "three weeks instruction is sufficient to teach most women to run a power machine, or to work efficiently on assembly jobs requiring only a single main operation."[48] At Small Arms Limited, makers of the Sten gun and the Lee-Enfield rifle, new female employees found themselves on the production line after only one day in the classroom. Instruction was limited to four basic machines, a milling machine, turret lathe, drill, and surface grinder, and, with some continuing supervision from patrolling instructresses, women who had had no previous industrial experience were found to perform well after the single day's training. As one woman recalled, "they showed you on your first shift" – that was the extent of her training.[49]

In general, war had necessitated a revolution in vocational training because, to meet the demands of war production, "Skill had to be created overnight." Justifiable only because the war emergency left no alternative, the crash training courses were seen as a radical departure from the "normal vocational training" that aimed at producing a well-rounded (male) worker with a wide range of skills. During the war, men as well as women underwent "hurried training in specialized tasks, but women's training was by and large the more hurried and the more specialized of the two."[50]

Women's access to skilled trades was also restricted by the job-specific training they received. One way in which the reluctance to hire women was overcome was through the designation of certain work processes as ideally suited to innate female traits. Women workers could then be concentrated in those "feminized" tasks. Improvement of machinery in the direction of increased automation and mechanization, which was fundamental to the subdivision and de-skilling of production also made possible the "feminization" of those operations.

It was widely believed that women were by nature more patient, more dexterous, and more capable of detailed, eye-gruelling work than men.[51] *Canadian Aviation*, for example, conceded that there were certain advantages to employing women: "Women thrive on routine, continued repetition of which would drive men to distraction," and "Women are faster than men at sorting small objects and any operations requiring digital dexterity."[52] Thus, women came to be regarded as eminently well suited for precision work in any kind of fine instrument assemblage, in electronics and optics, in various stages of aircraft, gun, or ammunition manufacture, and in the inspecting of war equipment. Thelma LeCocq wrote in *Maclean's,* for example, about the "deft-fingered" women who excelled at fine precision work in a plant that made airplane instruments, including finely adjusted meters to register voltage, current, and fuel. About 40 per cent of the workers in the plant were women. On the meters they did

> close machine work, winding wires only a few thousandths of an inch in diameter on tiny spools the size you'd find in a child's sewing set. They set jewels, synthetic sapphires hardly larger than a granule of white sugar, using fine tweezers to convey them to the lathe. They run machines that cut screws almost as delicate as the screws in a watch.

And to provide training for these jobs, management did not even have to draw on the War Emergency Training Program because the precision work could be learned by the women, given their natural endowments of "dexterity, patience and keen eyesight," in "only two or three days training right in the plant."[53] It was precisely the dull, repetitive, eye-straining jobs created by the greater subdivision of the production process that could be "feminized" and that women could be prepared for with a minimum of training.

Although the specific war industrial jobs for which women were recruited and trained extended into a large range of occupations formerly confined to men, the woman in the non-traditional job had probably received less extensive training than her male counterpart. The narrow, job-specific instruction that characterized women's training under the War Emergency Training Program handicapped any woman who desired to continue in a non-traditional occupation at war's end.[54] That narrowness of training was based in part on the assumption that women had come forward to work in machine shops out of patriotic motives and only for the duration of the war. As the Nova Scotia Director of Technical Education wrote of the women trained in his province, the general and theoretical aspects of the machine tool trade "did not interest them as much as the practical shopwork because they had no long-term ambition to become journeymen in order to continue in the trade after the war."[55] Whether such statements were based on facts or prescription, they nevertheless reflected a set of attitudes and practices that served to curtail any such "long-term ambition."

A minimum of training had brought the largest proportion of women war workers onto the production line at the lowest levels of skill where they could be concentrated in "feminized" tasks that depended for smooth performance on the allegedly superior female capacity for monotony and intricate work. During the war more than 50,000 civilian women had taken training for work in war industries, in addition to the women who had been trained for trades in the armed forces. The tendency of that training to be different and unequal prepared the way for the separate treatment of women in the rehabilitation training programs of the post-war world.

CANADIAN VOCATIONAL TRAINING AND REHABILITATION FOR WOMEN

However truncated and task-specific, War Emergency Training for women had extended into non-traditional trades. Rehabilitation training of women for the post-war world, in contrast, reverted to more conventional pre-war conceptions of labour suitable for women. As early as January 1943, when war employment was nearing its peak and a shortage of even women's labour was beginning to be felt, the Director of Training in the federal Department of Labour stressed, in a routine letter to regional directors, that in arranging for vocational training for ex-servicewomen, they should "keep in mind the employment opportunities as they may exist in the post-war period, and the likelihood that employment of women may be discontinued entirely or at least greatly diminished, in the metal trades and other heavy industries."[56]

It was estimated that at the height of women's involvement in war production in October 1943, 261,000 women had been recruited into war industrial jobs. Already by April 1, 1945, thousands of those jobs had been eliminated, resulting in the layoff of more than 80,000 women war workers.[57] In addition, approximately 50,000 women had served in the armed forces, of whom all but some Nursing Sisters faced discharge as the women's services were slowly reduced in strength after V-E Day until finally being disbanded in the second half of 1946.

Fears that massive demobilization at war's end would lead to a recurrence of post-war slump as after the Great War, or to a return to the dismal conditions of the 1930's, were counterbalanced by a heightened confidence in capitalism's ability to produce and in government's ability to plan.[58] As it was believed that planning in a democracy should not be arbitrary,[59] planners conducted surveys of post-war employment intentions. The 1944 Weir Report on post-war employment prospects in Canada sought to ascertain what type of occupation armed forces personnel were planning to enter or train for after discharge. With respect to servicewomen's preferences, "an extraordinary preponderance," as the Minister of Pensions and National Health expressed it, put stenography as the occupation of their choice. Even marriage, as indicated by the choice of "home-making," was "a poor second, followed by nursing, university courses, teaching, book-keeping and clerical work."[60] These results are not surprising, given the apparently sex-typed list of choices offered the servicewomen and the fact that the overwhelming majority of women in the armed forces had been trained as clerks and clerk-stenographers.[61] Furthermore, stenography was, after all, at the top of the hierarchy of clerical skills. Unfortunately, Weir did not survey the post-war employment preferences of the over 200,000 women war workers. There never was a reliable survey made of how many women employed during the war at non-traditional jobs would have wanted to stay in such work after the war.

On the equally crucial question of whether or not women wanted to stay on in paid work outside the home, the surveys came up with conflicting results. On the basis of questionnaires distributed among women war workers and interviews with employers and business experts, the 1943 government Sub-Committee on the Post-War Problems of Women estimated that between 45 per cent and 55 per cent of the 600,000 women who had entered the paid labour force since 1939 would be responding to "the normal urge towards marriage, and home, and family life" and therefore would be leaving their paid jobs once the war was over.[62] In contrast, one Labour Department survey of the "post-war working intentions" of 19,710 civilian men and 10,135 civilian women, conducted in 1944, showed 28 per cent of the women, as compared with 2 per cent of the men, intending to quit work after the war to take care of a home. That left 72 per cent wanting to stay in the work force.[63] A Gallup poll of the Toronto area found that 80 per cent of all women employed full-time intended to continue after the war and that one-half of the married women workers hoped to keep their jobs. Moreover, some unnamed but "large" trade union had recently surveyed 1,000 of its female members asking whether or not they would continue to work after the war, if a job were available. Eighty-four per cent of the married women, 95 per cent of the single women, and 100 per cent of the widows answered yes.[64]

Faced with such survey results and committed to the principle of freedom of choice, post-war planners might conceivably have done everything within their power to safeguard a woman's right freely to choose her occupation as well as whether or not to work for pay. The possibility for change in the post-war economy, including change in the direction of improving women's economic position, was enormous. Women's contribution to the war effort had been impressive and they had received recognition as capable workers in areas normally the preserve of men. Important also was the vision of a more egalitarian society that the war effort had generated. Dr. Olive Ruth Russell, appointed in January 1945 to the Department of Veterans' Affairs as an executive assistant, specializing in the rehabilitation of servicewomen, was fond of quoting Winston Churchill's claim that "'War had taught us to make vast strides forward toward a more complete equalization of the parts to be played by men and women in society.'"[65]

But undercutting any commitment to equality was the conviction on the part of most post-war planners that for most women the primary role should be the dual one of wife and mother, a role not to be combined, except in the direst circumstances, with paid employment outside the home. That belief coloured the major statements of reconstruction social policy that dealt at all with women, from the Final Report of the Sub-Committee on the Post-War Problems of Women to Leonard C. Marsh's Report on Social Security for Canada 1943. While asserting the principle of women's right to work, whether married or not, the government sub-committee nonetheless deferred to the contradictory principle of male economic primacy, regarding the creation of "sufficient well-paid employment for men" as of primary importance and as the necessary precondition for the best solution to the problem of women's crowding the labour market after the war – their withdrawal from wage work to devote themselves to home and family.[66] In its look at the post-war future, the Wartime Information Board based its "full employment campaign" in part on the expectation "that a good many *women* in the Services and in civilian jobs are looking forward to changing their tunics and overalls for aprons, as soon as the womanpower shortage is over."[67]

So, in spite of the vision of a more egalitarian society in the future and a professed confidence in the ability of government to plan for post-war full employment, there was no attempt in the post-war planning schemes to maintain the gains for women in social and employment policy that had been made during the war.[68] Rather, the aim was to return to a pre-war social reality, but without the disability of the pre-war economy, that is, without unemployment. The result was rhetoric that stressed the equal application of the training schemes to men and women; at the same time, a program was instituted that stressed women's traditional roles as paid or unpaid workers in the home and that reinforced the segregated participation of women in the labour force.

Government officials responsible for the post-war rehabilitation training program, initially designed for armed services personnel but extended in March 1945 to civilian workers displaced by the close-down of war industries, [69] were proud of Canada's progressive treatment of women. Dr. Russell doubted that any country had gone as far as Canada in "abolishing sex discrimination and the granting of equal status to women" in its legislation pertaining to ex-service personnel. [70] A Department of Labour booklet listed as one of the principles governing Canadian vocational training that "Women have equality with men in all opportunities for training." [71]

Equal opportunity, however, was not understood to mean the same opportunity or the same training. Commonly it was assumed that when women were given the freedom to choose, they would conform to traditional expectations. For instance, Dr. Russell told a Department of Veterans' Affairs counsellors' training course in February 1945 that it was unlikely women would "be interested in pursuing some of the training open to men," because of the "physical requirements, or other conditions of the job," although it would be "poor psychology to close any courses to them." She also quoted the advice of Mrs. Edgar Hardy, president of the National Council of Women, to the Training Branch of the Department of Labour: " 'Open all courses equally to men and women and you will find only very few women will enter what might be classed as courses typical for men.' " [72] Comments like these revealed a growing recognition that an "open-door" policy would not necessarily guarantee a return to pre-war sex roles. Therefore, deliberate steps were taken to ensure that the structure of the program limited the choice women could make: the selection process; the distinctly unequal treatment married women received in rehabilitation measures; and the designing of training courses specifically for women all served to make women's choice a narrow one indeed.

If interested in vocational training, an ex-serviceman or woman would consult an Employment and Selective Service office. From there an application for training would be forwarded to a District Rehabilitation Board, which would consider the individual's request for a specific type of training and approve it if the training desired conformed to what "would be most desirable in view of each applicant's background and aptitudes." [73] The District Rehabilitation Board was instructed to keep the following criteria in mind: (1) the trainee's physical condition; (2) previous education; (3) occupational experience prior to enlistment or while in the forces; (4) trainee's own preference and aptitudes; and (5) employment opportunities. [74] These criteria built the potential for discrimination against women into the selection process.

In addition, the unequal treatment of married women in provisions for subsistence allowances constituted another restriction on women's access to training. Unemployed civilians being trained in full-time classes were paid subsistence allowances at the following rates: $1.15 per day for a single person living at home; $1.50 per day for a single person living away from home; $2.15 per day for heads of families living at home; and $3.00 per day for heads of families living away from home.[75] The scale of maintenance grants to be paid to veteran trainees provided for payment of $60 a month to single men and women and $80 a month to married men. In addition, monthly allowances were to be paid for each dependent child up to six and for dependent parents. Although the language of the rehabilitation pamphlets issued by Labour and Veterans' Affairs was ambiguous on this point, it would appear that neither married female veterans nor married civilian women out of work were entitled to their own maintenance or subsistence grants while in training. It also seems reasonable to infer that, because servicewomen were not entitled to dependants' allowances for husbands or children while in service, they would not be as ex-servicewomen. Certainly in the case of the out-of-work benefit available to ex-service personnel, it was clearly specified that a married female veteran whose husband was "entirely or mainly capable of supporting her" was not eligible.[76] In post-war rehabilitation and reconstruction policy generally, married women with husbands deemed capable of maintaining them were not regarded as independent agents.

Equally insidious in the post-war world were the barriers being erected or re-erected to keep women out of certain jobs. The Re-instatement in Civil Employment Act of 1942 provided that ex-service personnel be given back their old pre-enlistment jobs with full seniority rights on discharge.[77] While this was to apply equally to ex-servicewomen and men, it tended to work to the disadvantage of women: not only were there many fewer female than male veterans, but also many civilian women had worked during the war in replacement positions.[78] Furthermore, a Civil Service Act provided that preference be shown in all Civil Service Commission appointments to ex-service personnel who had seen active service overseas or on the high seas.[79] As stated, the law placed ex-servicewomen at a disadvantage, since approximately 7,000 had been posted to overseas duty and none had seen service on seaborne vessels. But worse than that, there was an unlegislated rule that "'overseas veteran' means a male person." Indeed in employment placement generally, this was how the term had been interpreted by National Selective Service since 1943.[80]

Another significant barrier for women was the renewed enforcement of the civil service regulations barring married women from working for the federal government. Dr. Russell, in opposing this policy, argued that if the civil service set the example of refusing to employ married women, the government could scarcely blame other employers if they also refused to employ married women and pursued "policies of retrenchment based on fear, rather than policies of expansion based on courage, confidence and initiative."[81] But her protest was not enough to reverse this component of the post-war drive to return women to the home. The regulations barring married women from federal civil service employment were not rescinded until 1955.[82] Such barriers had a strong indirect effect on women's opportunities for training, since women were unlikely to be granted permission to train for jobs in which they were unlikely to be employed.

While women were technically eligible for all training courses, the government, through various surveys, predetermined what would be the best areas for women to train in. The surveys were notable for the extent to which the procedure prejudiced the information received. For instance, a 1945 Committee on Post-War Training carried out a special survey to ascertain what pre-employment vocational training programs would be appropriate for women given local employment opportunities across Canada. The questionnaire "guided" those conducting the survey by providing a list of employment areas, all classically female, to be looked into: (1) household employment; (2) hotels and restaurants (room service, waitressing); (3) hospitals (ward aides); (4) sales work; (5) stenography; (6) power machine sewing; (7) hairdressing; (8) dressmaking. The results of this survey were submitted to Canadian Vocational Training "to serve as a basis for further inquiry and planning."[83]

Across the country, the local offices of the National Employment Service, through the machinery of their women's divisions, regularly attempted to assess the projected labour demands for women. The monthly reports submitted to the head offices of National Selective Service in 1945 gave prominence to traditional women's trades: the consensus was that textile workers, nurses' aides, and domestic servants would be needed in the post-war period in far greater numbers than were likely to be supplied.[84] Local women's groups, still regarded by Labour Department officials as uniquely knowledgeable about "employment demands and opportunities" for women, were also of the opinion that chronic shortage of domestic labour offered a ready-made solution to the anticipated post-war problem of an excess of female labour.[85]

While during the war the shortage of domestic servants had been endured patriotically, the perception of this problem as acute immediately resurfaced once the pressure of war production priorities was eased.[86] The urgency of the problem was brought home in March 1945 to Employment Service officials in Toronto by the requests for assistance that poured in from prominent residents, such as senators, MPs, the U.S. consulate, and the chancellor of the University of Toronto, who had been without domestic help for six months.[87]

The demand for household training came overwhelmingly from women's organizations, prospective employers, and government officials. It had been one of the main recommendations of the Final Report of the Sub-Committee on Post-War Problems of Women. The other ready-made solution to a surplus of women workers on the post-war labour market was the departure of the independent waged or salaried female employee into marriage and economic dependency.[88] Herein lay the two-pronged thrust of Canada's rehabilitation training program for women, what Dr. Russell called the "special challenge for women in planning for the post-war period": "to develop ways and means of making employment in housework, waitress work, etc. 'attractive and desirable occupations'" and to convince married women that "*household management and the successful care and management of children is an art and a science that has endless possibilities and requires unlimited training and skill if it is to be managed successfully in the new world of to-morrow.*"[89]

The need to reconcile the private role as wife and mother with the more public role gained during the war was a prominent feature of post-war discussions of women's training. These, however, reflected no awareness of the fact that a rigid sexual division of labour that automatically and categorically assigned child-rearing and housework to women restricted women's access to paid jobs and limited the choices women could make. Dr. Russell is a good example. While she fought against sex discrimination in employment and for recognition of women's right to work,[90] and spoke up publicly for the women, including married women, who had found "a new, hard-won economic independence" that they did not want to lose,[91] she nevertheless argued women's "special responsibility for family life" and advocated a homemaking course for the brides and prospective brides among women leaving the services.[92]

Within the rehabilitation training program of CVT, provision

of household training initially was to begin "just as soon as sufficient requests are received from young women to justify the
opening of schools or special training centres."[93] But it soon became apparent that only a "very, very small number of service
women" had any intention of working as domestic servants
when they left the armed forces. Rather than abandoning the
scheme to re-establish home service training schools for women,
the Director of Training proposed expanding the program to include "not only training for home service work," but also
"training in home making" for those women being discharged
from the forces who were married or about to be married.[94] This
was the same idea that Dr. Russell had been pushing from within
Veterans' Affairs ever since her appointment. While various surveys taken of women in the armed forces and of those already
discharged indicated that there was no interest in training for
paid domestic employment, there did appear to be some interest
in a short course in homemaking among those women who expected to be running their own homes soon after discharge.[95] Because of the very different objectives of training in home management and training for household service, two distinct courses
were developed – a homemakers' course for brides and prospective brides and a home assistants' course for wage labourers.

The "brides' course" became a pet project of Dr. Olive Russell. Initially she envisioned a program involving both men and
women, thus putting "appropriate emphasis on marriage and
homemaking as a partnership," and which would last, at least
for the women, as long as a year.[96] As the discussions regarding
the course progressed, however, both suggestions were quietly
dropped. Dr. Russell stressed that these courses should "not be
confused with the pre-war youth training programmes, which
though admirable in many ways, are associated in many people's
thinking with depression years and training for 'domestics.'"
The intention was to focus the course on the more psychological,
emotional, and social aspects of marriage and family relations
rather than on the more physical aspects of housework, like
cleaning and ironing.[97] Under the title "Home Making and Family Living," the course for brides and potential brides among
ex-servicewomen was designed to last three or four months.
Toronto was the first place it was offered, starting in February
1946. By April home service training schools were planned or in
operation where the course could be offered in Vancouver, Calgary, Saskatoon, Winnipeg, Toronto, Montreal, and Quebec.[98]

All homemakers' courses followed a common outline that Dr.
Russell had invited Doris Runciman, president of the Canadian
Home Economics Association, to draw up. It had fallen to vari-

ous home economists connected with extension departments of provincial universities across Canada to develop the subjects suggested by Runciman's topical headings.[99] The Toronto home-making course operated out of a practice house at 216 Huron Street where ex-servicewomen took classes five days a week from 9:30 a.m. to 4:30 p.m. for four months at a stretch. There was instruction in interior decoration (with emphasis on "how to make a home beautiful on a limited budget"), meal preparation and nutrition, consumer education, home planning and management, and child care (for which "small guests" were "borrowed for observation and demonstrations"). In addition, trainees were given tips on entertaining and party refreshments. Once a week husbands and fiances were invited to attend "special" evening lectures on home life and family relations given by "well qualified speakers."[100]

Some, like Dr. Russell, believed that helping to "develop better, more happy homes" belonged in Canada's rehabilitation program every bit as much as training for gainful employment.[101] Others, particularly in the Department of Labour, had serious misgivings over including a "brides' course" in a program designed to train for paying jobs. When he finally got wind of it, the Deputy Minister exploded in a letter to Fraudena Eaton, National Selective Service Associate Director in charge of the Women's Division: "How in the world did we get into the training of homemakers? I thought we had enough responsibility without taking on the 'Instruction to Brides.'" His reaction is not surprising given his association with a Department of Labour that recognized only work for pay as labour and that was in the business of providing training only for paid work. From his perspective, therefore, training for unpaid domestic labour was not part of his mandate and unpaid housework in general, by departmental definition not labour, was not a matter of concern, except when advocating women's confinement to the home as a solution to male unemployment. In her response to the Deputy Minister, Mrs. Eaton even lost sight of this last connection, and condemned the brides' course for not being able to "solve any employment problem" as she saw the courses for paid household workers doing.[102] But other women officials in Labour, the Women's Services, and Veterans' Affairs had no difficulty accepting that the government should provide training in homemaking for ex-servicewomen. A Labour official warned the Deputy Minister that it was too late to "retreat on this training," for not only "Service women heads" and "D.V.A. women training people" but also "our own female training staff are 100 per cent behind this."[103]

Meanwhile there was unanimity among the leaders of women's organizations and government officials that the greatest unfulfilled demand for female labour was in the field of paid housework. The result was that the most ambitious and most widely touted training schemes for women centred on household service (training in the needle trades came in a distant second). No other training schemes consumed so much time and effort on the part of the planners or persisted so long in spite of obvious failure: among servicewomen and women war workers there remained pretty nearly universal and unvaried resistance to accepting paid work as maids and housecleaners.

This led women's organizations to recommend changes in legislation to improve the status of domestic workers and publicity efforts to make employers realize their responsibilities.[104] The National Council of Women at its annual meeting in July 1945 passed a resolution urging "the Dominion Government to extend the provisions of the Unemployment Insurance Act to include household workers."[105] The month before the National Council of the YWCA, in addition to having passed the identical resolution, had also resolved to "work to secure Provincial legislation establishing minimum wages, workmen's compensation, and maximum hours for household workers."[106]

In their repeated representations to federal and provincial governments to enact legislation that would regulate the wages and hours of domestic servants and have them covered by unemployment insurance and workmen's compensation, the women's groups of the post-war period went beyond their pre-war position. In a repetition of depression strategies to raise the status of household workers, women's organizations also undertook, with government urging, to launch educational campaigns among their own members about the problems and points of view of their household assistants. It was felt that the development of "a relationship of mutual concern, co-operative interest, and initiative on the part of both employer and employee in the management of the home" would be an important step toward improving the social status of household workers.[107] Another frequently recommended tactic was to avoid the term "domestic servant" or even "domestics."

From the point of view of the employers and government, which was more inclined to view the problem from the employers' than from the employees' perspective, training itself, of course, was thought to be critical to improving the status of household work. The push for improvements in wages and conditions of work could meet with success only when the quality of the supply of labour was guaranteed. This the government felt it could do if it could find enough women to train. Equipped with three- to six-month training courses (depending on the experience of the trainees) and proficiency certificates entitling them to recognition as skilled workers, household assistants, it was believed, could then establish their claim to the same respect and benefits as other workers.[108] The contradiction, of course, was that the precondition for enticing trainees into the program proved to be improved wages and conditions of work, while the objective of the program was to improve the quality of the supply of labour so that the conditions would improve.

Ultimately, no changes were made in protective legislation or in the eligibility of domestic workers for unemployment insurance and workmen's compensation. Nor did employers have need to worry about the wages of household help becoming exorbitant.[109] In spite of much publicity for the household assistants' training program, few women could be convinced to enrol in the courses. Even after the CVT rehabilitation training program was extended to civilian workers, the domestic workers' courses failed to draw.[110]

In the pre-war home service schools, women were trained specifically for live-in positions, and that type of training was resumed in the CVT home assistants' course. But by the post-war period, the construction of smaller houses, combined with a growing distaste among housewives for the lack of privacy and among household workers for the lack of personal freedom associated with being a live-in maid, led some planners to consider schemes to promote live-out household labour. Live-in domestics were still widely advertised for, but the new trend toward daytime, hourly work could not be ignored as a solution to the problem of domestic labour shortages. The most ambitious training scheme to stimulate the supply of this type of labour, especially among former war workers, was the "Home-Aide" project developed by Fraudena Eaton in the Women's Division of National Selective Service.[111]

In contrast to the CVT-sponsored course for brides and the home assistants' course for paid workers, which involved full-time training varying from six weeks to six months, the training provided by Selective Service's "Home-Aide" project consisted in only three or four one-hour lectures or films to supplement the practical experience to be gained on the job. CVT regional directors refused to incorporate the "Home-Aide" scheme into their program, because, as so little actual instruction was involved, it was "almost entirely a placement project rather than a training plan."[112] In the end, an inadequate supply of trainees doomed the "Home-Aide" project to failure, just as it had the other domestic training programs of the post-war period.

Although few women veterans responded to the government's

initiatives to push training for paid or unpaid work, of the almost 50,000 former members of the women's services, more than 25 per cent took advantage of rehabilitation training and education benefits, a higher proportion than that of the male veterans. Over 10,000 availed themselves of vocational training or high school courses to prepare for university or to meet educational requirements for a job. More than 2,600 enrolled in university, with what Dr. Russell regarded as "encouragingly large groups in Public Health, Social Service and Education."[113] Fully 85 per cent of those taking vocational training chose the following top five out of the ninety-one occupations in which women were taking courses: commercial (which included training for work as secretaries, stenotypists, clerks, and office machine operators); hairdressing; dressmaking; nursing; and pre-matriculation. At least half chose to be trained for one of the jobs under the heading "commercial."[114] The attraction to commercial courses persisted in the face of a decided attempt to deflect women from them in the belief that clerical jobs would not expand as they had in the past. Mrs. Eaton, for example, assumed that increasing automation, in the form of "the dictaphone, electrotype, and automatic calculator," was reducing the demand for clerical workers.[115] Counsellors were also instructed to warn trainees that more women were training as hairdressers and beauty operators than the market could absorb. The task of the counsellors, then, was to discourage large numbers of women from training in either area.

The only areas where women's demand for courses appeared to correspond to government's perception of where they should be finding jobs was in dressmaking and practical nursing. The demand for pre-matriculation courses, for example, was considerably higher than expected. Consequently, in some places, this training for ex-servicewomen was so over-subscribed that only those who needed it for university qualification were being accommodated, not those who required it for a purely vocational goal.[116]

Meanwhile, the courses for home assistants had gone begging. The main cause was that the occupation was one of desperation, only to be contemplated when all other employment possibilities were exhausted, a situation that did not materialize after the war. Unemployment among ex-servicewomen simply did not reach the proportions feared by some. The explanation, according to government officials, was that servicewomen enjoyed a reputation for efficiency and hard work.[117] This may have been partially true, but there is considerable evidence to show that government policy to eliminate both child-care services for working mothers and tax concessions for working wives was fairly effective in driving women from the labour force altogether, thereby also removing them from unemployment statistics.[118]

While government officials had been unsuccessful in their attempt to channel women's post-war training into the traditional field of paid housework, they enjoyed greater success in keeping the training sexually segregated and confined to occupations perceived to be appropriate for women. In February 1946, Canadian Vocational Training was offering training in over 100 types of trades in vocational schools and over 300 types under training-on-the-job schemes, yet women were to be found in only thirty-five types of trades in vocational schools and in only ninety-two under training-on-the-job schemes.[119] And even within this range, there was considerable concentration, as we have seen, with most training for women confined to a limited number of traditionally female occupations.

CONCLUSION

One of the myths about World War II holds that it broke down the sexual division of labour and removed the sexual barriers to occupations. Although not all evidence is in on this question, what we have learned from our examination of a decade of job training programs is that, while the demarcation lines were in some cases redrawn during the war, they remained distinct. In light of this, the re-emergence in the post-war world of the traditional, sexually segregated occupational structures becomes more understandable.

Underlying the fact that the extraordinary experiences of the war did not have dramatic repercussions in the immediate post-war period was a consistency in government ideology toward women's work that persisted throughout the years 1937-47. One unchanging assumption was that women had a special responsibility for and tie to the domestic sphere. Added to that was the related assumption that the male was the primary breadwinner and therefore should have his position in the paid labour force protected. Also unquestioned was the belief that there should be a sexual division of labour in the paid labour force and that this division of labour by sex should be hierarchical, with men at the top. Together with these was an acceptance of the existing class structure, which is evidenced in the fact that when in doubt government consulted upper- and middle-class women's organizations as to what would be appropriate for female labourers.

Members of these women's groups did not challenge the ideological structure but rather shaped their advocacy of women's interests to fit within it. These normative beliefs were so deeply entrenched that a female government offical was unaware of the contradiction between them and an espousal of equal opportunities for women.

The training programs reflected these assumptions. For instance, government-supported vocational training tended to be segregated by sex, even when women, as in the war, were sometimes being prepared for non-traditional occupations. Similarly, women were rarely trained to the same extent or to the same degree of complexity as men. In times of unemployment or fear of unemployment domestic labour was seen as most appropriate for women; but even in times of high labour demand, the threat of competition from women was to be avoided by the temporary nature of any non-traditional jobs for which women were trained or by the concentration of women in "feminized" work processes.

The extraordinary demand for female labour during the war generated a rhetoric of egalitarianism that made it look as if the sexual division of labour had been significantly modified in the direction of greater equality. In actuality, the rhetoric hid the fact that those changes were more apparent than real and were designed to be temporary. If the rhetoric of sexual equality had had any substance at all, one would have expected women's wartime gains to be consolidated in post-war plans. What occurred, however, was a use of the planning apparatus to confine women to traditional occupations more reminiscent of the pre-war period.

NOTES

We should like to thank Helen Lenskyj for editing the final version of this paper.

1. See *Business Week*, 21 June 1982, 137.
2. There were no sharp lines of demarcation separating these training programs. Indeed, there was always some overlap.
3. See Veronica Strong-Boag, *The Parliament of Women: The National Council of Canada, 1893-1929* (Ottawa, 1976).
4. *Labour Gazette* (May, 1939), 469-72. Home Service Training Schools were started in the late summer of 1937. During the first year all provinces but Prince Edward Island participated in the program and twenty schools were in operation. PAC, RG 27, Vol. 748, file 12-15-5, vol. l, "Dominion-Provincial Youth Training Programme – Home Service Training Schools – Report by the

Youth Training Branch of the Dominion Department of Labour,"
n.d., presents situation as at November 30, 1938, hereafter cited as
"Home Service Training Schools Report," 1938; "Training for
Household Employment – Dominion-Provincial Youth Training
Programme," Department of Labour, Ottawa, May, 1940, here-
after cited as "May 1940 Training for Household Employment."

5. The 1913 Report of the Royal Commission on Industrial Training
   and Technical Education mentioned specifically the National
   Council of Women, the Women's Institutes of Ontario, and the
   St. Jean Baptiste Federation of Montreal as "active in seeking for
   the inclusion of provision for the training of girls for housekeeping
   and home-making in the elementary and secondary schools."
   Royal Commission on Industrial Training and Technical Education, *Report of the Commissioners* (Ottawa, 1913), Part II, 364-78;
   Part IV, 1991-3. See also Strong-Boag, *Parliament of Women*.

6. Its other strong recommendation had been to educate country girls
   to an appreciation for rural domestic economy as a means of keeping young women on the land. PAC, RG 27, Acc. No. 70/382, Box
   75, "Final Report of the Women's Employment Committee to the
   Chairman and Members of the National Employment Commission," 10 December 1937.

7. *Ibid*.

8. The long-term trend toward women comprising an increasing proportion of the counted labour force continued in Canada during
   the depression despite the economic hard times. The number of
   women employed rose from 490,150 in 1921 to 665,859 in 1931 and
   an estimated 744,000 in 1937. Their percentage of the total labour
   force also grew, from 15.4 in 1921 to 17 in 1931 and 19 in 1941.
   "Wartime History of Employment of Women and Day Care of
   Children," completed before 24 August 1950, Part I, 1-5, PAC, RG
   35, Series 7, Vol. 20, file 19.

9. L.M. Grayson and Michael Bliss, eds., *The Wretched of Canada*
   (Toronto, 1971), vi.

10. The 1913 Royal Commission on Industrial Training and Technical
    Education (p. 376) had also argued that training and certification
    in housekeeping would increase remuneration for and remove so-
    cial stigma from domestic servants.

11. "Home Service Training Schools Report," 1938; "May 1940
    Training for Household Employment."

12. "Home Service Training Schools Report," 1938.

13. With respect to wage level, experience was more significant than
    training. For example, one live-in maid with three months' Home
    Service training was earning $12 a month, another $16 a month,
    while two with two years' experience were earning $20 a month
    and another, with four years', $25. PAC, RG 27, Vol. 748, file
    12-14-5, vol. 1, "Kitchener Household Employment Study Group
    Report," 26 March 1940; "Findings of Preston Study Group,"
    n.d.

14. Sara Diamond, "You Can't Scare Me . . . I'm Stickin' to the

Union: Union Women in British Columbia during the Great Depression," *Kinesis* (June, 1979), 16-17; Provincial Archives of British Columbia, Add. MSS 215, Vol. VIII, YWCA, Victoria Branch, Minutes of Board of Directors' Meetings, 14 December 1934, 11 January, 22 February 1935, 17 April 1936.

15. *Labour Gazette* (February, 1939), 167; "Findings of the Preston Group."
16. "Home Service Training Schools Report," 1938.
17. "Youth Training in Canada in 1938."
18. "Home Service Training Schools Report," 1938.
19. "May 1940 Training for Household Employment." In 1944, when there was talk of creating a similar institution on a larger scale for the post-war world, R.F. Thompson, Director of Training in the federal Department of Labour, anticipated that low demand from prospective trainees would be a problem because it had been difficult even during the depression "to obtain [a] sufficient number of applications to keep our two dozen schools filled." PAC, RG 27, Vol. 748, file 12-15-5, vol. 1, R.F. Thompson to Isobel Robson, the Local Council of Women, Winnipeg, 18 November 1944.
20. *Labour Gazette* (January, 1942), 34.
21. *Labour Gazette* (April, 1941), 427; "War Development of the Training Programme," n.d., presumed from internal evidence to be ca. mid-1943, PAC, RG 27, Vol. 744, file 12-14-16-12, vol. 1.
22. Such agreements were made with all provinces except Prince Edward Island, which lacked both training facilities and war industry. P.E.I. applicants were accommodated in Nova Scotia or New Brunswick.
23. *Labour Gazette* (January, 1941), 17.
24. Men who came within the age group liable to be called for compulsory military service (initially single men between twenty and twenty-six years of age) were not admitted unless they had medical rejection slips, and during 1942 ineligibility was extended to male farm and rural workers without special permits from National Selective Service. "Progress Statement in Training Programme, April 1st to December 31st, 1941," PAC, RG 27, Vol. 725, file 12-2-1; "War Development of the Training Programme."
25. *Labour Gazette* (May, 1941), 571.
26. *Labour Gazette* (April, 1941), 427.
27. R.F. Thompson to Minister of Labour, 3 November 1941, re Progress Report of the War Emergency Training Programme, PAC, RG 27, Vol. 725, file 12-2-1.
28. As early as April 1940, the decision of the Ontario government to close the Dominion-Provincial Home Service Training Schools in its province provoked a series of letters in protest from various women's associations. Ontario Archives, RG 3, Mitchell Hepburn Papers, General Correspondence, Public 1940, "Youth Training Movement"; 1941, "Labour Department."
29. Thompson to Minister of Labour, 3 November 1941.

30. "Progress Statement on Training Programme, April 1st to December 31st, 1941."
31. *Ibid.*
32. "War Development of the Training Programme."
33. Frederick Edwards, "Night-and-Day School," *Maclean's*, 1 May 1942, 16-17, 22-4.
34. See Ruth Roach Pierson, "'Jill Canuck': CWAC of All Trades but No 'Pistol Packing Momma,'" *Historical Papers*, (1978), 106-33; "Canadian Women and Canadian Mobilization During the Second World War," *Revue Internationale d'histoire militaire*, special issue prepared by the Canadian Commission of the International Commission of Military History (1982), 181-207.
35. Edwards, "Night-and-Day School," 16.
36. *Labour Gazette* (April, 1942), 405-6.
37. *Labour Gazette* (December, 1942), 1427-33.
38. *Labour Gazette* (September, 1941), 1103; (March, 1942), 299; "Training of Women Under War Emergency Training Programme," n.d., ca. mid-1943, PAC, RG 27, Vol. 744, file 12-14-16-12, vol. 1.
39. We are using "skill" and "skilled" in the traditional sense. The whole question of the nature and definition of "skilled" work is a complex one worthy of study. See, for example, Mercedes Steedman, "Sex and Skill in the Canadian Needle Trades 1890-1940," paper presented at the annual meeting of the Canadian Historical Association, Ottawa, 11 June 1982.
40. Speech reported in *Labour Gazette* (April, 1942), 414.
41. *Labour Gazette* (January, 1941), 15.
42. For similar practice in Britain during World War I, see Gail Braybon, *Women Workers in the First World War: The British Experience* (London, 1981), 51-65.
43. Leslie Roberts, "Fire Power," *Maclean's*, 15 May 1942, 13-14.
44. Thelma LeCocq, "Woman Power," *Maclean's*, 15 June 1942, 11.
45. The "powered fuselage conveyor assembly line," where all of the work was done by women, provided one illustration of this "fitting jobs to women." "There, and on the engine balcony, air driven wrenches and screw drivers, light weight electric drills and rivet squeezers are the rule. Special supports are used to hold jigs and assemblies, the weight of which would cut down the efficiency of women workers if they had to hold them as men did." "Women Workers – A Problem," *Canadian Aviation* (November, 1943), 78, 80.
46. R. Eric Crawford, "Ingenuity Pays Big Dividends Noorduyn Factory Men Find: Method Improvement Study Results in Many Clever Machines and Factory Ideas," *Canadian Aviation* (January, 1943), 39-43, 80.
47. *Labour Gazette* (November, 1942), 1292.
48. Edwards, "Night-and-Day School," 22.
49. Mary Oliver, "A Wartime Schoolroom," *Canadian Business*

(January, 1944), 69, 90. The instruction took place outside the War Emergency Training Program as any courses of less than two weeks were regarded as training on the job. "War Development of the Training Programme"; Gladys Ross, interview with Helen Lenskyj, Toronto, 25 August 1983.

50. Roberts, "Fire Power," 13-14. Roberts noted that men whose ethnic backgrounds would have been an obstacle to their admission to the ranks of skilled labour before the war also benefited from the wartime revolution in vocational training.

51. LeCocq, "Woman Power," 10-11, 40; Lotta Dempsey, "Women in War Plants," *Mayfair* (May, 1943), 93.

52. "Women Workers – A Problem," 78-80.

53. LeCocq, "Woman Power," 10-11, 40.

54. If she had directly replaced a man who had entered military service, her chances for holding on to that job at war's end were limited by other factors as well, a main one being the Reinstatement in Civil Employment Act of 1942, which guaranteed veterans their jobs back after discharge. See Department of Labour, "'Dismiss' but . . . what of a job?" October, 1944, copy at PAC, RG 27, Acc. No. 71/98, Vol. 1, file 22-5-1.

55. F.H. Sexton, Director of Technical Education, Department of Education, Nova Scotia, to T.D.A. Purves, Deputy Minister of Labour, Nova Scotia, 30 April 1943, PAC, RG 27, Vol. 605, file 6-24-1, vol. 1.

56. Routine Letter #141, R.F. Thompson, Director of Training, Department of Labour, to all Regional Directors, 7 January 1943, PAC, RG 27, Vol. 744, file 12-14-16-12, vol. 1. As the end of war came into sight, the emphasis in training shifted more and more in the direction of rehabilitation and post-war planning. By Order-in-Council PC 1976 of 21 March 1944, the very name "Wartime Emergency Training Program" was scrapped for one more appropriate to the post-war peacetime world: "Canadian Vocational Training." *Report of the Department of Labour for the Fiscal Year ending March 31, 1943* (Ottawa, 1943), 29; *Report of the Department of Labour for the Fiscal Year ending March 31, 1945* (Ottawa, 1945), 56.

57. "Wartime History of Employment of Women and Day-Care Children," Part I, 81.

58. See, for example, L.C. Marsh and O.J. Firestone, "Will There Be Jobs?" *Canadian Affairs*, 1, 18 (1 October 1944).

59. See, for example, Department of Labour, *DISMISS but . . . what of a JOB?* (Ottawa, 1945). An October 1944 draft of this pamphlet can be found at PAC, RG 27, Acc. 71/98, Vol. 1, file 22-5-1.

60. Anne Fromer, "Post-War Employment Field Graphed by Weir Report," *Saturday Night*, 22 April 1944, 6.

61. See Pierson, "'Jill Canuck.'" Also Routine Letter #141, R.F. Thompson to Regional Directors, 7 January 1943.

62. Advisory Committee on Reconstruction, *VI: Post-War Problems of Women – Final Report of the Sub-Committee*, 30 November 1943 (Ottawa, 1944). See also Gail Cuthbert Brandt, "'Pigeon-

holed and Forgotten': The Work of the Sub-Committee on the Post-War Problems of Women, 1943," *Social History/Histoire Sociale*, 15, 29 (May, 1982), 239-59.

63. "Post-War Working Intentions of Civilians as Indicated by Answers Given on D. L. R. 57-58 Forms Completed by 29,845 People in Canada," PAC, RG 27, Acc. No. 70/450, Box 14, file 208.

64. Janet R. Keith, "Situations Wanted: Female," *Canadian Business* (November, 1944), 74.

65. "Women To-Morrow," address by Captain Olive Ruth Russell to the University Women's Club, Dalhousie University, Halifax, 15 March 1944, PAC, MG 31, K 13, Vol. 1. At the time of this address, Russell was one of two personnel selection counsellors (army examiners) with the Canadian Women's Army Corps.

66. The government sub-committee also advocated a nursery school program that, because of its short hours (9 a.m. to noon), would have been a benefit only to the full-time mother and no help at all to the gainfully employed mother, struggling under the double burden of wage work and child care. In 1944 the sole woman on the Economic Advisory Board of the province of Quebec, Renée G. (Mme. Henri) Vautelet, produced a similar report on the post-war problems of Quebec women. It, too, bristled with unresolved tension between granting that women needed to seek employment outside the home and proposing policies that would "reduce industry's economic reasons for employing women in preference to men."

The change in provincial government in August 1944 had terminated the work of Quebec's Economic Advisory Board, and Vautelet's report might never have seen the light of day had it not been translated into English under the title *Post War Problems and Employment of Women in the Province of Quebec* and published by the Montreal Local Council of Women in August 1945. Copy at PAC, MG 30, C 175, Vol. 1, file #5.

67. Wartime Information Board, *Looking Ahead: Our Next Job*, Canadian Post-War Affairs: Discussion Manual No. 3 (Ottawa, 1945), 11. Similarly, Marsh made adult women fit into his social security scheme principally as wives dependent for benefits on "the husband as the chief wage-earner." Leonard Marsh, *Report on Social Security for Canada 1945*, with a new Introduction by the author and a Preface by Michael Bliss (Toronto, 1975), 195-232.

68. See Ruth Pierson, "Women's Emancipation and the Recruitment of Women into the Canadian Labour Force in WWII," *Historical Papers* (1976), 141-74; revised version in *The Neglected Majority: Essays in Canadian Women's History*, ed. by Susan Mann Trofimenkoff and Alison Prentice (Toronto, 1977), 125-45.

69. *Report of the Department of Labour for the Fiscal Year ending March 31, 1945*, 56.

70. The one minor exception to all this equality of status and opportunity that Dr. Russell acknowledged was the unavailability of out-of-work benefits to the married female veteran whose husband was deemed capable of maintaining her. Olive Ruth Russell, "Re-

habilitation of Persons from the Armed Forces with Special Reference to Ex-Service Women," address to the Business and Professional Women's Club, Ottawa, 13 March 1945, PAC, MG 31, K 13, Vol. 1.

71. *DISMISS but . . . what of a JOB?*, 29.

72. Olive Ruth Russell, "Rehabilitation of Women of the Armed Services," 19 February 1945, PAC, MG 31, K 13, Vol. 1.

73. War Emergency Training Agreement, Schedule "K" (1944-45), *Rehabilitation Training*, PAC, RG 27, Vol. 725, file 12-2-1. In rural areas local Canadian Legion branches provided the initial interviewing service.

74. *DISMISS but . . . what of a JOB?*, 28-9.

75. Appendix "Y" to Canadian Vocational Training War Emergency Training Agreement, Schedule "K" (1945-1946), copy at PAC, RG 27, Vol. 742, file 12-14-7-1.

76. Department of Veterans' Affairs, *Back To Civil Life*, 2nd rev. ed. (Ottawa, 1944).

77. *Ibid.*, 14.

78. A short story in a post-war issue of *Maclean's* took as subject the problem of what a veteran (male understood) was to do when he returned to find his peacetime job held by a "girl" "stubborn as well as beautiful." The story's proposed solution – "Marry her" – was meant only semi-facetiously. Ron Broom, "Marry the Girl!" *Maclean's*, 1 October 1945, 16-17, 22, 25-6, 28.

79. *Back To Civil Life*, 24.

80. Humphrey Mitchell, Minister of Labour, to A.D.P. Heeney, Clerk of the Privy Council, 10 November 1945, PAC, RG 27, Acc. No. 71/98, Vol. 2, file 22-5-6-7.

81. The Dominion Civil Service Circular Letter 1945-17, dated 17 November 1945, called for renewed enforcement of the pre-war discriminatory policy, which stated that: "'Any female employee in the public service shall, upon the occasion of her marriage, be required to resign her position.'" Quoted by E.L.M. Burns, Director General of Rehabilitation [drafted by Dr. Olive Ruth Russell], to W.S. Woods, Deputy Minister, 3 December 1945, Veterans' Affairs, PAC, MG 31, K 13, Vol. 1.

82. *Towards Equality for Women* (Ottawa, 1979), 5.

83. Employment Service and Unemployment Insurance Branch of the Department of Labour, Employment Circular, 17 May 1945, PAC, RG 27, Acc. No. 71/328, Vol. 2, file 90; Minutes of Conference of Supervisors of Women's Training, Canadian Vocational Training, Ottawa, 11, 12, 13 February 1946, PAC, RG 27, Vol. 748, file 12-15-5, vol. 1A.

84. 23rd Report on National Selective Service Operations, February, 1945, PAC, RG 27, Acc. No. 71/328, Box 3.

85. In a letter dated 10 April 1944, R.F. Thompson, Director of Training, Department of Labour, asked Mrs. E.D. Hardy, president of the National Council of Women, to contact women's organizations, particularly the National Council of the YWCA, for "sugges-

tions for various types of training which would afford reasonable assurance for employment" for women in the post-war period. PAC, RG 27, Vol. 744, file 12-14-16-12, vol. 1.

86. See, for example, "Will Maids Come Back?," *Chatelaine* (June, 1944), 21-2; Katharine Kent, "Crisis in the Kitchen," *Maclean's*, 15 October 1945, 10, 62.

87. Memo of March, 1945, to Mary Eadie, Supervisor, Women's Division, Employment and Selective Service Office, Toronto Branch, from Ombra Dill, Supervisor, Household Assistants, attached to letter of 15 March 1945, to Mrs. Rex Eaton, Assoc. Director, Selective Service, from Mary Eadie, for G.S. Collins, Mgr., Employment and Selective Service Office, Toronto Branch, PAC, RG 27, Vol. 748, file 12-15-5, vol. 1A.

88. Questioned on the problem of too many women in the labour force, Minister of Labour Humphrey Mitchell announced that women "have preferred – and I think this is a pretty sound conclusion to arrive at – to return to home-keeping." House of Commons, *Debates*, 1945, 2371. See M. Theresa Nash, "Images of Women in National Film Board of Canada Films During World War II and the Post-War Years (1939 to 1949)" (Ph.D., McGill University, 1982).

89. Russell, "Women To-Morrow," emphasis in original.

90. "Since woman's full right to work has been taken for granted in the war emergency and she has been able to prove her efficiency, is it not natural to assume that in the employment market after the war her claim to the right to employment should be based on her merits rather than her sex." *Ibid*.

91. Russell, "Rehabilitation of Women of the Armed Services" emphasis in original.

92. Whyard, "Dr. Russell – Rehabilitation," for *Saturday Night*, draft, 19 June 1945, copy at PAC, MG 31, K 13, Vol. 1.

93. R.F. Thompson to Miss Isobel Robson, Winnipeg, 18 November 1944, PAC, RG 27, Vol. 748, file 12-15-5, vol. 1.

94. R.F. Thompson, to A. MacNamara, Deputy Minister, Department of Labour, 20 March 1945, PAC, RG 27, Vol. 1523, file x5-12, part 1.

95. Rehabilitation Information Committee, Minutes of 11 July 1945, PAC, RG 27, Vol. 3575, file 11-8-9-9, vol. 1; Edith C. Scott, Lieut., Rehabilitation, Naval Service, Department of National Defence, to Marion M. Graham, Superintendent of Women's Training, CVT, 20 August 1945, PAC, RG 27, Vol. 748, file 12-15-5, vol. 11; A.C.P. Clayton, Group Captain, for Chief of the Air Staff, Air Service, Dept. of National Defence, to Training Branch, Dept. of Labour, 20 August 1945, PAC, RG 27, Vol. 748, file 12-15-5, vol. 1; Marion M. Graham to Bertha G. Oxner, Director of Women's Work, University of Saskatchewan, 6 September 1945, PAC, RG 27, Vol. 748, file 12-15-5, vol. 1.

96. Olive Ruth Russell to Mr. J. Andrew, Rehabilitation Information Committee, Wartime Information Board, 9 July 1945, PAC,

MG 31, K 13, Vol. 1; Fraudena Eaton to A. MacNamara, 18 February 1946, PAC, RG 27, Vol. 748, file 12-15-5, vol. 1A.

97. Olive Ruth Russell to Marion Graham, 5 September 1945, PAC, RG 27, Vol. 748, file 12-15-5, vol. 1. See also address given to the Winnipeg Local Council of Women by Dr. Olive Ruth Russell, February, 1946, PAC, MG 31, K 13, Vol. 1.

98. *Labour Gazette* (February, 1946), 196. The opening of such a school in the Maritime Provinces was not felt to be warranted. Routine Letter #388, R.F. Thompson to all Regional Directors, 3 April 1946, PAC, RG 27, Vol. 744, file 12-14-16-12, vol. 1.

99. Mary D. Slater, Superintendent of Women's Rehabilitation, Dept. of Veterans' Affairs, to Marion Graham, 13 November 1945, PAC, RG 27, Vol. 748, file 12-15-5, vol. 1.

100. Press releases "Homemaking" and "Homemaking Course" prepared for opening of the Homemaking and Family Living Course for ex-servicewomen in Toronto, 18 February 1946, PAC, RG 27, Vol. 748, file 12-15-5, vols. 1, 1A.

101. Olive Ruth Russell to Miss Bernice Coffey, Women's Editor, *Saturday Night*, 24 July 1945, PAC, MG 31, K 13, Vol. 1. Also PAC, RG 27, Vol. 748, file 12-5-5, vol. 1, Lieut. Edith C. Scott to Marion M. Graham, 20 August 1945: "Having the homes of ex-service people well managed by capable trained housewives will help greatly both in the re-establishment of the returning generation and in restoring a stable peace-time society."

102. A. MacNamara to Mrs. Rex [Fraudena] Eaton, 14 February 1946, PAC, RG 27, Vol. 748, file 12-15-5, vol. 1A. Eaton to MacNamara, 18 February 1946, PAC, RG 27, Vol. 748, file 12-15-5, vol. 1A.

103. A.H. Brown to A. MacNamara, 2 March 1946, PAC, RG 27, Vol. 748, file 12-15-5, vol. 1A.

104. *Labour Gazette* (April, 1945), 523.

105. Forwarded with a covering letter to Humphrey Mitchell, Minister of Labour, 2 August 1945, by Mrs. G.D. Finlayson, Corresponding Secretary, National Council of Women of Canada, PAC, RG 27, Vol. 748, file 12-15-2, vol. 1A.

106. Quoted in a letter of 25 February 1946 to Marion Graham from Mrs. C.D. Rouillard, Chairman, Public Affairs Committee, National Council of the YWCA, PAC, RG 27, Vol. 748, file 12-15-5, vol. 1.

107. *Labour Gazette* (February, 1946), 195.

108. Marion Graham to Chief, Legislation Branch, Dept. of Labour, attention Miss Mackintosh, 20 February 1945, PAC, RG 27, Vol. 744, file 12-14-16-12, vol. 1.

109. According to one review of rates as advertised in local newspapers throughout Canada, for general housework, live-in monthly wages were $25 in Nova Scotia, $40 in Vancouver and Quebec City, $40 to $60 in Toronto, $35 in Regina and Saskatoon. The prevailing rate for day workers in Toronto was 50 cents an hour with carfare and lunch. See the untitled report attached to Fraudena Eaton's note of 15 January 1946, that the "review was made on a date

within the month commencing December 7th, 1945." PAC, RG 27, Vol. 748, file 12-15-5, vol. 1.

110. Canadian Vocational Training Programme, Appendix B, For Women Veterans, Dept. of Labour, April, 1947, PAC, RG 27, Vol. 744, file 12-14-16-12, vol. 1.

111. See Ruth Pierson, "'Home-Aide': A Solution to Women's Unemployment After World War II," *Atlantis*, 2, 2 (Spring, 1977), 85-96.

112. R.F. Thompson to A. MacNamara, 11 January 1946, PAC, RG 27, Vol. 748, file 12-15-5, vol. 1. Routine Letter #346, Marion M. Graham to all Regional Directors, November, 1945; also the follow-up memo of 1 December 1945 to all Superintendents of Women's Training in CVT Regional Offices, PAC, RG 27, Vol. 748, file 12-15-5, vol. 1.

113. Women's Rehabilitation Annual Report, 1946-1947, draft prepared by Dr. Olive Ruth Russell, PAC, MG 31, K 13, Vol. 1.

114. Walter S. Woods, *Rehabilitation (A Combined Operation)* (Ottawa, 1953), 256-7.

115. Mrs. Rex Eaton's speech to a Regional Rehabilitation Training Conference in Vancouver, March, 1946, PAC, RG 27, Vol. 748, file 12-15-5, vol. 1A.

116. Mary D. Slater to Marion Graham, 15 April 1946, re: Visit of Superintendent to Vancouver District, 9-18 March 1946, PAC, RG 27, Vol. 744, file 12-14-16-12, vol. 1.

117. Canadian Vocational Training Programme, Appendix B, For Women Veterans, Dept. of Labour, April, 1947, PAC, RG 27, Vol. 744, file 12-14-16-12, vol. 1.

118. See Pierson, "Women's Emancipation and the Recruitment of Women." There is evidence that unemployed women, some of them displaced from insurable jobs in the offices and plants of war production, were denied Unemployment Insurance benefits if they refused to take jobs as domestics. See House of Commons, *Debates*, Stanley Knowles, 14 July 1947, 5636. Attention was brought to this debate by Nash, "Images of Women."

119. Marion M. Graham to Chief, Legislation Branch, attention Miss Mackintosh, 20 February 1946.

Readings in Canadian Social History